Praise for *The Unlikely Voyage of Jack de Crow* by A.J. Mackinnon

'A great travel writer and more importantly a great traveller' —*The Sydney Morning Herald*

'Not just an adventurer, but an artist, philosopher and keen observer of the world around him' —*The Canberra Times*

'Mackinnon's journey makes a lovely picaresque tale, one dotted with English literary references and wonderful descriptions of the English and European countryside' —*Good Reading*

'A marvellous adventure, and Mackinnon recounts it with humour and unflagging enthusiasm . . . a clever and entirely engaging read' —*The Melbourne Times*

'A wonderful idea for a book – a series of ever bolder improvisations . . . undertaken in praise of the spirit of adventure' —*Times Literary Supplement*

'A must-read for anyone planning to sail backwards through Europe. Epic, exciting and extremely funny.' —Tom Gleisner

Quaint Deeds

Also by A.J. Mackinnon

The Unlikely Voyage of Jack de Crow

The Well at the World's End

Quaint Deeds

Unlikely adventures in teaching and treasure-hunting

A.J. Mackinnon

Published by Black Inc.,
an imprint of Schwartz Books Pty Ltd
Wurundjeri Country
22–24 Northumberland Street
Collingwood VIC 3066, Australia
enquiries@blackincbooks.com
www.blackincbooks.com

9781760643690 (paperback)
9781743823354 (ebook)

A catalogue record for this book is available from the National Library of Australia

Cover artwork and design by Emily O'Neill
Text design and typesetting by Typography Studio
Internal illustrations by A.J. Mackinnon
Author photo by Stephanie White

Printed in Australia by McPherson's Printing Group.

Preface

> *'The best thing for being sad,' replied Merlyn, beginning to puff and blow, 'is to learn something. That's the only thing that never fails. You may grow old and trembling in your anatomies, you may lie awake at night listening to the disorder of your veins, you may miss your only love, you may see the world about you devastated by evil lunatics, or know your honour trampled in the sewers of baser minds. There is only one thing for it then – to learn.'*
>
> —T.H. White, *The Sword in the Stone*

At some point in my teaching career – I can't quite remember when – I was taken into a school office and interviewed by a man called Peter Althorpe. Peter was a relative stranger to me. He had been brought in as an educational consultant and motivational counsellor to assess staff, find out what made them tick, point out likely career paths and suggest suitable opportunities for promotion. He wore a blue suit, a smart tie in pinks and golds, and shiny black shoes. Despite all this, he was really a very amiable character and I had warmed to him over a few Common Room coffees in the previous week or so; he didn't fit the usual profile of a management consultant and we had shared a couple of laughs about the lighter side of education.

Thus it was that I felt really rather at ease as he chatted about the upcoming vacancy for the position of Head of English and a possible housemastership in the following year, both positions I felt more than ready to tackle. Peter sat there making notes in a small notebook and giving nods of encouragement, throwing in the odd compliment as to my suitability for the roles. Before long, I was confident that we had formed a bond of mutual liking and trust – which is when Peter leant forwards, smiled confidentially and asked the real biggie.

'So, Sandy, let's look at the broader picture. Let me ask this. Who are *you*? Who is the real Sandy? What have you always wanted to be? What's the dream?'

So relaxed was I that I gave him the honest answer.

'Well, Peter, I've always wanted to be a wizard.'

There was a long pause. Then a brief, tight smile, followed by a surreptitious scratching out of what he had previously written in his notepad – and the interview was over.

My application for the Head of English three weeks later was regrettably unsuccessful and I never did make Housemaster; not at that school at least. I later reflected that when a professional motivation counsellor asks for an honest answer in order to help clients achieve their goals, there are limits to their remit. But I recount this anecdote because that shared confidence was indeed my secret aim, and the following pages tell of the process whereby I have tried to live out that unworldly and ridiculous ambition. It has rarely been a deliberate and conscious programme, but now, as I find myself verging on retirement and a happy dotage, I am a considerable way along the road to wizardhood.

My publishers asked me some years ago to write another book, a follow-up to my two travel adventure books. In vain did I explain that I had not actually gone on any other grand adventures. Never mind, they enthused, write about your teaching. Write a book full of the wisdom and warmth that comes from a lifetime of engaging young minds. Be the James Herriot of the educational world, please, and we'll all make a tidy packet. After a decade or so of gentle persuasion, I have done just that, but find to my dismay that the book simply won't remain in the classroom. It won't even stick to school. It keeps harking back to childhood dreams, adolescent scrapes, early passions and pursuits – obsessions even. It relentlessly displays one characteristic overall: namely, an odious smugness at how jolly clever I have been in several ways. The book's subtitle could easily be 'Clever things I have done and how I did them'. A less obnoxious theme, however, has emerged behind this barrage of boasting. It is a hard one to put into a few words; indeed, it perhaps takes an entire book to express it with the subtlety it demands. But it has to do with magic in its many forms – yes, work-a-day conjuring and illusion, tricks, sleights of hand that baffle and delight, but also more ethereal forms: imagination that awakens things to life, serendipity of circumstance, daydreams coalescing out of the air in odd ways ... and, again and again, preposterous and inexplicable coincidence.

What has all this to do with teaching? Everything. The great wizards of literature have primarily been tutors: Merlyn to the boy Arthur, Gandalf to the young Frodo, Dumbledore to the pupils of Hogwarts. Almost all the enchantment that has happened in my life has come about because of the interaction with students that is the greatest privilege of a teacher's life.

> Let not young souls be smothered out
> Before they do quaint deeds and fully flaunt their pride.

So wrote the poet Vachel Lindsay. It has been my unceasing joy to see hundreds and hundreds of young souls over the last four decades resisting the world's smothering and sharing their quaint deeds with me, sometimes as their mentor, sometimes as their guide, but more often as a delighted spectator who has been lucky enough to be taken along for the ride. It is to them that this book is dedicated.

Chapter 1

How many goodly creatures are there here!
How beauteous mankind is! O brave new world,
That has such people in 't!
—William Shakespeare, *The Tempest*

I never thought I would be living out a portion of my life at the North Pole but there it was, plain to read, in faded inky letters. NORTH POLE. And who would have guessed that the North Pole had its own key? The North Pole was the name of the staircase in the south-eastern wing of the vast Victorian edifice that was Ellesmere College. My quarters occupied two sides of a very public corridor, along which the sixty or so boys of Lambart House thundered from dorm to dorm, or occasionally played impromptu games of scrum practice, indoor hockey or the rather jolly Hunt-the-Third-Former, a game also involving hockey sticks. My bedroom lay on one side of this corridor and the bathroom lay on the other. The latter was so antiquated in its plumbing and so cramped for space that it was impossible to change into a set of clothes without risking a sudden soaking from a showerhead that tended to belch into life on unpredictable whim. After my first experience of this eccentricity, I was faced with the daily dilemma of whether to struggle in and out of my clothes in the shower cubicle and hope the showerhead would refrain from gushing or to dash across the public corridor clad

only in a towel and risk being accosted by Crompton Major and his Sixth Form chums on a hunt for someone harmless and timid to humiliate – in which case their quest would have been complete there and then.

All this I was to find out later. I would also discover, over the course of the next few years, that the North Pole housed a nervous Welsh organist upstairs, a balding matron downstairs, a plague of emboldened mice, and not one but two resident ghosts, namely, a phantom cat and a spectral boy who appeared occasionally before flinging himself from a top-storey window. It only later occurred to me that these apparitions might have been responsible for both the nervousness of my upstairs neighbour and the baldness of my downstairs neighbour. The mice seemed wholly unconcerned about the phantom cat and danced hornpipes on my dressing table that first night, keeping me awake till the birdsong of dawn plunged me into a deep sleep. I woke several hours later, already late for my very first meeting in my new job at Ellesmere College.

Within a few weeks, I had become enamoured of this new place, largely because of the charm and eccentricity of a few of its senior boys. I had started my boarding career seven years earlier at an Adelaide private school which was predominantly a day school but catered for sixty or so lads from remote parts of South Australia or the Northern Territory. I was barely twenty myself at the time, as green and naïve as they come, so I was ripe for intimidation by that handful of boarders whose idea of a good time was to capture a live kangaroo in the home paddock, insert a shotgun into its anus and see what happened when you pulled the trigger – or so at least they would boast to one another in grunting troll-like tones as they gathered in dark corners of the boarding house. They were a terrifying bunch – pimply, vicious and uncouth – and an off-putting introduction to a career in boarding.

It was with some relief, therefore, that the first student I met at the College, wrapped in a navy duffle coat and a scarlet scarf against the gently falling snow, resembled the poster child for the King's College carols service. He introduced himself politely as something like Mungo Peverill-St Clair and on finding that I had just arrived, murmured, 'Really, sir. Welcome then … and look, when you've found your feet, you must pop around to Maldon House for a drink. Study Five on the left.'

He must have been all of thirteen and, such was his genially magisterial demeanour, I remember thinking that he was awfully small to be a Headmaster. What would be offered, I wondered. A small sherry before Evensong? A rather nice Bordeaux picked up on the last holiday in France?

Before long, I discovered a cohort of similarly civilised boys. Two of them in particular were straight out of a Wodehouse novel: Montgomery Cavisham and Henry Horton.

Monty was fine-featured, with curly dark hair, a gentle lopsided smile and dress sense from the Edwardian era. He was rarely without a waistcoat and cravat, and he sported an ever-changing set of cufflinks. His chosen summer sport was sailing, for which he wore spotless white trousers, a stripy blazer and a straw boater, looking for all the world like something out of *The Wind in the Willows* as he pottered around the mere in a dinghy. Monty took it upon himself to act as my personal valet. If he got wind that I was due to attend a dinner party or Common Room function, he would appear at my door with an array of silk ties, a set of cufflinks and sometimes even a small portable iron to crispen my collar and sleeves. He would insist on tying my tie in a correct Windsor knot, but I had to draw the line when on one occasion he arrived with a cut-throat razor, a cake of gardenia soap and a hand towel embroidered with the Cavisham crest, wishing to give me a gentleman's shave for my invitation to the Headmaster's house that evening.

His friend Henry was a stouter chap, red-faced and flop-haired; he could have been anywhere between seventeen and fifty-five. He'd often say things, with all sincerity, like this: 'Oh, sir, it's been a rather torrid weekend. I popped down to Horton-on-the-Wold to see Mummy and she asked me to have words with the Master of the Hunt. The bally fellow had allowed the hounds to go right through the Lodge garden and Nanny was in pieces. She's very proud of her sweet peas. What a kerfuffle … Still, he's a decent sort, the Master, and he'll see her right.'

Henry had stepped into his deceased father's place as local squire without seeming to realise the incongruity of being both landlord and schoolboy. He was, however, the first to admit his limitations. One evening he came to me deeply worried.

'Ah, sir. So sorry to bother you like this, but I'm in a bit of a pickle. May I come in?'

'Yes, of course, Henry. What's the problem?'

'Well, sir, it's like this. I've just been given – well, about a week ago – this rather splendid briefcase as a gift from Mummy. Look: she even got the family crest embossed on it. Two squirrels rampant holding up an acorn vert. Sweet, isn't it? At least I think they're squirrels. Or are they pine martens?'

'And?' I prompted.

'What? Oh yes. Well, look, the spiffy thing about this is that it's safe as houses. Look, these two locks are frightfully clever. They're what I think are called combination locks, sir. See. Tiny little numbers. You can set the code yourself even.'

'Marvellous,' I agreed. 'So, what's the problem?'

'What? Oh yes. Well, the fact is ... the fact is ... I had a hundred pounds in here last night and now it's gone.' He pronounced it 'gorn', to rhyme with 'horn'.

'A hundred pounds, Henry? What were you doing with that amount of money?'

'Well, I was going to buy a nice present or something for Nanny, because she lost her Bunty recently and she's pretty cut up about it, and I thought, *I know, I'll buy her a set of silver teaspoons because she uses teaspoons a lot.* She's a great tea drinker, you know, not so much coffee these days, mind, because it gives her – well, I shouldn't say it – but well, yes, *wind,* if you'll pardon the expression. So, spoons, I thought. Silver spoons – to make up for Bunty, you see. Bunty's a labrador, did I mention? Nanny doted on her. Got trampled by a horse. Bunty, not Nanny, of course. Still, sad, what?'

'Right. So, let me get this clear, Henry. You had a hundred pounds and you put it in this briefcase for safekeeping?'

'Absolutely, sir. Safe as houses,' said Henry as he patted the case affectionately.

'Yes, well ... evidently not. And you locked it?'

'Absolutely, sir. Locked it up tight. Good old bag. Er, this thingy. Not Nanny, of course.'

'And no one knew the combination?'

'Well, I did, sir.'

I took a deep breath.

'Yes, yes, of course you knew it, Henry – but did anyone else know it?'

'Absolutely not, sir. Top secret. Classified info. For my eyes only. Take it with me to the grave. Good old bag.'

'Right.' I examined the case carefully and noted that there were two clasps, each one sporting a three-digit combination lock of solid brass. Neither showed any signs of having been tampered with.

'Well, this is a mystery, Henry. Let's look inside then,' I said.

'Oh, you won't find the money in there, sir. I've looked. That's what alerted me to the problem, sir. Gone! Thin air. A complete mystery.'

'Yes, Henry, I know that, but I want to check if there's been some damage on the inside.'

'Brilliant, sir. Golly, sir, just like that Sherlock Holmes chap.'

'Quite. Now, let's focus. What's the combination, Henry?'

'Well, it's frightfully clever, sir, because you can set it yourself. You have to follow instructions, which were a bit tricky at first, to be honest, but you turn these little thingies *here* and then you push this thingy *here*, and the job's done.'

'So, the combination you chose is – what? Not your date of birth, I hope? Or your name spelt out as letters? Or something predictable like that. Something random, I hope.'

'Oh absolutely, sir. None of those things, sir.'

'So, what is it then?'

'Right, let me think. Umm …' Henry closed his eyes in ferocious concentration. 'Right. It's … zero, zero, zero … umm … zero, zero … ah, zero.' He opened his eyes and smiled with relief. 'Yes, that should do it.'

'Zero, zero, zero, zero, zero, zero?!'

I sighed as I imagined the anonymous opportunist finding the case and casually, idly – playfully even, and without the slightest hope of success – trying out the base setting on each lock. And their incredulous delight as it snapped open to reveal a hundred pounds for the taking.

'*Zero, zero, zero, zero, zero, zero*, Henry? What were you thinking?' I asked, shaking my head in despair.

'Well, umm,' said Henry, with disarming humility, 'you see, sir, to be honest, I didn't think I could remember something more complicated.'

I do like a chap who knows his intellectual limitations. I believe Henry is a Member of Parliament now. Or does he work for the Treasury? Either way, Britain is in safe hands.

Chapter 2

By nature, an auction is kind of a wholesale beast anyway.
—Paul Brown

Magic doesn't happen often – not once in a blue moon . . . I expect there isn't another magic ship like this one in the whole world.
—Hilda Lewis, *The Ship That Flew*

Delightful though the company of such students was, I cast around for some adult friendships – but initially without much success. Arriving at the same time as me were six other teachers, most of whom would later become firm friends, but at first it seemed as if this would not be the case. Several had young families and were torn away every spare minute by the demands of infants and spouses; one promising chap called Ross Bassenthwaite, a lanky Yorkshireman with a curt manner, seemed to disappear at every opportunity in his battered red panel wagon laden with climbing ropes, crampons and kayak paddles and return on Monday morning having circumnavigated Iceland in a bathtub or something. Being at that time without a car, I found myself maundering about the College on weekends on my own – on my own, that is, until I was taken under the wing of Mrs Pamela Pinkerton.

Mrs Pinkerton was married to Stanley Pinkerton, a school porter from Staffordshire of whose utterances I understood not one word. He was a friendly chap, often stopping in the midst of his duties for hours at a time to regale me with long, incomprehensible tales about ... well, I was never sure what. The Staffordshire accent is one of the thickest in Britain, making even Glaswegian sound as polished as Henry Higgins' shaving mirror, and Stan's conversation – in all likelihood about nothing more out of the ordinary than the ups and downs of his beloved Tottenham Hotspurs – could for all I know have been a treatise on the sex life of wood-voles. I would exclaim 'Gosh!' every few minutes and waggle my eyebrows in appreciation and even nod eagerly from time to time, wondering what exactly I was assenting to.

'Horrid door,' he'd say cheerily. 'Worrit garn a puff fleck, eh? Noah got the liddy sauerkraut, eh?'

'Absolutely!' I'd agree and then ask when he and his maintenance pals might get around to removing the five locked filing cabinets that took up most of my sitting room and had been there since I'd moved in six weeks previously.

'Ah,' Stan would say sagaciously and wink at me in a conspiratorial manner. 'Them lark hornets? Buzzard's not hoary boat cross-larks. Chizdee, eh? Chizdee artichoke.' And off he'd go, disappearing into the bowels of the College with a nod. Mentioning the filing cabinets or another job that demanded urgent attention was the only way to stem the flow; he'd invariably respond by remembering there was a kettle on somewhere that needed attending to.

Stan's wife Pamela, on the other hand, was of a different breed. She invited me over one Sunday afternoon to her spotless little apartment above the Sanatorium and plied me with pikelets and cream and slices of Victoria cake as light and tasteless as a bathroom sponge. We drank tea out of tinkling little cups, and I was asked to admire her collection of fine silver sugar tongs and porcelain cream jugs. She confided to me on that first Sunday a certain loneliness in her life at the College. Some of the other matrons were, well, salts-of-the-earth, no doubt, but regrettably ill-informed about matters of culture and art and the wider world beyond the College gates. She always kept an eye out for bachelor gentlemen arriving at the school who might need a little intelligent company, especially those from foreign lands. How she loved travel, she enthused, but Mr Pinkerton had never been one for travel, more one for the football and the lotto and a pint or two at the Black Lion most evenings.

I was her newest lifeline to a world beyond the duties of a College matron and was invited weekly to intimate tea parties for two. Each week, Mrs Pinkerton would endeavour to keep me there beyond the allotted hour by engaging me in conversation about Australia, and she clearly felt her questions had to be suitably sophisticated for an educated gentleman like myself. Thus, she would ask me things such as the population of South Australia (umm?) or the average income of blue-collar workers (er?) or who the current Leader of the Opposition was. 'Umm … Paul Keating?' I would hazard, and Mrs Pinkerton would say with mild surprise, 'I think he's your Prime Minister, dear. Isn't he? I'm sure he was on the news last night.' 'Harold Holt?' 'Dead and drowned these last twenty years, dear,' she'd say, offering me another piece of Battenberg cake scented with eau-de-cologne and possibly wondering if she'd picked the right bachelor for her project of cultural enrichment. Occasionally, to my relief, there would be a question about sailing on Sydney Harbour, to which I would respond with enthusiasm. And one brief enquiry about Australian birdlife had me happily launching into a paean of praise for the brilliance of firetail finches, the treasure-troves of satin bowerbirds and the rapturous mimicry of the lyrebird, and allowed me to perform my celebrated rollicking kookaburra impression – at least until Mrs Pinkerton remembered something that needed urgent attending to in the kitchen. But such opportunities were rare and I spent most of these interminable Sunday afternoon teas wondering how I could politely extract myself. I might never have succeeded in escaping were it not for the charity auction.

One afternoon, Mrs Pinkerton told me in a fit of pink delight that there was to be an auction at the Boathouse that evening, to raise funds for a local orphanage. She was terribly excited, as there were always some good bargains to be found – something to add to her collection of silver sugar tongs perhaps. In vain did I try to explain that I had never been to an auction before, that I wouldn't know the first thing about bidding. 'Then you shall watch and learn, young man,' she said firmly. 'I shall be right there to give you a few tips.'

She always managed to get a good bargain, she told me. Some of the choicest items I had seen in her parlour had been snapped up for a trifle at this annual event, in fact. It struck me that it might be a good opportunity to purchase a few ornaments to enliven the somewhat Spartan décor of the North Pole sitting room once those filing cabinets were removed. It was arranged. She would pick me up at seven and we would show the locals how it was done.

That evening, over a pre-auction sherry at the Boathouse, Mrs Pinkerton pointed out a shady character in a mothy fur coat and leather gloves. This man, Sideboard Sid, was renowned in the district as an unscrupulous antique dealer. An expert eye would allow him to bid aggressively for a number of treasures, knocking local well-wishers out of the running and getting things for much cheaper than they were worth. Sure enough, there he was now, turning over a few items on the table and feigning indifference. However, I saw his interest quicken infinitesimally over a battered but handsome silver cigarette box – before he caught me looking and tossed it back amid the clutter. Behind me, Mrs

Pinkerton radiated prim disapproval and semaphored with her eyebrows the iniquity of it all. It may have been the sherry, but I too caught myself flushing with indignation. This was meant to be a charity event, keeping the local orphans fed at nights. I thought I might give this man something to think about.

When the auction got underway, I displayed my ignorance of strategy by taking a front-row seat. Only when I glanced around and saw Mrs Pinkerton lurking in the shadows of the back row did I realise that hers was the spot for a serious bidder. Sideboard Sid had taken a canny position as well – halfway back and just a little over my left shoulder. Sure enough, as soon as the bidding got underway, I glanced over to see him flicking his gloves every now and then to bid on a particularly interesting item. In the first ten minutes he had won the bidding on at least six items and was looking smug. In the meantime, I had my eye on one or two lots of my own. There were a few bundles of silver-plated cutlery and bone-handled knives, a set of dinner plates gaily painted with nasturtiums and a charming little silver Viking ship: not real silver, of course – probably not even silver-plated, judging by its yellowing patina – but it reminded me irresistibly of just such a ship in a long-forgotten children's book from my childhood and I was determined to have it. There was also a rather splendid stuffed fox, which I thought might look sporting in my College digs and establish me as a would-be country squire.

As well as bidding for these items, I kept a weather eye on Sideboard Sid. In fact, once I had successfully purchased the ship, the dinner set and the fox, I decided that he needed a little competition. The next item he bid on was a pair of candlesticks in which I had no interest, but just as the auctioneer was going to award the purchase to Sid for a paltry five pounds I upped the bidding to ten. A furtive glance over my left shoulder showed that the raccoon-like scowl had deepened, but, sure enough, there came a flick of his fingers as he bid fifteen pounds.

'Twenty,' I bid, and there was a stir in the room.

'Twenty-five,' came back Sid.

'Thirty,' I said nonchalantly, giving the impression that both my funds and my expertise in candlesticks were fathomless. I could tell people were wondering who this stranger was in their midst – certainly someone in a very different league from the timid pensioners who made up most of the crowd. An anonymous viscount perhaps? An Australian cattle baron? A man of extravagant and refined tastes, it was certain – why, look how he had homed straight in on the stuffed fox.

'Thirty-five,' came through clenched teeth.

'Forty.' Tra-la-la ...

There was a long pause and I wondered if I had overplayed my hand. Perhaps the candlesticks would be mine after all. Never mind. I would find a place for them somewhere, perhaps to adorn the Blue Sitting Room in the east wing.

'Going, going ...'

'Forty-five!' – and a gasp susurrated through the crowd.

At that point, I shook my head and the auctioneer let it be known that the candlesticks had gone to the irritable gentleman in the fur coat. In the hiatus that followed, I caught the eye of Mrs Pinkerton and gave her a cheery wink. She dimpled back at me, and I felt a warm glow of pride. Sideboard Sid had got the candlesticks at nine times the price he'd expected to pay and the orphans would eat well for another week.

Three more times that evening I played the same game, conscious each time of Sideboard Sid grinding his teeth over my left shoulder as I hiked the bidding higher and higher. Indeed, after the third time, I rather fancied that I could read the man like a book, telling to within five pounds how much further he was likely to go. At any rate, I managed to bump up the bids to a substantial price each time, and each time the rascal found himself forking out treble or quadruple what he might otherwise have paid. The final item in the auction was none other than the silver cigarette case that I had seen Sid take such an interest in at the beginning of the evening. Sure enough, the bidding started high and fast, just over my left shoulder. I could practically hear the flap of leather gloves as each bid was made.

'Thirty,' called the auctioneer. 'I have thirty for this fine cigarette case.'

I lifted a hand surreptitiously in the time-honoured manner of a professional.

'Thirty-five,' called the auctioneer. 'Thank you, sir. Do I hear forty?'

A creak of gloves. 'Forty pounds, thank you, do I hear forty-five pounds?'

Flick. 'Forty-five pounds. Fifty, do I hear fifty?'

The room had fallen silent, apart from the eager crescendo of the auctioneer. I stared straight ahead, hardly daring to envisage the snarling, hollow-eyed face behind me.

Creak. 'Fifty!!'

And so it went on, the bidding signalled in strained silence, fifty-five, sixty, sixty-five, a bold leap up to seventy-five, quickly and smoothly topped by ninety. Ninety!

Now there really was a pause. I sat frozen, staring straight ahead, uneasy for the first time that I might be about to purchase a cigarette case I didn't want for a whacking ninety pounds. Perhaps I would take up smoking to make the purchase worthwhile.

'I have ninety pounds from the cattle baron in the front. Ninety pounds? Do I hear a bid? I have ninety pounds; do I hear a hundred?'

The auctioneer's eyes darted about the room, seeking that higher bid.

'No? Going, then to the young viscount with the stuffed fox, going, going ...'

His eyes flicked. 'We have a hundred! A hundred pounds! Do I hear a hundred and ten?'

As casually as I could, I signalled out. Let the Raccoon have the damn thing. A hundred pounds it would set him back, a hundred pounds rather than the expected thirty. And that would make him think twice about sliming along to charity events like this and besting the genteel amateurs. Ha! I turned in my seat to give my admirer in the back row the biggest thumbs-up yet and a wide, conspiratorial grin, just as the auctioneer declared the winner.

'So, sold for a magnificent hundred pounds,' cried the auctioneer to the applauding crowd, 'to the lady at the back.'

Lady ...?

I froze. There was no sign of Sideboard Sid – I later learnt that he had left some fifteen minutes earlier – but a tight-lipped Mrs Pinkerton was writing out a cheque with such quivering irritability that the pen must surely have gone right through the paper. The glance she shot at me was in no way mollified by my thumb still perkily aloft. With a visible effort, the venom of the glance melted to a merely hurt look, one more in sorrow than in anger. This was my gratitude for a month of afternoon teas, a month of pink iced cakes among the collectable silver, a month of proffered friendship. I was no better than the rest of her bachelor projects. I suspected – and was proven right in due course – that the Sunday invitations would cease forthwith and counted that not least among the gains from that night; in fact, it was almost up there with the stuffed fox.

*

As for the little silver Viking ship, that became the seed for something that was to sustain me throughout my time at Ellesmere. It started with Edwin Appleby, one of the first students to come to my attention. Edwin was a quiet, bespectacled Sixth Former, a skinny boy with fine hair and almost translucent skin who sang as a tenor in the Chapel Choir. He had on one or two occasions stopped after Evensong to chat about the evening's choral repertoire, and I had been pleased to find a fellow enthusiast for church music. He had stopped me one evening after the service and taken the trouble to show me something I otherwise would never have noticed, namely that each oaken hymn-board was carved with a wooden mouse, as was the large eagle-spread lectern in the centre aisle. I loved these little touches about Ellesmere; they added to the whimsical eccentricity of the place, so different from the bare utilitarian décor of the Adelaide college where I had started my teaching. He also pointed out the beautiful stained-glass window in the Lady Chapel where Saint Oswald was depicted robed in cerulean blue, his compliant raven held aloft on a raised wrist. I also became aware that he was a good friend to some of the junior boys in the school who appreciated the fact that he was one of the few seniors who didn't treat them as rodents that needed a dose of the hockey stick to keep them in their place.

A few weeks into term, I was approached by two such younger boys who marched straight up to me and said, 'Yes, please. We'd like to join the Philosophy Club. When is it on?'

I was puzzled. I wasn't running a Philosophy Club – perhaps, I suggested, there was some other teacher with a similar name who ran such a thing. The lads looked sceptical but wandered off. The next day, another trio of boys approached me and registered their interest in the Philosophy Club I was going to run. When I denied any knowledge of such a club, they assured me that Edwin Appleby in the Sixth Form had told them I was going to run a Philosophy Club and had urged them to come and see me. Again, I apologised but told them that there must be some mistake. Were they sure it wasn't Mr Mackenzie in the Design and Tech Department he was referring to? A glance among the trio spoke volumes about the likelihood of Mr Mackenzie running anything remotely philosophical. The only philosophies they heard expressed in the Design and Tech Department were generally accompanied by visual clues involving a mallet and chisel and were along the lines of what the Tory government could do with itself.

After several more approaches along similar lines, each delegation quoting Edwin Appleby as the source of this disinformation, I sought the Sixth Former out. 'Edwin,' I said. 'I'm a little puzzled. Students keep coming to me to ask if I'm going to start a Philosophy Club. They tell me you've been telling them so.'

'That's right,' said Edwin equably.

'But I've not mentioned anything like that to you, have I? My memory's not what it was, but I'm sure I would have remembered.'

'No,' said Edwin, 'but I knew you'd like to. Wouldn't you?'

'Well, er – yes, now I come to think of it, yes, I would. But that's not the point. How ...'

'So, I thought I'd get things started, sir. We meet tomorrow night in the North Pole flat, if that's okay with you. I've let the others know.'

And while I stood gaping and trying to think of some sort of lecture on the sin of presumptuousness, Edwin sauntered off

down the corridor, humming a Purcell anthem to himself. So, I ran a Philosophy Club.

Before the dozen or so students arrived that evening, I lit some candles and tried to make the sitting room look as much like a Cambridge don's study as possible, or what I fondly imagined such a venue to be. At the last minute, struck by inspiration, I placed the little silver Viking ship on the coffee table in the centre. This, I explained, was just like Skillibladnir, the ship of the Norse legends. It was made by the dwarves for the god Frey and could travel anywhere through time or space. Moreover, it was so finely constructed that it could fold up small enough to slip into a pocket. It seemed to me that this was an admirable symbol for philosophy; a vehicle to take us safely across the vast ocean of ideas, to the far reaches of enquiry, back in time to the beginnings of thought and out into the dark and starry spaces of wonder and surmise – and yet, it could fold away and tuck into the space between our ears, taking up no more room than a little model ship.

A corny idea, perhaps, but the boys took to it and named our group the Skillibladnir Club. Sessions always started with the lighting of the candles and each pupil lightly touching the gleaming sails of the little silver ship in our midst. These sessions were informal affairs and not held particularly regularly but for me were a source of great satisfaction and delight over the years. The Skillibladnir Club tended to attract those students who were a little at odds with the prevailing culture; daydreamers, oddballs, misfits and curious gentle souls. It was often astonishing the depth of ideas we covered. Indeed, I have found that fourteen- and fifteen-year-olds make some of the very best philosophers. No idea is yet stale to them. Rarely have they read existing theories and adopted them as dogma. In fact, I made a point of not overtly teaching past philosophers and their ideas. We would start with some idle question, often offered shyly and tentatively – something along the lines of whether what I saw as red – a strawberry, perhaps – was actually seen by someone else as blue or yellow, but because we both used the word 'red' we assumed we were experiencing the strawberry the same way. Something like this would lead to whole discussions of consciousness, sentience, the nature of perception, the reality or otherwise of the world, all couched in everyday language and peppered with concrete examples. This made for a far more fulfilling exercise than introducing time-worn philosophies and the esoteric language of the textbook.

On occasion, there would be an insight or a breakthrough in thought that was truly unique and brilliant. I remember one long evening of discussion in which we were debating whether something like the multiplication table was a real thing – that is, whether it had an existence independent of human thought. If every brain in the universe died out tomorrow, would the notion that three times four equalled twelve still in some way 'exist'? And would yellowness exist if every eye in the universe went blind or ceased to function? The debate raged fiercely as we all tried to claim some greater reality for certain elements of the world than others. 'What is more real? Irish stew, the number two or the colour blue?' as Edwin summed it up.

Round and round in circles we went, until a boy called Lewis, who had spent most of the evening staring hard into one of the candle flames, seemingly miles away, quietly offered this astonishing insight. 'I think the problem,' he said, 'is that the single word *exists* is inadequate. It's a bit like arguing endlessly over whether skateboarding is a sport when some of us define sport as having to be competitive, like sprinting, and others define sport as something that is simply skilful and active, like sailing, say, and others again say a sport has to have rules, like tennis or soccer. The one word *sport* isn't helpful in an argument like that. We can only start talking sensibly about skateboarding if we bring in other words, like *game* or *skill* or *pursuit*. In the same way, I think we really need three different words to use for the different ways things can – well, exist. So, let's make up three words, something like … I dunno … *physate*, *mentate* and *sensate*. Then we can say that an acorn or a rock or an atom or an x-ray or a bowl of Irish stew *physates*, because it has physical existence; it's made of atoms or energy and exists somewhere in time and space. And something like the number two or $E = mc^2$ or equality or fairness *mentates* – that is, it exists as a concept, quite free of matter, time and space. And finally, that something like the colour blue or the smell of mint or the sound of a French horn or the sensation of cold *sensates* – exists as a sensation attached to, but quite different from, the *physating* atoms of light waves and our optic nerves or neurons. How would that be?'

I think you will agree that for a fourteen-year-old such an insight into the power and usefulness of language – and its propensity to obscure or clarify an issue – was pretty impressive. And that is just one example of the many bold explorations we made in the little ship Skillibladnir on those evenings high up in the North Pole where the candle flames stood up pure and golden and warm and lit the thoughtful smiles and flashing eyes of young souls a-thinking the world into shape.

Chapter 3

'Destiny guides our fortunes more favourably than we could have expected. Look there, Sancho Panza, my friend, and see those thirty or so wild giants, with whom I intend to do battle . . .'

'What giants?' asked Sancho Panza.

'The ones you can see over there,' answered his master, 'with the huge arms, some of which are very nearly two leagues long.'

'Now look, your grace,' said Sancho, 'what you see over there aren't giants, but windmills, and what seems to be arms are just their sails, that go around in the wind and turn the millstone.'

'Obviously,' replied Don Quixote, 'you don't know much about adventures.'

—Miguel de Cervantes, *Don Quixote*

One of the students who made the greatest impression early on was, like me, a new arrival. Huw Davies had come from the Welsh valleys to start in Third Form, or Shell, as it was mysteriously called. (English private schools are full of such arcane slang. *Tell Davies, that pie-job in the Shell, he has to report to Biggers for a leftie.* That sort of thing. You get used to it.) He was a dark-haired boy with a white face, huge black eyes and the air of a border collie ready for adventure. In the very first week of term, I had cornered him and four other new students and asked if they wanted to help me explore some of the surrounding countryside that coming weekend. *Ooh, yes sir, thank you sir, we'd love to sir,* they chirruped like baby gerbils, but come that Sunday, all but young Huw had found better things to do. I assumed that Huw would also want to duck out of the prospect of a walk now that his friends had absconded, but he turned up after chapel in a pair of enormous boots, a poacher's jacket several times too large for him and a bundle of Ordnance Survey maps.

'I've had a look at the map, sir,' he said, 'and I think we could make it to Whittington Castle and back before lunch.'

'Good-oh,' I said breezily, 'I'll follow you.'

Three hours later, I was up to my knees in the cloying mud of a ploughed field and Whittington Castle for all I knew was still several leagues to the west. Huw, I had discovered, took an adventurous approach to rambling, choosing to use rabbit tracks, badger runs and holes in hedges rather than the well-marked footpaths that seam the English countryside. He was small and nimble enough to duck under barbed-wire fences, skim across soggy pastures and scramble through holly hedges like a graphite otter, and his sturdy poacher's jacket protected him from spikes, thorns and nettle stings. I, in contrast, felt about as agile as a Black Angus in gumboots and was frequently two hundred yards behind attempting to disentangle myself from a strand of barbed wire while Huw was perched cheerily on a distant stile calling out, 'This way, sir! Mind the nettles now!'

'We should be able to see the castle any minute now, sir. If only we could get up higher, isn't it?' Huw was lilting. 'Climb a tree, like.'

'My dear Huw, I seem unable even to move from this spot, let alone shinny up a tree. I'm stuck.'

It was true. Both boots had sunk deep into the winter mud and any move I made to extricate one foot simply sent the other gurgling deeper into the mire. Huw was dancing from tussock to tussock a few yards away, anxious to help but unable to get closer without risking getting stuck himself.

'Perhaps if I weave a rope, sir,' he suggested hopefully. 'Didn't they make hemp rope out of nettles, sir? In the olden days, sir?'

'I'm not sure we have time to set up a cottage industry, Huw.'

'Or how about carving some duckboards. I've got my Swiss Army knife with me, sir.' He pulled from one of a dozen pockets a shiny red knife.

'Again, dear chap, I don't think we have the requisite time. I've sunk another bloody three inches in the last minute.'

Perhaps it was hearing a teacher swear that did it, but as I watched, Huw's eyes opened wide in alarm and he started backing away. 'Hell's bells,' he said. 'Sorry, sir, but I need to find that tree!'

Now I really was cross. The boy had no sense of the urgency of the situation. Then, glancing over my shoulder at a strange whickering noise, I realised he had a better grasp of the situation than I had. Approaching rapidly from behind was the largest black stallion I have ever seen. It was coming at full gallop across the field, pausing now and then to rear up in a Hi-Yo Silver pose, scream defiance and thrash its forelegs around like a ninja helicopter.

Huw, all his Boy Scout instincts abandoned, was haring across the field to a lonely ash tree as I tried vainly to wrench a congealed foot from the fudge-like grip of the mud. Suddenly, I felt hot sulphurous breath on my neck and my collar seized in a mighty grip. A strangled glance over my wrenched-up shoulder revealed a set of teeth resembling an ancient piano keyboard and a pair of eyes red with imperious wrath. The stallion plucked me from the bog with one heave of its coal-black neck, shook me crossly as it trotted over to a nearby stile, and dumped me over the fence in a startled heap. Then it galloped off as sharply as it had appeared, presumably patrolling the boundaries of its domain to see if there was any further riffraff to be seen off the premises.

A few seconds later, Huw reappeared with eyes like saucers in his pale face. He picked me up, dusted me down, said 'Gosh' and 'Sorry, sir' a lot and in general behaved with the abject shame of a young squire who has just abandoned his knightly master at the first ford crossing. I eventually calmed him down by relating what I had seen in a glimpse while being tossed over the stile – namely, the tower of Whittington Castle rising above the landscape just three fields away. 'So, let's get on, young Huw, and hear no more about it.'

Huw glanced down, evidently still ashamed. 'But, sir—' he started.

'Now, now, none of that,' I said briskly. 'We're going to have to hurry. Lead the way.'

'It's just that . . .' he said.

'Yes?'

'Won't you be needing your boots?'

I, too, glanced down. Both boots were missing, left behind in the quagmire when the stallion had uprooted me.

'Ah, yes, quite. Good observation. Just duck over and fetch them for me, there's a good chap.'

And while my new squire trotted off to excavate my footwear from the bog, I sat down again and seriously started shaking.

*

On the way back, we paused for a breather in a little copse. Whittington Castle had been a charming place for a lunch-stop, a quiet ruin half surrounded by a ruffled moat where a swan couple drifted in silence in the winter sunshine. We had clambered over

the crumbling stonework and Huw had surprised me by producing a packet of squashed jam sandwiches from one of his countless pockets. 'I made enough for two, sir.' A nearby plaque announced that this castle had been the stronghold of one Fulke FitzWarren in the tenth century. Again, Huw seemed remarkably knowledgeable. 'A Robin Hood figure, he was, Mr Mackinnon. King John hit him with a chessboard, he did, when Fulke won the game they were playing – and the King banished him from his castle and took away his lands. But Fulke didn't give up, not a bit of it, sir. He rode around the land with his men, harrying the sheriff and the abbots and the King's men, and finally won his castle back.' As he chatted on happily of kings and knights and holy saints and noble outlaws, I pondered on the Welshman's natural love of story, romance and scholarship, harking back to a time before the uncouth Saxons had come tramping over the fields with axe and fire. If Huw was a taste of what was to come in the way of Ellesmere pupils, I suspected I would be happy here.

Now in the little copse, Huw left off being the dreamy poet and scholar and reverted to poacher mode with a thump. His eyes lit upon a number of pale ashen things lying in the undergrowth. Wood pigeons. Eleven of them, dead as dodos but evidently freshly slain. Huw picked one up and cradled it in his hands, trying to ascertain how it had died. He stroked the lovely dove-grey feathers and admired the purple-green sheen on the neck. Then his eyes lit up in holy delight. 'I've had a brilliant idea, sir! I'm taking four of these beauties back to school, sir, and I'll present them to Mr Pebmarsh. He can make a pigeon pie, sir! That will be a grand gift, won't it?'

I was none too sure about this. Mr Pebmarsh, Huw's housemaster, was a man I had then barely met but he had struck me as a neat, fastidious little man more at home in a library, museum or tea shop than as a putative poulterer. His closest connection to fowl was a tendency to turn turkey-cock red when affronted by a blotted textbook, dog-eared essay or slopped tea-saucer. With his immaculate suits and pernickety turn of phrase, I couldn't quite see him up to the elbows in pigeon feathers. Nevertheless, Huw could not be dissuaded from employing another four pockets of his jacket to carry four fat corpses, and we wound our way schoolwards, arriving home just as darkness fell.

It had been a delightful day, but after a long, hot bath, a stiff drink and a good night's sleep, the wood pigeons had faded from my mind. Until Morning Assembly, that is. After the usual business of assembly – announcements for the day, congratulations on a good start to the school year, commiserations for the loss of a rugby match against Grimslade – the otherwise genial Headmaster's voice took on a sterner note. He wished to invite Mr Pebmarsh up to the stage to talk about something very serious and most disappointing that had occurred over the weekend.

Mr Pebmarsh strutted up onto stage and from the way the hall fell silent I could gauge the nervousness of all present. I would learn later that Mr Pebmarsh was a brilliant teacher of History and high-achieving students considered themselves lucky to have him as their A-Level master. But his insistence on immaculate standards, his sharp tongue and his scathing wit put some of the more oafish offside, and there was that year an undercurrent of dislike from a small and boorish coterie among the students. Now, even these were silent as the little red-faced man strutted onto stage, lips pursed, looking angrier and icier than I have ever seen anyone look before or since.

Ten minutes the lecture lasted, ten minutes in a voice no louder than the hiss and sweep of a whip thong slithering across the floorboards before the deadly crack. It was difficult to believe, he said, that such uncivilised behaviour could exist in such a community – clashes of personalities between masters and students were, of course, inevitable, but one hoped one could always sort out differences with a civil word – that never in twenty years of dedicated service to Ellesmere had he been on the receiving end of death threats – impossible to believe that this outrage could be anything but some sort of sick threat – four bloodied and verminous corpses deposited on his doorstep overnight – a sickening and disturbing sight – immediate confession from the perpetrator or perpetrators expected – sad and sorry day . . . and so on.

No one dared move. But out of the corner of my eye, I could see Huw Davies, newest of new boys, shrinking, shrinking, shrinking inside his school blazer that was already two sizes too big for him, his face the colour of feta cheese and his dark eyes like saucers of watery ink. He was beginning to gulp and hiccup. Only his ears were red as maple leaves. Of course, he had not found Mr Pebmarsh at home the night before but had left the birds on the doorstep, confident in the obvious nature of the gift – plump fresh pigeons for the making of a good poultry pie. And had inadvertently started his school career by issuing a death threat to his housemaster. That and, for no apparent reason to anyone not in the know, suddenly vomiting unexpectedly all over the hall floorboards at the very first assembly of the new year.

Despite that shaky start, Huw went on to thrive at Ellesmere. Within weeks, he was establishing himself as a gentle eccentric who pursued his own quiet path, and he won the hearts of all who took the trouble to know him. A fortnight after the pigeon incident, a flagstaff appeared projecting out of a window high up on the third floor of the North Pole wing. Watchers below in the Quad would gaze in puzzlement as a green and white flag sporting the scarlet Welsh dragon would flutter up the flagstaff and back down again at intervals. Huw had contrived it such that every time someone opened and closed his study door, the flag would shoot up the pole and down again – Huw's quiet salute to his beloved Wales. Huw was one of the first to come to the newly formed Philosophy Club; indeed, in five years, he never missed a single session. Mind you, I don't think I ever heard him say a word either – he was content to sit and listen intently to the ideas sparkle and shift around him, gazing all the while at the flame of the candle that he always took upon himself to light to signify the start of the meeting. Then, at the end, he would always be the last to leave. He would snuff out the candle, thank me for the evening and invariably add, 'Interesting, all that,' before vanishing down the darkened corridors with his light poacher's tread. He took up very little room in the world, did Huw Davies.

Chapter 4

I know a bank where the wild thyme blows,
Where oxlips and the nodding violet grows,
Quite over-canopied with luscious woodbine,
With sweet musk-roses and with eglantine:
There sleeps Titania sometime of the night,
Lull'd in these flowers with dances and delight

—William Shakespeare,
A Midsummer Night's Dream

In later years, Huw joined the school's army cadets. As far as I know, he had not the slightest interest in things military but he loved the exercises that involved going out at night, heavily bedaubed with camouflage make-up, and seeing how close he could get to the enemy without being detected.

We later learnt that he would often sneak out of the boarding house on warm spring nights to do the same thing, except that his quarry was the badger cubs over in Bluebell Wood, or love-lorn hares leaping in the moonlight beyond the canal. He also took great pride in seeing just how close he could approach, undetected, groups of illicit smokers enjoying the privacy of the woods. On some nights he would lie for hours within a yard of them, hearing every word of gossip and intrigue before melting away again like a wood shadow, but never repeating a word later to show off his skill. For Huw, it was all about simply doing, never boasting of it – hence the anonymous pigeons left on Mr Pebmarsh's doorstep in that first week. And his love of woodcraft never left him. Many a night in spring or summer, Huw would trot off illicitly into the blue-silver-shadowed woods to snare a rabbit. This he would cook up over a little campfire, along with some carrots or onions filched from a farmer's field. As far as I know, he never bothered with the temptations explored by his cronies dotted about other parts of the woods, which must have made the bosky shadows seem like one of the more hectic scenes from *A Midsummer Night's Dream* – a gang of hardened smokers in that dell, a bottle of vodka being passed around down that thyme-wild bank, a couple of madly snogging Lysanders and their loves entwined like ivy under the chestnut trees. Huw was content to play a sober, watchful Oberon, a shadow of a different sort, and make love only to the rising morn.

Speaking of the *Dream*, this was one of the plays I directed while I was at Ellesmere, and possibly one of the most enjoyable productions I've ever overseen. It is best done out of doors, of course, but the date was set for February and even the hardiest of audiences would have baulked at sitting in the frost and frozen murk of a February day – so we staged it in the little school theatre. Determined to bring the freshness of a springtime wood to the stage, I bought out the Ellesmere florist's entire stock of violets, daffodils, jonquils, primroses and narcissi. These I bedded down in banks of moss and troughs of water, concealed between dozens of ancient hessian gym-mattresses that turned the bare boards of the theatre into a hummocky, humpy forest floor, perfect for the soft landings required by the gymnastics of the characters.

To make a gnarled forest tree, I tied three thick gymnasium climbing ropes, four long bands of hessian and a couple of lengths of camouflage netting from the lighting beams above the stage and then plaited them into a woven column to make the trunk.

Huw appeared at the last moment with a great swathe of ivy and a rambling rose, which we wrapped around the tree trunk to complete the picture. What with the banks of yellow daffodils and primroses, the scent of jonquils and violets and a vast painted background showing a pastoral scene under a sunset sky, the staging was the prettiest I have ever worked with.

The plaited tree had a special purpose. Before the show, the boy playing Puck, a superbly gymnastic – and somewhat stoic – student called Toby Larkin, would unwind the tree a little and then wind himself into it, like a mummy in a shroud. There he would stay motionless, disguised as an integral part of the tree trunk, throughout the first few scenes set at the Athenian court. Then when Puck first appeared, the audience was astonished to see a single arm shoot out of the twisted trunk – then a leg, then another arm, writhing as though an enchanted tree limb had come alive – and finally the entire goblin shape of Puck shake itself free from within the tree.

Even then, the audience rubbed their eyes at the strange, misshapen figure before them, a stunted bodiless head perched on two ungainly legs, for all the world like the Magic Pudding. As this odd creature waddled about the stage, it seemed to change and grow in alarming ways. Suddenly it was twice as tall, but still oddly deformed, its limbs misjointed. Finally, with a flourish, it would change for the last time – and there stood the impish, bulldog-featured Puck, human at last.

These remarkable transformations were the brainchild of Toby Larkin himself, aged all of thirteen. Not content with my simple idea of emerging from the tree trunk, Toby decided to do so bent double, with his bottom displayed to the audience. This was dressed with a goblin mask, so he looked for all the world like a mythical dwarf whose legs went all the way up to its chin. The next transformation was achieved merely by whisking the bottom mask away and standing upright, but still with his back to the audience. A similar goblin mask clapped to the back of his head fooled the audience that this creature was facing them – but with oh such oddly jointed limbs, all of which seemed to bend the wrong way. Finally, Toby simply stood upright, having discarded both masks, and showed his own face and stature. That this face of his was wonderfully goblinish itself, even off stage, was an extra bonus.

The whole production seemed to have an air of magic about it, but never more so than in the effect of that little western flower that causes all the mischief. In the play, Lysander is enchanted by means of this flower to dote hopelessly upon the maiden Helena, who wants nothing to do with him. In real life, Mungo, the handsome but very junior boy playing Lysander, fell madly in love with Briony, playing Helena. She was three years his senior and quite definitely out of his league – Mungo was thirteen at the time – but long after the play was over, the enchantment was still strong. Briony tried everything she could to shake her besotted Lysander from his purpose – kind words, strong words, forthright letters, threats to call in her pitchfork-wielding dad if he persisted – but nothing would break the spell.

In one unguarded moment, Briony gave out on the last day of the Lent term that she could only ever love a chap with a good singing voice, and as Mungo at best sounded like a strangled crow he must accept his lot and look elsewhere. Mungo was undaunted. Enter Huw Davies, with a lovely Welsh singing voice and similar enough in looks to Mungo to fool Briony on a night of half-moon at a distance. Mungo sent Briony a letter informing her that he had taken singing lessons over the holidays. Naturally, he wrote, he was a tad shy about showing off his newfound baritone to the other chaps for fear of ribbing but for her ... *ah, for her* ... he would risk anything. If she would look out of her second-storey window that night at midnight, he would prove the earnestness of his passion and serenade her in person.

Short-sighted Briony, flattered perhaps by this young squib's insistence, duly looked out that night to see Mungo in the moonlight below her window. After some initial whispered words of longing, he announced he would now sing her heart to his. A brief shuffle ensued as Mungo appeared to fall backwards into a nearby hedge, but soon he was on his feet again, a dark shape in the mazy moonlight, standing as tall as ever – even a fraction taller, if possible. Then the singing started, a throbbing melodious baritone. The music filled the night, woke several other girls from the surrounding dormitories and perhaps woke even Briony's cold heart to the possibilities of a fling with this romantic boy who was prepared to do anything. The only thing was … she couldn't understand a word of what was being sung.

Not surprising, really. In his haste to organise his Cyrano de Bergerac substitute, Mungo had failed to check what aria Huw might be singing. He never suspected it would be in pure Welsh.

Once the singing had stopped, Huw melted away into the darkness with his customary ease and Mungo stood forth again, waiting for Briony's reaction.

'Lovely song, Mungo. What was it all about though?'

'Um … Welsh. A love song. Yes, a love song.'

'Ooh, I'd love a translation.'

'Um … right, well, basically, um, it's … um … Your hair is like an ash grove, where blackbirds are singing and the bluebells of … um, Wales … will … get there before ye … For my love is like a red, red rose … for the sake of Auld Lang Syne … um … diddly-diddly aye. Sort of thing …'

Suspicion shivered in the moonlit air.

'So, you learnt singing and Welsh over the holidays, then?'

'Ah, yes, that's right, my bluebell …'

'Ooh, I love Welsh. Go on. Say something, Mungo, my love.'

Mungo knew the jig was up, but he would go down fighting.

'Um ... Abergavenny?'

There was a slamming of windows from above.

... pause ...

'Boyo?'

And the purple flower's spell was, perforce, laid to rest.

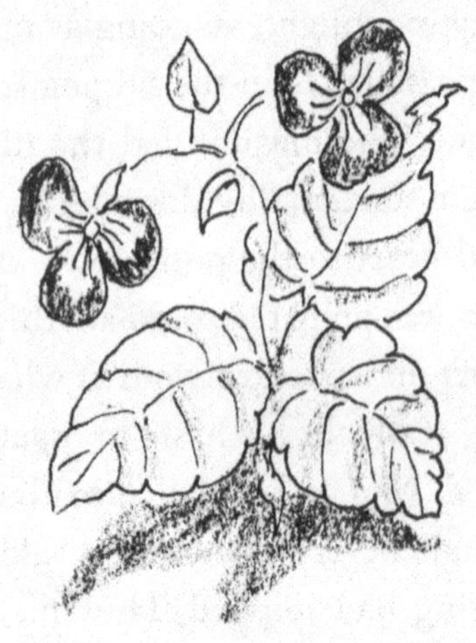

*

Private schools in England, confusingly called public schools, fall into two categories, major and minor, and even the staunchest fans of the place would admit that Ellesmere College fell firmly into the latter category. It sat a mile and a half from the little North Shropshire market town of Ellesmere, renowned for its sprinkling of lakes and meres in the nearby countryside, and very much a centre for canals and narrowboats. The College itself was set in spacious grounds surrounded by pastures where Friesian cows grazed placidly so that the faint tang of cow manure lay as a background perfume to all that went on there. The main building was a vast

H-shaped edifice of red brick, topped with slate roofs, ornamental pinnacles and clock towers, whose four storeys housed the four main boarding houses, a splendid chapel, a dining hall, Big School (the customary name for an assembly hall) and a warren of brick-lined passages and tunnels where a casually opened door might reveal anything from a morose blacksmith – Brian the Iron – to a faintly harassed Headmaster trying to placate the local bishop as to the choice of hymns for the upcoming Confirmation Service.

At that time, the College catered for about 450 students, mostly boys between the ages of eleven to eighteen. A cohort of around twenty girls in their A-Level years occupied a separate building, St Oswald's. It was a common custom at the time for all-boys' schools to take in a number of girls in their senior years as the first cautious step towards embracing the complexities of full co-education, often as a way of convincing the older members of the Common Room that their Latin classes would not be contaminated by such abominations as hair scrunchies or sanitary-pad disposal bins.

The College staff were mainly housed on campus, some in houses dotted around the site but single bachelors usually in small apartments in the main building, cheek by jowl with the boarders. The year I started, there had been a large influx of younger staff, mostly male, who were eyed with deep suspicion by some of the senior staff members, many of whom had been there for over thirty years. We were collectively called 'the Young Turks' – and it was widely thought that, as an Australian, I was most likely to be the rabble-rouser among them. Little did they know that I had spent my life wishing for nothing more than to live out the traditions of *Tom Brown's School Days* and had not the temperament for tearing down old, fossilised institutions.

For there was certainly an element of fossilisation in this place. David Du Croz, as a relatively new Headmaster, had his work cut out to bring the place out of the 1930s, which he did with a gentle manner that some mistook for insipidity. I have rarely met a more decent man, nor worked under someone so patient, kind and shrewd. He was nothing like his somewhat bombastic predecessor, and there were enough gown-clad, pipe-smoking old diehards on the staff to make his job an uphill struggle. The whole place was a parody of itself. At my Adelaide school some years earlier, I had directed the classic Whitehall farce *The Happiest Days of Your Life*, set in a stuffy, rundown boys' school in the '30s. I had deliberately dressed the Common Room set to be as fusty as possible: mustard-coloured hessian walls stained with pipe smoke, sagging leather armchairs, a moulting stag's head above the mantlepiece and pigeonholes bulging with dog-eared exam papers, confiscated cricket balls and the odd bottle of cheap whisky. To my astonishment, the Ellesmere College Common Room was identical.

But for all these anachronisms – or perhaps because of them – I found on the whole a very happy school where a relaxed attitude towards supervision allowed a cordial relationship between students and staff. Teachers were given free rein to pursue their own interests, so that at any time in the week a visitor might have witnessed a small group of boys being taught falconry behind the shooting range by the hawk-mad Mr Rufus, or learning the chemistry of vodka distillation from Stinky Gillespie behind closed doors in the labs, or marching off – armed with rifles – to a distant copse with Colonel Judd to recreate the Battle of the Bulge with live rounds and the odd grenade as a way of helping the old fellow relive his youth.

In fact, it was a place whose gentle chaos and lackadaisical approach to health and safety provided a rich humus where magic and enchantment could thrive.

And speaking of such things, there was of course the arrival of Jack de Crow.

Chapter 5

> *For there is an upstart crow, beautified with our feathers, that with his Tyger's heart wrap't in a Player's hide supposes he is as well able to bombast out a blank verse as the best of you.*
>
> —Robert Greene, *A Groatsworth of Wit*

From the moment I arrived at Ellesmere College, I was struck by the prevalence of the crow motif that imbued the place.* Six huge Scots pines at the front of the school were clamorous with rooks, every rooftop and gable chimed with the *chack-chack-chaow* of jackdaws, and a pair of murderous carrion crows patrolled the banks of Spyglass Hill behind the chemistry labs, on the lookout for an ailing lambkin or a poorly Shell weakling. Many people would find such a congregation of the *corvidae* menacing, but I have always loved these birds and the legends that surround them – the ravens in the Tower; the jackdaw of Rheims; the spymasters of Odin, Huginn and Muninn, who flew through the world on sable wings and reported back nightly to their master on all the doings of the world. The College itself celebrated its own crow legend, displaying in the chapel that beautiful stained-glass

* I have written of these things in an earlier book, but it now seems fitting to expand on the events surrounding the arrival of Jack de Crow into my life.

window depicting Saint Oswald, King of Northumbria, and the raven that returned his episcopal ring to him in the heat of battle, pointed out to me by the gentle and scholarly Edwin Appleby. Even the Headmaster's name, Du Croz, was pronounced *du crow.*

It was undoubtedly all this that helped form in my mind a daydream of a most unlikely and romantic sort, namely to own a tame crow. I saw myself in vivid detail cycling around the countryside, crow perched on my wrist or flying along overhead to be summoned by a whistle, or crossing the quadrangle on a night of storm and lightning bright, academic gown sweeping out behind me like an enchanter's cloak, calling my dark familiar to my outstretched hand. So vivid was this daydream in my mind that I had conjured up a name for the bird. The name was – wait for it – Jack Micawber Phalacrocorax Magister Mordicorvus de Crow. I'd even shared the name with Huw Davies, who was suitably impressed until he found out that this bird was merely a figment of my overactive imagination.

He was almost as surprised as I was when, two days later, Jack arrived.

By extraordinary coincidence, I had confided this daydream to an old friend of mine, a vet, who, the very next day, had come across a tame, slightly injured jackdaw on a farm in Worcestershire. As this bird had a tendency to scare the living daylights out of visitors to the farm by landing on their heads with a thump, the farmer had asked my friend to take it away before he wrung its bloody neck. Two days later, Jack was delivered to Ellesmere College in a box, and I found myself realising that daydreams can be awkward things if they come true.

For a start, Jack de Crow (as I called him for short) was by no means as tame at first in my company as he had been on the farm. When I released him from his box, he launched himself into the air and flapped frantically around my sitting room, depositing white splashes of fright with every wingbeat. He finally subsided in a panting bundle of soot on the top of the dresser, feathers awry and a look of panic in his eye. Several times he made for the window and dashed himself against the glass in an attempt to flee to the blackness beyond, and after the third attempt to concuss himself I grabbed him in a tea-towel and placed him safely inside his cardboard box. I realised then that I would have to spend the next few days – weeks? months? – keeping him confined until he became accustomed to my face, my voice, my smell.

Now it happened that a fellow new teacher, a soldierly chap called Michael Barton, was still waiting for his apartment to be completed by the school builders and had been billeted with me on a temporary basis in the meantime. It suited me to have good company, and Michael was certainly that: wry, sharp-witted and with the orderly mindset of a military man. I later came to know him as being almost obsessive about domestic tidiness and hygiene, but at that time I barely saw anything of him; we were both working hard during the day and Michael spent most extra-curricular hours visiting his wife and infant daughter, who were staying near Shrewsbury until the apartment was finished. Thus, Jack had been flying loose in my apartment for a whole weekend and I had not yet had the opportunity to warn Michael of our new avian flatmate when he returned unexpectedly one late Sunday afternoon.

Jack was loose in the sitting room and I was trying yet another dish to tempt him down to my hand. All weekend I had been trying various things – a plate of untouched cat food sat on the floor; half a loaf reduced to crumbs and soaked in egg yolks occupied the coffee table; and in the kitchenette, a tea caddy of live woodlice and spiders collected that afternoon sat on the draining board. Jack had turned up his little slaty bill at all these attempts. My latest idea was maggots, and I had just come back from town with a large

tub-full bought from the local fishing shop down by the canal.

I arrived to a disheartening sight. Jack, although still on hunger strike, had revived in spirits sufficiently to occupy himself during my absence with attempting to singlehandedly disembowel the stuffed fox in pride of place atop the dresser. How he had gone about this I do not know; all I know is that Jack was perched triumphantly on the fox's scalp and the sleek russet fur of Reynard now sprouted a strange fungus resembling the tufts of spotted hair on an ailing hyena. Jack had presumably stabbed through the skin and attempted to pluck the yellowed stuffing out from within. Moreover, a glass eye had been half-wrenched from its socket and now stared crazily at the ceiling, and a foreleg, always a little fragile, had given way completely so that the whole beast lurched sharply to one side.

Not content with subduing the stuffed fox, Jack had also taken issue with the sofa cushions and had demolished several of these; duck down drifted across the room in swathes and billows. Something about this exercise had clearly loosened the jackdaw's bowels, because the whole place smelt of guano, even above the familiar odour of rancid cat food.

I had only a moment to take this all in, standing there with the tub of maggots in my hand, before I heard the familiar smart *tap-tap* of Michael coming up the stairs at his usual headlong trot.

'Mackinnon? You there? I'd like to introduce—'

'Don't open the door!' But it was too late.

'Christ!' he exclaimed as he burst in. 'Have we been burgled? And what happened to the fox?'

Before I could explain, a dark shadow swept down from the curtain rail and with a shrill *cha-cha-a-ark*, swooped low over Michael's head as it made for the open doorway. 'Christ!' yelped Michael again, arms up to shield his eyes, and stepped backwards into the dish of cat food.

It was fortunate, I suppose, that as he stumbled backwards he fell safely enough onto the sofa, disappearing gently into a cloud of loose feathers. Less fortunate was the fact that, as I now noticed, the whole headrest of the sofa resembled the Cuillin Hills after the first light fall of winter snows. Ah. Here was the source of the guano smell, hitherto hidden by the dusting of white feathers. When Michael sat forwards again, the back of his head was plastered with creamy white streaked with yellow and grey, and loose feathers were adhering to the nape of his neck like the plumy ruff of some exotic waterfowl.

'What the fuck was that?' he cried, swiping at his neck and trying to dislodge lumps of congealing cat food from his polished brogues. But I had other things to worry about. In a lunge to slam the sitting-room door before Jack could escape, I had abandoned the tub in my hands and now there was a writhing heap of yellow maggots in the middle of the floor. Already, some were making a spirited dash for freedom and several had already vanished under the sofa. Others were humping their way across the carpet at surprising speed and beginning to vanish into cracks in the wainscoting. In the meantime, Jack was circling the lightshade like a demented bat, sending confusing shadows whirling about the room like a pandemonium of devils newly escaped from Pandora's box.

'Christ!' intoned Michael.

'Er, sorry about this.'

'I've got Donna outside. And in here, you've got ...'

But I never did find out how he was going to describe the carnage. There was a *yoo-hoo* and the door was pushed open. In stepped a tall woman, beautifully dressed.

'Shut the door!' Michael and I roared in unison, but Donna barely flinched. She calmly reached behind her and pushed the door shut. Jack, feeling outnumbered perhaps, ceased his panicky gyrating and flew to his perch on the ravaged fox's scalp. Now with one damaged leg unable to support it properly, the fox toppled slowly and somersaulted to the floor with a thud. Several maggots changed direction at yet another gift of carrion falling from the heavens.

Michael's wife seemed unruffled by the state of the room. 'So you must be Sandy. Michael has told me so much about you. I'm Donna.'

Then she sat down carefully with great poise in a cleanish chair and held out a welcoming finger to Jack. 'He never mentioned this charming jackdaw, though.' And at that, she picked up a passing maggot and held it out for Jack, who accepted it with a gracious nibble and a pleased *chac-chaw*. 'And a stuffed hyena? How unusual.'

I did not make the best of first impressions, crawling across the carpet to sweep up absconding maggots and return them to the tub. It was a hopeless task. The floor was now off-white with the creatures, all swarming at a speed that was astonishing for creatures as legless as jellybeans in sleeping bags. It was Donna who came up with a solution. She went to my desk, rummaged around for a glue stick, took a wodge of tissues from her handbag and smeared them liberally with glue and then – dab, dab, dab – lightly blotted all the maggots up from the carpet in a sticky mess and handed the captive mass to Michael to flush down the loo. Three repeats later and the last of them had either been dispatched or vanished into the ancient wainscoting. Soon Michael had managed to clean up himself, his shoes and the sofa with a similar application of tissues. All that remained was to put the kettle on for a pot of tea to accompany the homemade chocolate brownies that Donna now produced.

'You two stay here,' offered Michael, 'and I'll make the tea.' He stalked out, scowling around the room and giving his foot one last cat-like shake.

Donna smiled at me. 'He does so hate mess. I'm sure it's not usually like this. It's very good of you to put him up like this until the flat's ready. And it's good for him to cope with a little mess now and then, now that Bess is on the scene. Children aren't naturally tidy.'

Already I liked Donna. She seemed a calmer, softer counterpoint to Michael's military temperament. She also seemed genuinely interested in Jack. 'What is he feeding on?' she asked.

'Well, as you can see – and smell – I've tried cat food, and the maggots were the latest experiment.'

There were homely sounds coming from the kitchenette. The kettle being boiled, china mugs being placed on a tray, the clink of a teapot fetched down from its shelf. Teaspoons. Tea. The gentle grunt as Michael struggled with the too tight lid of the old tea caddy.

'You should try woodlice,' Donna said. 'Jackdaws adore them.'

'Oh, I have though. They're …' I paused, remembering. 'Oh Christmas, excuse me!'

I headed for the door. Too late.

'CHRIST! Not again!'

There was the clang of the caddy hitting the floor – 'more fucking wildlife!' – and Michael danced back into the sitting room swatting woodlice and spiders from his shirtfront. I was quicker this time. I deftly removed the cat-food saucer from under his stomping foot and Donna dug into her bag for another wodge of tissues.

'Glue again?' I asked.

'Glue again,' she replied and went to help Michael remove most of his clothes and shake them free of the cascade of arthropods.

But Donna was right. Jack, his appetite whetted by all this excitement, or perhaps by his resounding victory over the fox, descended to the floor and pecked and hopped, waddled and pounced, snapping up woodlice and spiders by the beakful. Soon he was back on the top of the dresser, happier than I had seen him yet. Perhaps it was the bountiful supply of edible wildlife, perhaps it was seeing the mischief and mayhem his presence could wreak in a single afternoon; whatever the case, Jack de Crow was happily ensconced in his new home.

(I should add here that after this inauspicious start Michael and Donna became my very best friends at Ellesmere. Donna was gracious, warm and intelligent and Michael, when not under attack from homicidal crows, proved to be good-humoured and hospitable in the extreme. Once ensconced in their own apartment, the family had me round for dinner or drinks far more often than I deserved. I watched young Bess grow into a lively, cheeky girl, soon to be joined by a little brother, Seb, a golden-haired baby whom I am proud to call godson. I might have somewhat taken the family's hospitality for granted. One evening I turned up for an impromptu visit and the door was answered by Bess, then about five years old. I heard Donna call out, 'Who is it, Bess?' Back came the reply, 'Oh just Sandy again, begging for food.' A very red-faced Donna and Michael hastily appeared to reassure me that Bess had certainly not picked up that particular phrase from them – but I did try to limit my visits after that, especially around mealtimes, to just once a week.)

In the meantime, Jack was a daydream come to life, but it must be confessed that the reality was sometimes less comfortable than the dream. Although he came to live out my fantasy by responding to my call and spiralling down out of the sky to perch on my outstretched arm, he also had a disconcerting habit of waddling up my arm, nibbling gently at my earlobe and then, without warning, pecking straight into my ear with considerable force as though spying a particularly delectable morsel buried deep within. On one occasion, he lodged a small acorn deep into my inner ear and it took a trip to Sick Bay and some handy work by Matron with a pair of tweezers to remove the item.

Jack also had a dreadful habit, shared by all the *corvidae* tribe, of stealing anything bright, glittery, gleaming or – in Jack's case – papery. Within the first few weeks, the housemaster under whom I worked lost a gold fountain pen and his car keys. He also severely reprimanded his seven-year-old daughter for having played with her mummy's jewellery – this after several stern warnings that this was not to happen – and only later believed her tearful protestations of innocence when he witnessed Jack sitting on his wife's dressing table rifling through her jewellery case and making off with a pair of ruby earrings. These were never recovered. The Director of Studies, a large, bearded man with all the natural sweetness of a gout-inflicted grizzly bear, came to inform me testily that Jack had been responsible for demolishing an entire set of mock exam papers sitting on his desk, reducing them to so much papery straw. The P.E. Master told me of his exasperation when an important hockey match was delayed when Jack insisted on swooping on the ball and picking all the stitches out of it mid-game. Any attempts by the players to shoo him away with a hockey stick simply had him fluttering aside only to land once more and continue with his unpicking.

On one occasion, Jack de Crow split the Common Room neatly down the centre. Our hall was hired out on occasions to the local Freemasons. Half the staff held this group in the deepest suspicion, accusing them of nepotism, high-level corruption and, in their secret rituals, something bordering on Satanism. The rest of the staff were either Freemasons themselves or agnostically practical and grateful for the funds the cost of hiring the hall brought to the coffers. On the occasion of the meeting, the Grand Master, or whatever he is called, stepped out of the hall after the ceremony into the open air and Jack promptly landed on his head, confirming for all the protestors that here indeed was proof that the school hall was being used for the Dark Arts. From that time on, the Freemasons were asked to convene elsewhere.

Unfortunately, Jack seemed to delight in tormenting Mr Pebmarsh in particular. Mr Pebmarsh lived high up in an apartment of the North Pole wing, and for some reason Jack chose his bedroom window as a favourite pre-dawn perch. There he would sit at about five in the morning and peck a rapid tattoo on the window pane, arousing Mr Pebmarsh from slumber. In vain would Mr Pebmarsh open the window to shoo the wretched bird away. Jack would simply topple off the sill, execute a graceful plunge and upward swoop through the quadrangle and return to the sill to continue his wake-up-call duties. Extraordinarily, Jack also especially sought out Mr Pebmarsh's classroom window to perform the same trick. The steadiness, industry and sobriety of many a history lesson, of which Mr Pebmarsh was rightly proud, would be sabotaged by the cheeky Jack tapping on the window and uttering his ringing *chac-chaow* every few minutes, delighting the pupils within but rendering Mr Pebmarsh apoplectic.

In the end, Jack's only remaining fans were the laundry ladies, the saintly Headmaster and his wife – flattered by the pun on their surname, perhaps – and myself. Indeed, it soon got around that several teachers had put a hefty price on Jack's head, and when I caught one student pursuing Jack down a corridor with a tennis racket in hand, he informed me that he was merely trying to claim the five-pound reward offered by Mr Pamirs for Jack's corpse.

There came a day when Jack no longer seemed to be around. Several wagers were laid by some of my more disgruntled colleagues as to the fate of the creature. Attached to a brick now resting at the bottom of Top Pond was one supposition. Plastered to the front wheel of Mr Pebmarsh's Volvo perhaps. Heartily strangled by the Director of Studies and fed to his cat? No one seemed to know for sure. But over the next few months, the laundry ladies would tell me of a tame jackdaw that had been seen strutting about the playground of the primary school over Tetchill way, or further afield near Oswestry. A pearl brooch had been snatched from a lady's coat in the beer garden at the Cross Foxes. A spate of petty pilfering had broken out in Welsh Frankton. Who knows? But Jack's memory lingered on among the rooftops of the College, the pine-tree hollows stuffed with shredded exam papers and Mr Pebmarsh's habit of flinching wildly at shadows that took him more than several years to shake off. And much later, before I left the College, Jack de Crow's name was gloriously revived in a double reincarnation that would allow him to become, if not immortal exactly, a particularly long-lived specimen of the jackdaw tribe. But for now, that was far in the future and there are other enchantments of which to write.

Chapter 6

There's a breathless hush in the Close to-night –
Ten to make and the match to win –
A bumping pitch and a blinding light,
An hour to play, and the last man in.
And it's not for the sake of a ribboned coat.
Or the selfish hope of a season's fame,
But his captain's hand on his shoulder smote –
'Play up! Play up! and play the game!'
—Sir Henry Newbolt, 'Vitai Lampada'

One of my colleagues – the Head of English in fact – was a tall man called Felix Arne. Felix had all the lazy grace of a panther on a long weekend. He was sophisticated, erudite, amusing … and somewhat disdainful of those members of the Common Room, and there were many like this, who tended to run up and down the sidelines in rugby matches bellowing imprecations at butter-fingered Third-Formers. The nearest Felix got to the playing field was in a spot of cricket umpiring in a linen jacket, a Panama hat and – if he could get away with it – in a deckchair. I liked Felix immensely but was rather in awe of him for various reasons. In one of our English meetings early on, Felix was explaining to me what I should be teaching my junior classes. As he ticked off various items on the list he had handed me – *figures of speech, verse forms, alliteration and assonance, of course – Manly*

Hopkins is the best poet for that, you'll agree – oh yes, metaphor, simile, ogzimmeron – all the basic stuff – I inwardly quavered. *Ogzimmeron*? What the blazes was *ogzimmeron*?! I was meant to know this stuff.

Felix must have sensed my doubt. 'Ogzimmeron? Fourth from the bottom. On the list,' he pointed out kindly. I scanned the sheet in front of me. Fourth from the bottom. Hang on. 'Oxymoron.' The penny dropped. I sighed with relief. I knew what 'oxymoron' was, of course – the poetic use of contradictory terms for effect, such as 'cold fire', 'brawling love' ... or 'uneducated English teacher', for that matter. So, I could teach it all right. The problem was that all my life I had been pronouncing it incorrectly. Like the uncouth ocker Adelaide boy I was, I had grown up pronouncing the word to rhyme with 'lock-si-door-on' and only now had learnt the correct, proper, Oxford-educated way of saying the damn word. '*Oxymoron* ... to rhyme with *shimmerin*.' I blushed at my ignorance and wondered how many other shameful gaps in my education would be brought to light by Felix's erudition.

It was only after three years of dutifully teaching the students under my care the correct pronunciation of *oxymoron* – 'Yes, boys. It's spelt like that but it sounds like *ogzimmeron* ... rhymes with *shimmerin*, and don't let anyone tell you otherwise' – that I overheard Felix tossing off the strange terms 'di-alla-goo' and 'apper-strofes'.

Again, Felix must have sensed my faint tremor of alarm at yet another couple of unfamiliar terms. 'Yes, dear boy. Die-aller-goo. Apper-strofes ... and remembering not to put the um-farcies on the wrong suh-larbel.'

Good God. I didn't know any of this stuff! So much for an Australian education. I certainly hadn't been teaching any of this high-falutin' Greek rhetoric stuff over the last few years, and it was probably going to be in the exams. All I'd been doing was bloody apostrophes …

Oh, hang on. Apostrophes. Ap-o-strophes. Apper-strofes. Di-aller-goo? Dialogue.

Felix had been playfully putting the emphasis on the wrong syllable … or – I groaned – the 'um-farcies on the wrong suh-larbel', as he had just put it. I breathed a sigh of relief, and it was only much later that night that I sat up in bed with a sudden realisation. He'd been playing with mispronouncing technical words for years, starting with those 'ogzimmerons'! There is now a whole cohort of boys from a small backwater of Shropshire who have been mispronouncing 'oxymoron' for years now. And no doubt, on discovering the fact in later years, blaming it on that Australian teacher who didn't even know the basics of the English language. Plaguey idiot …

Poxy moron, even …

*

It will come as no surprise to my readers that when it comes to any form of competitive sport, my heart really isn't in it. Early exposure to P.E. teachers whose knuckles scraped the ground and whose loftiest ideal of teaching ball skills was to throw medicine balls heftily at my chest as an eleven-year-old and go 'hur hur hur' when I toppled winded to the ground – extra points for knocking over the Headmaster's wimpish son – had left me incapable of taking the slightest interest in any of the manly sports espoused by the British education system. I had, it is true, been forced to participate in rugby by my father who, as both the Headmaster of the school and the sole rugby coach, had some considerable sway in the matter. This team was cobbled together by my father as a way of mopping up all the boys who for various reasons were unsuitable for the rigours and fanaticism of Australian Rules football. These reasons included morbid obesity, mental frailty, incurable aversion to physical exertion or, in my case, simple lack of enthusiasm for ballgames. As such, we were a ragtag crew who never won a single match. My dad nevertheless trotted up and down the sidelines week in, week out, exhorting us to tackle, scrum up, pass the ball, go wide and occasionally fling ourselves tactically to the ground and shield the ball with our bodies so a ruck could form – and tried not to let his exasperation boil over when any of us observed how unpleasantly wet and muddy underfoot it all was. I still remember the expression on his face when Ormsby (the only team member with any physical talent for the game, but also an alarming shortage of brain cells), was well on his way to scoring the first and only try in the team's history . . . but stopped to pat a rather adorable Labrador on the sidelines that had caught his eye as he was sprinting for the line.

It didn't help, I suppose, that his own son could frequently be observed trying out a new Monty Python routine with his like-minded pal Tim Leckie while the ball went by unheeded. Trips home in the car after matches were frequently characterised by silence – apart from the occasional dreamy observation from me about how very spectacular the clouds had been that afternoon. 'Did you notice, Dad? There was one huge white one like a castle – and another that looked exactly like a unicorn. You get such a good view from a playing field, don't you?'

All of which goes to explain that much as I love the schoolmaster's life, one of the elements that enthuses me less is the compulsory coaching of sports expected of all staff. In my first Lent term at Ellesmere, I was drafted to coach rugby – in an effort to appear willing, I had explained to the Master-in-Charge of Rugby that yes, I had indeed dallied with the game in my youth.

Fortunately, there were enough staff with a genuine enthusiasm for the mud, the grunting and the icy sleet of a February afternoon to coach the major teams, but there was also a small cohort of talentless boys who made up the Under XIV Fifths and had the dubious privilege of having me as their coach. In the first session, things went rather swimmingly, I thought. It was mercifully a bright autumn day with snowy clouds gathering in a crisp pale sky. With vague memories of Dad's coaching techniques, I got all the boys to warm up by trotting around the field several times. I also taught them a few techniques for passing a ball – you sort of swing your arms and let go – and I also remembered my father's advice about catching a ball by clutching it to your chest. All well so far. Then there was scrum practice and line-out drill. I really was quite surprised by how much was coming back to me. Finally, we started to put it all together. I got them lined up at one end of the field, handed the ball to a bushy-tailed lad at one end of the line and instructed the squad to run the length of the field, all spread out, passing the ball to each other down the line. Dad would be so impressed.

Off they went and my careful coaching seemed to have paid off. The ball glided effortlessly from one boy to the other, all the way down the line and back again. Just one thing puzzled me.

'Okay, lads, gather round, gather round. Look, well done. Good passing. Watkins, remember to use both hands – and, Puckeridge, no need for the victory dance after each catch.

But boys, boys, boys,' I sighed with mild exasperation at the perverse illogicality of thirteen-year-old boys. Still, I was here to set them right. 'Boys, boys, boys,' I repeated, 'it's no good passing the ball backwards, is it? That makes no sense at all. Now let's try that again – and properly this time.'

It was some time before I worked out why I so completely and suddenly lost the confidence of every lad there – apart from Winterbottom, of course, who hadn't heard a word I said, gazing dreamily as he was at the huge white unicorn in the sky.

*

Word must have got back to the Master-in-Charge of Rugby because shortly afterwards I was relieved of my coaching duties and handed over to cross-country running. This was difficult to muck up and afforded me many delightful opportunities to explore the lanes, woods and fields around the College and add a few new birds to my list – redwings, fieldfares and a bunting or two, spotted in the bare purple hedgerows that fenced in every narrow laneway.

But when the summer term rolled around, I was approached by the Master-in-Charge of Cricket, a wizened chap called Ernest Wimborne, who lived and breathed the sport. He was delighted to have an Aussie on the staff – he pronounced Aussie to rhyme with 'horsey' – as he was convinced that every one of my compatriots was born in cricket pads and spent each waking moment lobbing a cricket ball hither and thither, knocking koalas out of the local coolibah trees and into nearby billabongs with the force of their delivery.

'Splendid,' he said, as he bought me a pint in the Common Room bar. 'An Orsey! We'll have you coaching the First XI and give St Edmund's a run for their money this year. Bonza, as I think you Orsies say, what!'

In vain did I try to explain that I had all the cricketing expertise of a Swedish lemming. 'Oh, you Orsies! That dry sardonic sense of humour. Crocodile Dundee to a tee! I'll put you down to umpire the Cheltenham match next Saturday. Drink up, cobber, and get another pint inside you. I expect you'd prefer a stubbie.'

I soon found to my horror that he really had put me down for umpiring a major match at Cheltenham College that weekend. In vain did I plead my ignorance as I boarded the coach. In vain did I try to tell anyone who would listen that I seriously knew not the slightest thing about the game. In my youth, cricket had been simply a terrifying and mystifying pastime; on the few occasions I had been forced to play, the only aim of the game I could see involved the bowler trying to concuss the Headmaster's offspring with a hard red ball hurled at lethal speeds in the direction of his head.

Finally, in the last few miles before arriving at Cheltenham College, I managed to persuade a senior student called Chadwick sitting next to me on the bus that I really needed to learn some of the rules of cricket in a hurry.

'Well,' Chadwick started doubtfully. 'I wouldn't give LBW too often ...' he said tentatively. 'Of course—'

'Stop right there,' I said, holding up a hand and allowing some calm desperation to pervade my voice. 'Understand me very clearly, Chadwick. Let me put it this way. Tell me, how much do you know about training armadillos to perform Olympic diving?'

'What? Er ... nothing, sir. Umm ...'

'So, if you wanted to learn from scratch … and you only had twenty minutes to master the art … and you asked me to teach you, you'd be a bit put off if I started with some obscure acronymic advice such as "Try to avoid an ASD in the first trimester," wouldn't you?'

'ASD?' Chadwick realised he was a little out of his depth.

'Armadillo Swan Dive. Not important. Concentrate.' I looked him hard in the eye. 'You need to start from the very beginning. I have never played cricket. Ever.'

Chadwick looked bewildered. 'But you are Australian, aren't you? Don Bradman and all that.'

'Pretend I am American. Start from scratch.'

'Well,' he said, taking a wary breath. 'Every over has six balls, of course.'

'Simpler still.'

Finally, Chadwick got the message. As the coach rolled into the outskirts of Cheltenham, I received what was possibly the quickest and most comprehensive rundown of the rules of cricket ever delivered. I listened intently and with increasing astonishment at the sheer complexity of the game. As the coach pulled up beside the elm-lined ovals of Cheltenham College, Chadwick rounded the explanation off. 'And so, when the final batsman is either run out or bowled out or gets LBW—'

'Leg before wicket,' I chimed in proudly. 'To be given only sparingly. Got it.'

'Well done, sir – then the team with the most runs is declared the winner. And I think that's covered everything.'

'Goodness gracious me,' I said admiringly. 'Astonishing! And to think, they do all that on horseback?'

'What? No, no …' The startled look on his face was worth it.

'Only kidding. An old joke I heard on Michael Parkinson once. Never mind. Thanks. Now to put the damn thing into practice.'

And so it was that I umpired my first cricket match on the hallowed fields of the stately Cheltenham College, regency jewel among the Greater Public School set, and somehow got away with it. True, there was an awkward moment when I was so intent on identifying a green woodpecker flying from elm to elm – that characteristic bounding flight – that I couldn't respond as confidently as I might have to a distant 'Howzat?!' from the lad bowling at the time. I opted for caution, gave a 'not out' signal – to a few low growls of discontent from the Cheltenham crew – and the game went on.

Forever, it seemed. I think a game badly thought out if it involves standing for up to ten hours in motionless solitude in the middle of a wide-open field in the blazing summer sun. A game like that, I submit, lacks a certain snap, a certain zinginess of forward momentum – or so at least I came to believe over the next eight umpiring engagements that followed over the ensuing weeks.

One thing I definitely learnt was that a quick game is a good game, and I soon abandoned the caution urged on me by Chadwick about employing the LBW rule. As time went on, in fact, my decisions were made less on any fine Wisden-esque judgement of ball-play than with the sole aim of getting a whole side briskly out before afternoon tea so we could toddle off home. In fact, so heartily sick of umpiring did I get that I used to stand and fervently pray for a miracle shower of rain or a lightning strike to call off the match.

And then, finally, my prayer for a heaven-sent miracle was granted in a rather strange way. It was the final match of the season and was being played at Rhyll College, a grim Welsh school set on a clifftop above the Irish Sea. It was all the grimmer that day because autumn was nearly upon us and the weather had turned grey and louring, with a bitter wind whistling off the scudding sea. A few windblown gulls hung above us in the fitful sky but they were just ordinary herring gulls – nothing like a rare kittiwake or fulmar to distract me from the endless tedium of a game that had already been going for several decades. I was frozen to the bone, leg-weary and bored witless – and the blasted match showed no sign of ending. The Ellesmere side were in and were chasing 97 runs by the impressive Welsh side. Pritchard and Pratt were our last two batsmen, passionate about the game and doggedly making up for the lacklustre performance of our previous nine men. Neither of them was a fan of mine; I think they knew me for an impostor when it came to umpiring. But for all their dour cow-like stolidity, they seemed to be unshakeable. In vain did the Rhyll bowler try to knock the bails off the stumps; each time, Pritchard or Pratt drove the ball into a distant clump of rhododendrons from which it seemed to take an inordinate time to be retrieved by a trio of junior boys – and another four runs were gained.

I clearly wasn't the only one wishing the game over. Some of the Rhyll fielders had started shouting out a half-hearted and spurious 'Howzat?!' from time to time with no clear reason why it would be granted.

And yet the game slogged on, the wind growing icier, the daylight fading to murky grey – and still our last two batsmen held their ground, creeping towards the desired number of runs needed to secure the match. 'God,' I prayed under my breath, 'for the love of Moses, let this game end before I die of exposure … or old age. You're in the miracle line, aren't you?' I muttered. 'Plagues of frogs, loaves and fishes, that sort of thing. Lightning bolts from the sky. Anything!' I hunched deeper into my jumper.

Suddenly, from the depths of my misery, I was aware of a 'Howzat?!' from the Rhyll wicketkeeper – not one of the half-hearted expressions we'd been having at intervals, but one with a ring of surprised conviction. I snapped to attention. What? Where?

The wicketkeeper was pointing at the ground near the stumps, and, sure enough, the bails were lying on the ground. 'Howzat??' he called again.

I was puzzled. I was certain the ball had gone nowhere near the stumps. It was once again sailing the hundred yards to its accustomed home among the sodden rhododendrons where the retrieval party had now set up a permanent camp and appeared to be toasting crumpets on a modest fire. But indisputably the bails were off.

I approached to have a closer look and found the evidence of my desired miracle. Lying on the ground near the dislodged bails was a small silver herring, flapping intermittently at the indignity of finding itself hoicked out of its native element by a compliant deity. And in its fall, it had dislodged the bails. Glancing up, I saw a possible explanation. Two or three herring gulls were wheeling and squabbling above me; one of them even had a small fish of its own wedged in its bill while the other two were attempting to force it to drop its piscine prize. Such might have been the case with the flapping herring on the pitch.

A veritable miracle. That old classic, in fact – a shower of fish! Well, fish singular rather than fish plural, but who's counting: a miracle is a miracle. Even with only seven runs to win the game for Ellesmere, it was an easy decision. A ball had been bowled. The bails had been dislodged. The rules were hazy on the legitimacy of aquatic interference, so the umpire's judgement was called for.

'Out!' I called – and to the glowering Pritchard and Pratt, who questioned me with a hostile look, I gave a calm, dignified – and hastily improvised – explanation. 'Australian regulations. Bradman vs. Stockwell. 1953. Ask Mr Wimborne. Hard luck.'

They must have done so. A few evenings later, I waltzed into the Common Room bar to find Mr Wimborne having a muttered conversation in the corner with the Master-in-Charge of Rugby. Neither seemed inclined to offer me a drink, Fosters or otherwise. Ernest's stock of jovial Aussie clichés had quite dried up.

The miracle of the fish was still working for me in other quiet ways, but the results didn't manifest itself until the start of the following summer, when I discovered that my services as an umpire were no longer required. With rugby coaching and cricket umpiring removed from my orbit, I would have to find some other way of fulfilling my co-curricular duties.

Chapter 7

Oh, Life's richest Treasures are not overseas, but here, every day, close at hand . . . And Treasures there are, like – A walk with a friend; a garden; the spire of a church . . . our Life is a Treasure-Hunt right to the end, if only we'd join in the search!

—Marjorie G. Hellier

Sometimes it looks like I'm dancing, but it's just that I walked into a spider web.

—Demetri Martin

When I was about eight, I read a children's book called *Spiderweb for Two.* It ought to be better known, because it was ingenious, realistic and charming and it set me on a course that has influenced me to this day. It concerned a family of four children living in rural New England. The younger brother and sister are despondent at having been left at home while their older siblings have gone off to boarding school and life looks a dull prospect. But then they are sent a clue, written in verse, and this becomes the first of many in an ingenious treasure hunt devised by a mysterious setter. Each clue is a riddle that needs to be solved, each one leading them to hiding places that are many and varied – inside old clocks, frozen into the ice-cube tray of the freezer, attached to the weathercock above the stables, among others.

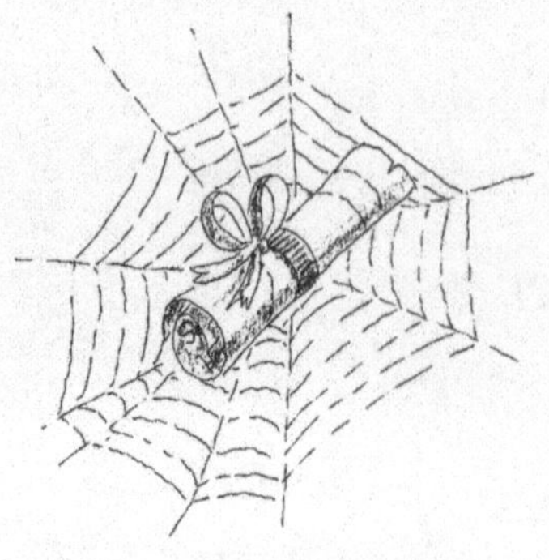

From the moment I read that book, I became obsessed with treasure hunts – and indeed everything associated with them: puzzles, riddles, clues, adventurous questing and so on. Now I reflect upon it, I realise that I had had this germ inside me from an even earlier age. As an infant, I would often get into trouble from my exasperated parents because I was in the habit of hiding things – Mum's purse, Dad's car keys, my sisters' toys – but none of them realised that I was not simply hiding these things out of mischief or spite. No. I was actually, even as a four-year-old, setting my beloved family a rudimentary form of treasure hunt. I would hide Dad's car keys in the laundry basket, but – here's the clever part – I would cunningly take out a single dirty sock from said basket and place it adroitly right in the spot where the keys had been sitting. This was a clue, of course. An observant puzzler would have noticed the sock, sniffed it, realised it was soiled and drawn the connection between the missing keys and the laundry basket.

Where my plan to provide joyous entertainment for my family generally fell down was that rarely was the recipient of my treat aware that they were cast in the role of a keen-nosed Sherlock Holmes eager to cry, 'The game's afoot!' All they knew was that their keys were there, right *there* a minute ago, and now they were not, and *I'm already running late for an important meeting and Sandy, Sandy, where are you? You've gone and hidden my keys again, haven't you?! Where are they?!*

In vain would I nod knowingly at the tell-tale sock and smile, Sphinx-like, rolling my eyes towards the laundry basket as a helpful hint. The appertaining rage would usually be so fierce, I'd burst

into tears, deny everything and flee the room, leaving the family to turn over the entire kitchen and living room like a pack of truffle-hunting baboons.

As I grew older, I learnt to be more judicious in my setting of treasure hunts – until only one victim remained. This was my dear, long-suffering friend Tom, for whom I kept setting, as special birthday treats, hunts of greater and greater complexity, never once realising that putting someone in a situation that involved them walking vast distances in strange terrain, baffled by ambiguities in the clues and rather wishing that they'd got a $50 book voucher instead might not have been the engaging delight it was intended to be.

Sometimes these treasure hunts inadvertently ended up characterised by moments of acute embarrassment and even potential danger for poor Tom as he stumbled from clue to clue. On one occasion, I had devised a treasure hunt to be done in the wee hours of a moonlit night up Brownhill Creek, a local nature reserve in a deep valley that was our boyhood playground. There were several ingenious clues. One such clue directed him to climb a familiar oak tree a little way up the valley. Racing ahead, I had climbed to the highest pinnacle of the oak with an archer's arrow clenched piratically in my teeth, jammed it into the bark pinning the next clue to the tree, and swung down gracefully out of the branches to escape before he came toddling along the moonlit path.

In fact, it wasn't as smooth as that in its execution. On descending from my mission up the tree, I found the arrow lying on the ground with the note still affixed to it; the wretched thing must have come loose and beaten me to the ground. Shoving it once more in my mouth, I clambered up the tree again – up and up and up – jammed it once again, with renewed vigour, into the tough oak bark and again made my descent . . . where I found the arrow waiting for me yet again at the foot of the tree, innocently lying there as if to say, 'What kept you?'

So, for a third time, I scrambled up that bloody oak tree – swing, clutch, grab, pant, heave – and hammered the bloody arrow a full inch into the bark – and then heard Tom coming along the path, feet rustling through dead leaves. My descent from the tree on that occasion was more a tumbling plummet, such as might be executed by an orangutan that has just been clubbed heavily over the head with a brick. I bounced from bough to bough before thudding to the ground and sprinting off into the darkness to avoid giving Tom a chance to say, 'Sandy, thank you so much for this treasure hunt – another one, gosh! – but can I just go home now? Please?'

The final clue I was particularly proud of and had taken some setting up. I had placed sparklers at intervals, marking a trail to a cave which was to contain the final treasure. The idea was that on seeing one sparkler off in the darkness, Tom would be drawn towards it – and then would see another flare further up the hillside, and, as he approached it, see another one ignite – and so, like a traveller from old tales being lured to the faery hollow by a dancing will-o'-the-wisp, Tom would come slowly but surely to the final prize.

But how was I to know when to light the first one?

My cunning idea was that the chain of clues after the oak tree would lead to a bridge across a moonlit stream where I had placed a small silver box, and in it a whistle with a clue suggesting that this was the enchanted horn that would lead the way to Fairyland. On hearing it thus blown, a hundred yards up the valley, I would light the first sparkler.

But I had failed to take one thing into account. I had arranged for Tom to be propelled into this midnight hunt via the offices of a mutual friend, who had agreed to inveigle Tom from his house on some pretext, drive him the four miles or so to the mouth of the valley and, thrusting the first clue into his hand, suddenly propel him from the car with a cheery 'Good luck!' before speeding off into the night. So far, so good. All this had happened without a hitch. What I hadn't foreseen was that Tom, all unawares of what the night had in store for him, had been lured out clad only in his pyjamas, slippers and a thin dressing gown.

So, standing there by the bridge at one o'clock in the morning on a cold July night, ill-clad for such a nocturnal adventure and not knowing how long this was going to go on for, Tom was a tad fed up. At that point, he noticed a white car parked some yards up the valley in the Seven Pines layby. And it happened to be precisely the same model as the car owned by Jonathan, a close crony of mine. Ah, thought Tom. So this is what will happen. I will dutifully blow this whistle. Jonathan and his smirking mates who are sitting there in the car will hear it. They will drive off and I will be expected to follow it at a brisk trot, looking like a complete idiot as they accelerate out of reach, and there will be Sandy and his chums all watching as I play along with their little game. Well, stuff this.

With a grim set to his jaw, Tom walked up to the darkened car, leaned in the open window and blew the whistle at a piercing blast twelve inches from the figures who lurked within.

Only at that point did Tom realise that it was not Jonathan's car at all. Inside were a young couple with the seats down, taking advantage of the midnight seclusion of the valley to indulge in a bout of vigorous copulation. They had certainly thrown modesty and caution to the winds; for a fraction of a second after the piercing blast of the whistle, the gentleman's buttocks were visible in the moonlight as a fleshy double globe before the enraged paramour struggled to pull up his trousers and extricate himself from the car, ready to give this night-stalking, whistle-blowing pervert the thrashing of his life. It surely didn't help matters that Tom was in his nightwear.

Thankfully for him, before he could be pummelled to a pulp, Tom had spotted the first sparkler flaring into life a hundred yards up the road. Uttering a hasty apology – 'Sorry, sorry. Carry on!' – he sprinted towards the sparkler at a speed that would have impressed an Olympic-grade cheetah.

Well, all ended happily, and I like to think that the final prize – a candlelit cave, a bottle of cheap port and a near-death experience – were all one could want for one's twenty-first birthday, so it is surprising that Tom later begged me not to feel I had to organise a treasure hunt for every birthday. 'Or indeed, any birthday, Sandy, thank you very much. A pair of socks or a punch in the head will do just fine.' So of course, I solemnly assured him – no more birthday treasure hunts. The end of an era. A line drawn under it. Say no more.

A promise is a promise. There were no more treasure hunts for his subsequent birthdays: my only recourse was upping the ante on the treasure hunt stakes a few years later when Tom asked me to be his best man and I had a stag night to organise. Yes!

I was a bit cross, to be honest. Tom had been my best friend throughout school and university; I had thought my companionship was all he could have wanted – days of exploring mines up Brownhill Creek, cycling around the Adelaide Hills, singing in the local church choir, inventing exciting games about the Holy Grail, bird-watching on the Coorong and sharing a love of literature – both favourite childhood authors such as T.H. White and C.S. Lewis and the texts we were studying as part of our Old and Middle English studies at university. And then suddenly he was seeing way more of some girl called Kitty than was reasonable – and now, a mere three years on, announcing his incomprehensible decision to marry her. Still, deeply puzzled by this unreasonable course of action though I was, I gratefully accepted his invitation to be best man and started planning out something rather splendid.

I knew that Tom was not the faintest bit interested in a traditional stag night – beer bongs, strippers, lap dancers and getting wasted (though he let me know afterwards that he wasn't in fact totally averse to a traditional lap dancer or two). Be that as it may, I knew that this would be the last chance to give Tom an adventure before the shackles of matrimony closed about him. I told him mendaciously that I had arranged a stag night for the following Thursday at a certain hotel in the city, but in the meantime, that Sunday, why didn't we arrange – just the two of us – to go for a picnic and one last long ramble through the September spring sunshine of the Hills?

The Adelaide Hills, for those not familiar with them, are a treasure for walkers and ramblers, gourmets and gardeners alike. They form a wrinkled maze of little valleys, dusty roads, hidden orchards, vineyards and almond groves, tiny farmsteads and winding creeks seamed between forests of tall eucalypt and black wattle ringing with birdsong. For me, one attractive feature – an anathema to ecologists, I realise – is the riotous mixture of plants from different cultures around the world: English cottage garden, Mediterranean maquis and Australian bush. So tall ribbon gums will shed their great strands of tan and cream bark on swards of grass starred by wild freesias and orange cape tulips. Here is an old sandstone quarry where fig trees grow sprawling against the ochre walls, their splayed leaves smelling like coconut in the warm sun. In the midst of a pasture grazed by kangaroos at dusk where the bush orchids grow thickly underfoot, a solitary apple tree glimmers like a white cloud of blossom in the twilight. The reedy creek beds between massive redgums are tingling with mint and lemon balm growing in great fragrant swathes, and the tall frondy fennel perfumes the dusty roadsides with its smoky aniseed. Around every corner, a new vista opens out; a grove of silver-green olive trees dotted down a dust-red hillside; a lonely road wandering to a hill's crest against the sky. It was this landscape that I wanted as a gift for Tom – spiced, of course, with clues and adventures galore.

It all began with Tom sitting through the Sunday service at a little parish church in one of the Hill villages, wondering where the blazes I had got to. I had arranged to meet him there, explaining that this particular church had an exquisite choir that was worth listening to.

There was no choir. There was no sign of me either. But when Tom went up for Communion, he found that as the wafer was being thrust into his hand by the administering priest it was accompanied by a tiny slip of paper. This was the first clue of what Tom now realised – with a sinking heart, perhaps – was another bloody treasure hunt. So, after the service, off he set on his unlooked-for quest.

As a setter of treasure hunts, I have always striven to make the clues as elegant as possible, employing references to literature, poetry, music, history and legend. Thus, one of the earlier clues was simply the divine description of the god Pan from *The Wind in the Willows* in the chapter entitled 'The Piper at the Gates of Dawn'. But what could the clue mean? It was then that Tom spotted a large and regal-looking billy-goat in an adjacent field. Could it be? Surely not. But yes, around the creature's neck seemed to be some sort of collar and attached to that a capsule. That was the first of his trials – pursuing and wrestling to the ground a large, frisky goat in order to extract the clue I had asked the goat's owner to attach there. It didn't help matters, as Tom explained afterwards, that the goat had been unusually amorous that morning and Tom's interest had aroused it in more ways than one. Just as Tom had wrested the pill box free from the hairy brute's collar, nature took its course and the goat ejaculated wildly and copiously in Tom's direction, drenching him with seminal fluid. (I later learnt that there is nothing quite so musky and ripe as the emissions from a randy member of the caprine tribe, and Tom's encounters with members of the public for the next few hours were characterised by people suddenly backing away hastily, hands clamped firmly to mouth and nose.)

This was on my part an unforeseen element of adventure, but there were other parts of the treasure hunt where I wanted Tom to find his adrenaline pumping, and I had laid plans accordingly. For example, at one point, he found a bicycle for his use. The problem was that it was chained with a combination lock to a high cyclone-wire fence surrounding a gracious manor. An envelope, obviously containing the combination, was pinned to a tree just out of arms' reach on the other side of the fence, and between Tom and the envelope were two large German Shepherds roaming the grounds. At Tom's arrival, they set up a barking and snarling that put him in mind of the bloodier passages of *White Fang*, and it took all his dexterity with a long stick to dislodge the envelope and drag it within grabbing distance while the two hounds snapped and snarled and reduced the stick to saliva-bedewed splinters. It possibly didn't help that Tom was still reeking of goat-musk.

And so the adventure went on. In fact, Tom recalls the next few hours with something almost approaching fondness. The long downhill glide on a bike through the warm spring sunshine down lanes lined with almond trees in bridal white and a blue sky above; this was very heaven ... and a clue in his pocket was leading him to Camelot.

One of the astonishing features for me of this treasure hunt is the way the landscape seemed to open up unlikely possibilities just for the wishing. As I set out to explore the Hills, I discovered to my delight a wealth of hidden places – and people – that provided precisely the legendary flavour for an enchanted adventure.

One such place was Camelot Castle, a wedding reception centre with parapets and towers of honey-coloured stone set in beautiful gardens by a stream. Beyond the stream was a path through a little wood to a tiny but exquisite chapel. Above the stone altar rose a bell tower with a Germanic tiled steeple, and a

long bell-rope led up to a large bronze bell high above. This was perfect for my purposes. One of the medieval texts Tom and I had studied at university was *The Legend of Saint Kenelm*, a murdered boy-saint whose death is avenged when a miraculous dove fluttering from heaven appears to a holy knight when he is praying in a solitary woodland chapel.

Or in this case, an origami dove with a message in its bill, perched precariously by the aid of a long pole on the lip of the bell, ready to flutter down the moment Tom, my holy knight, pulled the bell-rope. A spot of pre-dawn trespassing that morning and my nifty work with the pole had the dove ready in place for Tom's arrival. Hopefully he would be in and out of there before anyone noticed. It was sheer bad luck that somehow the first tentative ring of the bell by the wary Tom failed to bring the dove toppling. He tried again, harder this time. Still no luck. Peering up the shaft of the belltower, Tom could see something white perched up there and guessed that this was what he was trying to dislodge ... so he gave the bellpull a good hard yank. *Dong!* It sounded very loud in the hushed and tranquil air of the garden.

Still no luck. Nothing for it then. He'd just have to ring until it fell.

Dinggg! Dong!!! Clang!! Donggg! Dinggg! Donggg! The chimes rang out as though announcing the end of a major world war. Three gardeners appeared, sprinting across the immaculate lawns to see who the hell was playing silly buggers with the bell. They didn't look too happy, and it occurred to Tom then that I might not have gained permission for this escapade – as was indeed the case.

Dinggg! Clangggg! Donggg! ... and at last, the dove dislodged and came fluttering to the altar. Tom pounced on it like a starving goshawk and fled out the chapel door and through the woods as the gardeners came thundering up the path, pruning shears at the ready. But before long, Tom was half a mile away on his trusty bike, waiting to see where the message would send him next.

To be honest, it is all a blur now thirty years on. I know there was a dangerous foray into a field where a flock of savage geese resided, presided over by a cranky goose-lady who had a stern way with trespassers. And there was the Excalibur moment where a wooden sword tied to a floating buoy out in the middle of a secluded dam needed to be fetched. Then there was the episode where Tom inadvertently stole a car. You see, at one point I needed to get Tom to walk up a hill to get him from Point A to Point B. At the top of this hill, I had been delighted to find a few weeks earlier a quaint white cottage, and in that cottage an even quainter little old lady. At my request, she had agreed to give my friend a cup of tea to revive him and a Scotch finger biscuit or two, along with the next clue. She was so perfect for the part that in a literary vein I christened her Mrs Tiggy-Winkle, after the sweet-natured hedgehog washerwoman in Beatrix Potter's books who takes in laundry and offers strangers cups of tea.

To that end, I wrote a clue directing Tom to her cottage that went something like this.

Now neither linger, rest or stay!
Two miles uphill now make your way
Until there comes in
plainest sight
A cottage small and snug
and white,
And there you'll find, her
eyes a-twinkle,
Kindly Mrs Tiggy-Winkle.

The night before, I rang everyone I had contacted to make sure they were all set to be at the right place at the right time.

Message tied to goat's neck? Check.

Bike chained to railings? Check.

Savage hounds released? Check.

Mrs Tiggy-Winkle to expect Tom at about four on the morrow? Yes, dear. How lovely. Check.

I even dropped around personally that morning to ensure she was still happy to proceed.

'Oh yes, dear. Look, there's the teapot all ready to go. I've chosen the willow pattern, dear. Doesn't it look nice with the cornflowers I've picked fresh from the garden this morning? What fun!' And she twinkled at me with that sweet little-old-lady smile I knew would charm Tom when he knocked at her door after a long thirsty walk up the road.

So, I have absolutely no explanation as to why, when Tom arrived at the white cottage at four that afternoon, clutching his clue and trying to predict who Mrs Tiggy-Winkle would be, the twinkling old dear was nowhere to be seen.

Of course, Tom didn't know what to expect. He knocked and knocked, but there was no answer. Puzzled, he went around the side of the house, looking for a telltale envelope containing the next clue. Nothing. At the back, he found the kitchen door open so he wandered inside, calling *yoo-hoo* tentatively – but to no avail. A little frustrated now, he started to explore the cottage, lifting cushions, peeking in drawers, peering behind picture frames.

Eventually he came out into the front garden baffled. At which point he noticed a car in the driveway. A white Mini Minor. Hmm. Could this be 'Mrs Tiggy-Winkle'? A cute British name for a cute British car. He reread the clue. Ah. Her eyes a-twinkle? Headlights, of course!

But no. Sandy couldn't possibly have arranged for a car as part of this ... could he?

Test to see if it's unlocked.

It is.

But it's no good without keys so, no, this can't be it.

The keys are in the ignition.

In a daze of doubt, Tom climbs into the driver's seat. *This really can't be it – besides, what I am meant to do? Drive it where?*

At that point, past the end of the driveway, a red car flashed by. Although it was going at speed, Tom recognised it instantly, and this time he was correct in his car identification. A bright crimson Citroën, belonging to a friend of ours, Sean. (Unbeknownst to Tom, Sean had been dragooned into helping me with surveillance to make sure things remained on track. His rapid passing of the white cottage just as Tom was sitting in the Mini Minor was an entirely unintentional coincidence. However ...)

Tom made up his mind. The hunt was on. The game was afoot. The Mini was his. Starting up the engine, Tom edged out of the drive onto the country road and turned in pursuit of the car speeding off into the distance.

Now Tom is a modest and cautious chap in all he does. Behind the wheel, he is the sort of driver who checks all mirrors twice before any manoeuvre, usually proceeds under the speed limit and makes careful hand signals whenever he intends to turn. None of this was going to help him keep up with Sean, whose driving occupies the opposite end of the caution spectrum. Tom found himself hurtling along the dusty lanes, swooping up the hills, plunging down into steep little valleys and screaming around bends in an attempt to keep sight of the oblivious Citroën ahead.

After about twenty minutes Sean noticed that a little white Mini had been following him, and way too fast. Regarding himself as a man of action and mystery, Sean accelerated and whipped unexpectedly down a tiny side lane between two orchards. After a minute or two, when the Mini still seemed to be following, he clenched an imaginary pipe in his teeth and let the engine rip.

Five miles later, the Mini was still pursuing when Sean hit a patch of sealed road, giving him a chance to look back and do a double take.

'Good God!' Sean said, slamming on the brakes. 'I think that's Tom!' There was an echoing squeal from behind and the Mini rocked to a standstill. Out climbed a shaken figure, pale as the dust that was settling around them.

'Hello, Tom, old chap. Where did you get that car from?'

*

Half an hour later, after a much more sedate return drive to the white cottage, Tom parked the Mini exactly where he had found it and wiped his fingerprints from the steering wheel, the gear-stick and any mirrors he may have touched, and polished clean the dusty car. If, as we later surmised, the old lady's failure to appear was because she had been bumped off by an opportunistic burglar – 'Come in, dear, first a cup of tea and then the clue. Goodness, what a big crowbar, dear' – and was now curled up lifeless in the bathroom linen cupboard, we felt it fair not to further confuse the investigating constabulary with a second set of prints.

And so the long afternoon wore on. Sean was able to point Tom in the direction of the next clue, revealing that he had to get to Norton Summit and find the 'solemn pillar of the dead, and letters there each etched in red'. Tom groaned. It was getting late and Norton Summit was all of six miles away along roads steep and winding and weary. It would take him two hours of walking.

But just then, in the apple-lit dusk, he heard the *clip-clop, clip-clop* of horse hooves behind him. Black Riders? Another threat? But no. This was the final treat I had organised. Farmer Maggot in a horse and buggy heading home to Norton Summit and offering a lift to our poor footsore hero.

Tom bowled along through the blue spring dusk, the air cool on his damp brow, clutching his hat to stop it blowing off, watching the lanterns come on in the houses and the small white stars prick out among the apple trees and poplars in a pearl-green sky. Hopping off at the tiny village square of Norton Summit, he looked around for a 'pillar of the dead'. Ah. Easy. The village War Memorial, a tall stone etched with the names of those who had fallen in battle. And yes, faint but clear, some recent hand had picked out eleven letters in what could have been blood – or perhaps red nail polish. S-U-M-M-I-T-H-O-T-E-L.

And sure enough, there it was behind him: the Norton Summit Hotel, perched on the very edge of the hills and looking down over the plain of the city to the far-off sea fading in the west to molten umber. And inside, a bed and bathroom booked and a set of clean clothes – then friends, drinks, a meal, good music and a retelling of the day's adventures over a pale ale or two – or three – before the welcome embrace of bed and a night's slumber.

*

I cannot resist adding a sort of epilogue to this chapter of events, partly as a way of explaining how I seem to have slipped sideways in space and time from the cricketfields of Ellesmere to the haunts of my youth. The fact is that on the way back from that first cricket match at Cheltenham, the one where Chadwick was so very helpful in explaining the duties of an umpire, I had been dozing in the coach only to become aware of an eager conversation going on between two young lads in the seat across the aisle. One of them was recounting with great relish a tale which sounded oddly familiar. It involved a tussle with an amorous goat, a reluctant dove, an inadvertent car theft from a hedgehog – here the narrator sounded a little unsure of his facts – and various attacks by chained mastiffs or vicious geese. To my astonishment I gradually realised that this was an account of the very treasure hunt I had set for Tom three years previously and on the other side of the world. It transpired that the boy telling his companion about this had lived briefly in Adelaide and had been fortunate enough to have had Tom as a teacher. At some point, I gather, Tom had decided to forgo the planned lesson for that day – apostrophes? media analysis? – and instead regale the class with his adventures over the weekend, possibly to explain the various bite marks and nervous twitching that he had acquired since the Friday before. It seems quite incredible to me that this student should have chosen just that moment on the coach to entertain his friend with the quest while its architect was half-dozing two feet away in the next seat. And it was especially satisfying, as the boy faltered in trying to remember the conclusion to the treasure hunt, to be able to lean over and say, 'Yes, I think you'll find that the last bit was a pony trap ride to Norton Summit to discover the red letters on the war memorial and a slap-up dinner to follow at

the Summit Hotel,' before resuming my nap and leaving the boys gulping like junior goldfish in puzzled astonishment.

This was not the only time I discovered that treasure hunts have a peculiar way of generating the most astonishing coincidences, sending out gossamer threads in a glimmering web through the ether of time and space to make connections that defy belief. This is something I was to discover in spadefuls in my time at Ellesmere and many times since – but such marvels must wait their turn as I make my way back to the more prosaic pastures of education.

Chapter 8

It is noble to teach oneself, but still nobler to teach others – and less trouble.

—Mark Twain

Like most teachers, my career launched in my salad days, when I was, to quote the Bard, a tad green in judgement. In my very earliest days of working in the Adelaide boarding school, for example, I had been desperate to prove myself a wonderful mentor to the boys under my care. To my eyes, the housemaster seemed to lack any finer feelings and was about as pastoral as a physics textbook. I would make it my job to be a welcome contrast. To that end, I was almost skipping with delight when a new boy called Angus knocked on my door one evening, eyes red with tears and snuffling miserably. He felt terribly homesick, he explained through hiccups, and didn't know how he'd be able to cope.

These days, with more experience, I always say the same thing. I explain that homesickness is like the common cold. It's rotten, it's miserable, there's no cure for it – but most importantly, like a cold, it doesn't last very long. It will be over in three days, mark my words. Cold comfort at the time, no doubt, but true.

Back then, however, I took a different approach. I invited the blubbing Angus in and sat him down on a sofa in my living room. I lit a dozen candles around the place and played a tape of Allegri's *Miserere*. The candlelight, the pure soprano voices, as pure and radiant as the candleflames themselves, the shadows flickering gently on walls and ceiling: how could such things not soothe the tortured soul and bring peace to a troubled mind?

It is quite a lengthy piece of music. Long before it had finished, the puzzled and slightly fidgety Angus had clearly had enough of this weirdness and asked if he could leave. A little hurt at his lack of receptivity to my pastoral experiment, I shooshed him gently and indicated that he should go on listening. The best bit was coming up … ahhh! Now! I closed my eyes in absorbed rapture to drink in the beauty, oh, the beauty.

I opened my eyes a few moments later to hear my front door closing behind the discreetly departing victim of my pastoral approach. I was later to discover that Angus was a simple boy from a cattle farm in the Northern Territory. Previous bouts of homesickness at his former school had been dealt with by allowing him to ride his dirt bike at top speed in the back paddock. He wasn't quite ready for Allegri by candlelight. One thing it did ensure, however, was that any boy experiencing homesickness in the boarding house over the next few years made a point of seeking a remedy elsewhere – anywhere, in fact, rather than Mr Mackinnon's door.

*

The proper relationship between a student and a teacher is a vexed and complex issue. Indeed, the playing field of opinion in this matter is an ever-shifting one and can be as treacherous as the shifting sands of Dee. I vividly remember in one of the very early lectures at teachers college the tutor saying, with forbidding emphasis, 'And gentlemen, ladies, I hope you are under no apprehension that you are entering the teaching profession to be *liked* by your students.'

My fellow graduate Tom and I glanced at each other surreptitiously and with some dismay. That is *precisely* why we wanted to be teachers. We had both been lucky enough to have had a class teacher at our high school whom we liked enormously: a brilliant, passionate, funny, authentic Scotsman called Dr McWhae. He was strict and demanding. He had a temper that would occasionally see him fling errant students bodily from the room – such students were said to have joined the Flying Club – and he would let us know in no uncertain terms if we were being arrogant or unkind or lazy. The rest of the time, the vast majority in fact, he filled simply with being wonderful to be around. He gave out that he found our company stimulating, our jokes funny, our ideas fascinating and worth pursuing, our ambitions noble. We loved him and I know that many of us keep in touch with him to this day, forty years on. So, to be told that a principal tenet of teaching was not under any circumstances to seek to be liked by our students was a bit of a blow to our young idealism.

Of course, I know what that lecturer meant. There are a few young teachers who make the mistake of wanting simply to be friends with their students and not play the mentoring, and therefore sometimes disciplinary, role that is so important. But he should have added – and would nowadays, I suspect – that the key to being a good teacher is to form a genuine relationship with each student and one that is built on mutual liking, respect and enjoyment of each other's presence. Without at least some rudiments of liking, all the instruction in the world will amount to nothing.

There are further complexities, however. A timeworn piece of advice given to teachers in an all-boys school at the start of a school year is not to smile until Term 2 – and there is some sense in it. It is certainly true that any group of boys, when faced with a new situation, will be acting at a primal level not dissimilar to a pack of prairie wolves. It has been said that a teenage boy is a role-model-seeking missile. They are deeply programmed to seek out a pack leader who is worthy of their loyalty. If the new teacher shows signs of indecisiveness, poor judgement, unfairness or frivolity, a class or dormitory of boys will be lightning-quick to be dismissive and disrespectful and look elsewhere for leadership, usually among their own number. That is why Dr McWhae was so successful. His clear demands for good behaviour early on and his preparedness to bare his metaphorical teeth showed us a strength we were all happy to follow. The rewards – funny classes, stimulating lessons, brilliant stories – were the portions of deer-shank handed out by a confident wolf-leader to his loyal and obedient followers.

Put like that, it sounds awful. Obedience has become a dirty word. We have seen too many films and read too many stories where a strong and ruthless gang leader alternatively terrorises and rewards his followers until they blindly eat out of his hand. And it is true that obedience can be coerced like that to terrible effect. But the fact is that boys will be obedient to *someone*; it is in their nature. If it is not to a good teacher, it will be to the class thug.

One Headmaster I worked under told me that having a weak or ineffectual classroom teacher in a school was more detrimental to morale and discipline than having an incompetent administrator or two. I was surprised by this at the time, but have since found it to be true. As students pass through the vacillating Mr Snipe's French class, for example, and find that they can lounge, snigger, demand and needle with impunity, they leave with the taste of blood in their mouths and are emboldened by it. They adopt a new swagger as they saunter off to the next class draped in a confidence that, with a little time and effort, the weak points of other teachers might be winkled out.

Trying to maintain that fine balance between developing warm relationships with students and maintaining the strength of a wolf-chieftain is a tricky endeavour and one that comes with experience and time. To add to the complexity, there is the possibility that students might develop a crush on a teacher they admire. I have found this a mercifully rare phenomenon in my case; any burgeoning crush towards me over the years has probably been quickly stifled by my tendency to take any interest shown and misinterpret that as a desire on the part of the dewy-eyed pupil to have Boolean algebra explained to them at great length over a plate of assorted creams.

One such student comes to mind, though. While at Ellesmere, I had under my care a frail little French boy with a mop of flaming red hair and a smattering of freckles. Aurelian was very young for his age, with a piping voice and a sweet innocence that was in marked contrast to his fellow Third Formers; he took a ragged teddy bear called Pepitôt with him everywhere he went and had a tendency to skip around talking to passing butterflies and clouds. Aurelian would often seek me out to have long conversations in the House study about homesickness, his pet hamster back home, his uncle's chateau in France and how much Pepitôt was missing the morning croissants and hot chocolate. During these conversations, Aurelian would edge closer and closer on the old leather settee until he was snuggled up under my armpit, piping plaintively like a little bird beneath my tweedy wing. Nowadays, if such a situation arose, I would ensure the study door remained wide open and that there was sufficient passing traffic in the corridor to forestall any thought that I was seeking privacy for pastoral chats like this. Back then, however, I was so early in my career I was unaware that there could possibly be any inappropriate affection directed from a student to his mentor. If such thoughts ever did intrude, I brushed them off as ludicrous.

One evening, we were just about to start Chapel Evensong. As the organ music swelled, there was a bustle and a flutter behind me. It was Aurelian, his flaming hair awry, having arrived late from somewhere and at a hasty trot. His pew was right at the far end of the Chapel and he clearly felt uncomfortable at making the long solo walk under the glare of various staff members perched like elderly black-clad cormorants along either side of the aisle. As the Head and the Chaplain took off at a solemn pace down the aisle and I readied myself to follow them, Aurelian whispered to me, 'May I walk you down the aisle?'

I nodded a curt agreement but inwardly smiled to myself at the unfortunate turn of phrase; no doubt this little French lad had no idea of the usual purport of those words. But five paces into our slow march, I heard quite distinctly above the drone of the organ a high piping hum from my left elbow. Aurelian had a dreamy faraway look on his face and was humming the Wedding March from Lohengrin as he did indeed walk me down the aisle in the fullest sense of the phrase. After that, the study door stayed firmly open and there was a large pile of workbooks to be marked on the sofa next to me whenever Aurelian came for a chat.

*

Although in many ways as a young teacher I was hopelessly naïve and idealistic, there were some elements of my instinctive care for youngsters that I now recognise were better than the standard practice of the time. Not that I knew that, of course. I was anxious to follow in the footsteps of my elders and betters, even when I didn't really understand their reasoning.

For example, when it came to dealing with bullying, standard wisdom dictated that the complainant and the victim be kept

separate at all costs. If little William Howlett came to me and told me that Mark Fogarty had poured sour milk all over his pillow, and that this was a common occurrence, the instructions on how to deal with this were very clear. First and foremost, don't let Howlett Junior and Fogarty Senior be in the same room together. Ensuring that young Howlett is safely out the way, call in Fogarty and present him with the accusations made against him. Moreover, try to do this without giving the slightest hint of who made those accusations – the theory being that if Fogarty knew the squit Howlett had raised such calumnies against him, he'd hunt him down and lose no time in flushing his head down the nearest loo.

This recommendation was fraught with difficulties. There was, of course, the problem of bringing up the charges without being specific about the chap on the receiving end. 'So, Mark. Tell me. Have you made use of any milk recently ... sour milk, for example ... used for purposes other than that which its Maker intended?'

'What, like making yoghurt, sir?'

'Er no, er, no, er, more bed-linen-related activities, er ...'

'Are you mad, sir?'

'What? No, look, it has come to my attention ... that is, I've heard rumours, whispers if you like ... that you ... or possibly not you, but no, definitely your name was mentioned, so yes, you ... might have poured some sour milk on a pillow somewhere.'

Instant outrage. 'What, me, sir? It's that little weed Howlett, isn't it, sir? He spilt it there himself, sir, I swear to God, and said he was going to blame it on me because I won a conker off him fair and square in a game of cards, sir. I bet he hasn't told you about the time he put a frog in Trevelett-Jones's bed, sir.'

The next step recommended was to dismiss Fogarty Senior and track down Howlett Junior before Fogarty and his mates did. Then the interview would go something like this.

'So, William, I've spoken to Mark Fogarty and he seems to think that you spilt the sour milk on the pillow yourself. What would you say to that?'

'Oh no, sir, well, not really, well, I did have a cup of hot chocolate in bed, sir, and I did spill a tiny bit, and then Bartlett said I should clean it up before it went sour, and I said I'd do it later, and then he said I was a pig, and that's when Fogarty came in and hit me with a conker he'd stolen off me, so I threw my hot chocolate at him by accident and he then went and got some sour milk, and Bartlett threw my pillow at him and it landed on the floor, and then Fogarty poured the sour milk all over it, and then he called me a crybaby, and I swapped the pillow with Trevelett-Jones's pillow because of the frog incident last week and … and that's really what happened, sir, and it's all so unfair.'

And so it goes. Following the policy of never allowing the plaintiffs or accused to speak to one another, one would find oneself involved in a week's worth of interviews, uncovering more and more stories and counter-stories, having to bring in more and more participants in the drama, and being presented with a tissue of lies and evasions that would tax even the great Hercule Poirot. I found the process frustrating, time-consuming and ultimately fruitless. And in the meantime, late at night in an unsupervised bathroom, the flushing mechanisms of the toilets were getting a thorough workout as the boys administered justice in their time-honoured style.

From very early in my career, I couldn't help thinking the best way to proceed was to get all involved in a room together – and, importantly, get a whole crowd of uninvolved bystanders included in the conversation as well, and lay all cards on the table. When I suggested this, I was told by various housemasters and senior teachers that this was sheer madness. How dare I compromise the anonymity of the complainant? How dare I force the victim

to converse with his tormentor? No, the more the left hand didn't know what the right hand was doing, the better for all concerned. If it was good enough for homicide detectives, it was good enough for us.

After decades of watching this procedure fail badly, I finally had the confidence to try out my radical idea of allowing a supervised conversation take place among all parties. As I had suspected, it worked a treat. The presence of neutral bystanders was a game-changer. The fact that everything had to be said in an open forum meant no one could get away with lies or evasions; more often than not, it was Fogarty's own friends who ensured this.

Almost always, victim and accused learnt something about each other: that Fogarty's parents were in the middle of a messy divorce, or that Howlett was genuinely scared of the dark. And they would leave with a mutual respect for each other's vulnerabilities. These meetings also had the knock-on effect of killing dead any chance of private retribution. If, later on, the boys saw Fogarty winding up to get his own back on Howlett, they could step in and remind him that he had publicly assured everyone the matter was now closed and amends had been made and accepted. The broad daylight of public inquiry had a wonderfully sanitising effect on proceedings and outcomes.

Of course, my idea to deal with things in this way was subject to a lot of experiment and adjustment over the years. Early attempts were not always completely successful. One thing I did which made a huge difference was to teach those involved certain ways of couching their grievances. Rather than say, 'Fogarty, you're a mean bully and just horrible the way you speak to me,' I'd tell a boy that it was better to phrase things in terms of how Fogarty's actions made him feel. For example, 'Fogarty, when you call me Blubber-Bog, I feel a bit small and helpless. It makes me sad.'

The genius of this is that no one can argue with a statement about somebody else's feelings. Although Fogarty can react with outraged denial at being called a bully, he can't very well respond to a statement like 'You make me feel sad' with 'No, I don't!' Almost inevitably the reaction to someone telling a bully his actions or words makes them feel sad or small or helpless or angry will be, 'Oh crikey. Do they? I didn't realise that. I'm really sorry to hear it.'

I am pleased – one might almost say smugly pleased – to report that this way of dealing with things has now become common practice in most schools. It goes by the name of restorative justice and is even beginning to find its way into our courts and legal system.

*

But one way of circumventing all this hoo-ha, to stop the bickering and bullying before it begins, is to give the buggers something else to think about. And for that, we must turn to fairyland for inspiration.

Chapter 9

Oh, grown-ups cannot understand,
And grown-ups never will,
How short the way to fairyland
Across the purple hill.

—Alfred Noyes

Midsummer's Eve. A huge harvest moon, yellow as a grapefruit, hung in the summer night and I was sleepless. Looking westwards out of my high window, I could see the Shropshire plain etched out in warm silver – the winding canal across the playing fields a glimmering thread, the spire of Welshampton Church a needle of black and gold, and the air heavy with the scent of mown grass and mid-May's eldest child, the dreaming eglantine trailing in every hedgerow from here to Whittington Castle. Midsummer's Eve – a time for magic – and there a mile distant, a hill crowned with beech trees, solitary on the plain ...

When I was about thirteen, some blessed soul bought for me as a birthday present a book called *Faeries*, written and illustrated by Alan Lee and Brian Froud. Many such books were popular at the time; *Giants, Gnomes, Dragons*, all beautifully illustrated, often with hand-written text, each one pretending to be a set of naturalist's notes on these mythical creatures. None was as exquisite or as haunting as *Faeries*, though. Even the archaic spelling, now so familiar, was new to me and spoke of a world entirely removed from the tinselly Disney-esque creatures I understood fairies to be.

More than almost anything else, that single book informed my imaginative appreciation of the wild, haunted character of the landscape. At first, I was more attracted to the illustrations by Brian Froud: mischievous, humorous watercolours of earthy leprechauns and scrunched-up gremlins seemingly made out of seed pods and potatoes, squash-nosed, twinkling-eyed, clad in leather overcoats and wide-brimmed hats, twirling on knobbled thorn sticks or jigging madly in drifts of autumn leaves. But soon my admiration turned to the more subtle watercolours of Alan Lee, which gave a haunting sense of menace and sorrow. Here I met Jenny Greenteeth, a balding Gollum-like figure with duck slime plastered across her scalp, reaching out of a black pond for a small child's ankle. (I later discovered that Jenny Greenteeth originated from the meres and pools around Ellesmere.) Here, also, were pictures not of the denizens of Faery itself but of the signs they left in the landscape: three twisted hawthorn trees on a mound, a shapeless stone on the edge of a field, a red ribbon around a ragwort stem. I think what was so powerful about the book's illustrations was their naturalness. The artists had chosen not to glamorise the magic world by adding in haloes and sparkles and improbably twisted trees or impossibly pointy spires of rock; every pine cone or river stone, every blackberry spray or striped snail shell was exactly like the ones I had seen with my own eyes in the countryside. This made me think that had I just looked a little closer, I too would have spotted the garnet eyes or root-like fingers hidden there.

When I visited England at the age of nineteen, I had found myself camping near the Snowdonian mountain village of Capel Curig. In the late afternoon light, I had set off to explore the valley below the campsite. From the very start, my skin had prickled with a sort of gleeful terror. Here were elements in the landscape straight from Alan Lee's *Faeries*. In a steep copse of hazel and ash, a stack of boulders took on the lumpy contours of a stone troll clad in ragged raiment of lichen. On the border of a meadow, a flooded ditch held the drowned body of a ewe, its fleece pulpy white in the stagnant water and green fingers of slime throttling its foolish neck – the fingers of Jenny Greenteeth in person. On the other side of the meadow, bristling with ragwort, five goblin crows hopped and pecked at something in the long grass – a dead lamb, its eyes picked out by those stabbing spears. Fleeing back into the woods, I found a precipice with a deep cleft in it, a cave of sorts, and there in the darkness at the back was a white slab of quartz – the pale hollow-eyed face of a blind hermit. And finally, just as the last light faded from the landscape, I stood in an open glade amid tall oaks while all about me and high above came the sweet piping from a dozen elfin throats – but wherever I turned my eyes to see the hidden singers, there was nothing but a flicker of bright colour, flashes of gold, azure, crimson, leaf green, no sooner glimpsed than vanished again in the canopy.

So, the geology and fauna and flora of a Welsh farming community on the edge of a national park – a couple of ill-fated sheep, some opportunistic carrion birds, an exposed seam of quartzite and a flurry of woodland songbirds – chaffinches most likely, and blue tits, and perhaps even a rare goldcrest – singing the last of the daylight out. Not magic at all. And yet . . .

By a wide pool under alder trees, I hit upon the way to think about this experience. Yes, these visions were imagination, and knowingly so. There was not the slightest hint of hallucination. Never for one moment did I see a hominid goblin form instead of the avian figure of the carrion crow. Never for one second did I see anything but duckweed draped across the maiden-white neck of the drowned ewe.

However – and this was the big insight – the act of creative imagining is usually a voluntary one, a private game of 'Let's Pretend'. One willingly opens one's mind to the possibility of seeing that bent thorn tree as a hag or that toadstool as a goblin face. Here, however, in the valley of Capel Curig, it seemed that the act was *not* voluntary. I was not 'opening my mind'; it was being *forced* open. It might still be just imagination – it *was* just imagination – but there seemed in this corner of Wales to be very little choice in the matter on my part. All the work was being done *through* me but not *by* me – and if not by me, by what or whom?

And that meant, to my youthful philosophising at least, that there was something about that valley that was doing the forcing. Perhaps this was what Faery was. Perhaps the enchantment of Faery – what used to be called 'glamour' – was this propensity: to compel the imagination of a wandering mortal to see with the inner mind the beauties and terrors of the faery world.

Such were my musings as I stood there by the rushing river in the twilight. Then I remembered one particular sketch in the *Faeries* that had caught my attention years ago. A drawing of a giant toad-like creature with wide bat-like wings, a trailing pterodactyl tail and needle-sharp teeth in its gaping maw, accompanied by the terse handwritten note, 'Water Leaper – preys on Welsh fishermen'. Realising how effectively the rushing torrent would mask the long, slow sweep of approaching wingbeats, I judged that further musings on the nature of Faery could wait. I hurried up the hill to a somewhat shaky supper of cold baked beans in a tent that remained firmly closed against the perils and dangers of the Welsh night.

But now, on this Midsummer night and under the madness of the grapefruit moon, perils be damned. Slipping into some clothes and grabbing my tin whistle, I stole out into the night and trotted westwards, across Parry's Field and through a gap in the hedge to the banks of the canal. The night air was full of the clanking cry of a thousand frogs; tall cream spikes of meadowsweet filled the air with a heady scent. Surely, if Pan were abroad, or Oberon and his shadowy hosts, tonight of all nights I would meet them. Crossing the canal by a humped brick bridge, I came to a wheatfield, shadowy gold under that colossal moon. Beyond it was the fairy hill. Waist deep, I waded across the field, the silken tassels brushing my fingertips and painting my hands with a sticky sap. The going was harder than I had imagined, a hundred stiff stalks crackling like musketry against my thighs as I waded onwards. Looking back at one point, I noticed with some alarm just how dark and wide a swathe I had cut through the crop on my pathless pursuit. I hoped that the farmer, if woken from his slumber by the noisy progress through the field, might attribute it to alien crop-circle action and stay cowering under his bed rather than come looking for a terrestrial trespasser.

The hill was crested with beech trees, silver grey in the moonlight. I sat against one of these and, as my breathing slowed, the silence of the summer night stole over me once more. Before me at the foot of the hill, the canal curved in a tight bow, almost in the manner of a moat. So still was the night that I could hear the gentle *scrunch-scrunch* of cows feeding in the pasture beyond the canal. Somewhere over towards Whittington, a fox barked to the moon.

No fairy revels then? No distant sounding of elf horns or dwarf drums? No dancing in madcap circles by quaint waistcoated figures whose faces were made of toadstools and puffballs? Nothing but the warm night breeze and the smell of hawthorn and fast-fading violets, covered in leaves. Nothing for it then. I drew the tin whistle from my pocket and begin to play.

For years I had been learning to play on this tin whistle – or flageolet, if you are in some posh orchestra – and I knew dozens of folk tunes off by heart. But at times such as these no known tune seemed to fit the occasion, so instead of piping out 'Drowsy

Maggie' or 'Lanigan's Ball' or 'The Battle of Aughrim' – all fairy tunes without a doubt – I found myself playing a tune of my own devising. Tentative at first, a fitful piping like a reed warbler deep in her sedge thicket, with many a pause, a jump, an experimental run, a weak trill followed by another silence to allow me to hear if an enraged farmer was storming across his desecrated wheat-field … But soon, encouraged by a small wind that sprang up and set the beech-leaves rustling above me, the tune grew bolder, more certain, and took on a strange rhythm that echoed the jumpy beating of my pulse. High and low it jumped, pittering and pattering, maddening the blood and setting hidden feet a-dancing. Sometimes it changed, slowing to a deep breathy note, hollow as panpipes, wavering on a long-held note that fell as it died … and it seemed to me that even the cows in their pasture had stopped chewing to hear the low piping from the hill.

I do not know how long I played for, jigs and airs and laments pouring from my little pipe as though drawn out by the enchantment of the night, but when I finally finished the moon was low over the Welsh hills and there was a paling of the eastern sky behind me. Oberon, if he were there, had declined to appear to mortal senses but remained a King of Shadows – and the dawn was coming. I got to my feet stiffly, the imprint of a beech buttress firmly planted in my back for days to come, and made my way down the hill in a weary frame of mind. My experiment had failed. There had been none of that enforced imagining that had been pressed upon me in the valley of Capel Curig twelve years previously. Perhaps I had grown up at last. Or perhaps this was a sign that I had to grow up. *When I became a man, I put away childish things. But now I see in a glass darkly …*

That day seemed a particularly long and tedious one. It perhaps didn't help that I had only snatched a few hours' sleep before having to get up and teach lessons, mark essays, supervise lunch in the Dining Hall, umpire another interminable cricket match, run a play rehearsal and deal with the case of Billy Bagworth (Third Former) vs. the Tuckshop in the matter of some stolen Cheezels. But at the end of the day, as I was crossing the quadrangle, I was approached by a Sixth Form boy whom I didn't recognise. He had tight curly hair of a light golden hue and a pair of large spectacles on a pale face.

'Mr Mackinnon?' he said. 'Sorry to bother you. I don't think we've met properly. I'm Daniel May. Can I ask you a slightly odd question?'

'Er, yes. Yes, I think so. Daniel, is it?'

'Yes sir.'

'So, what's this odd question then? If it's anything to do with the LBW decision I gave against your House this afternoon, I can only claim temporary distraction by what I think was a passing wryneck—'

'Oh no, sir,' said Daniel. 'I try not to get in the way of the keener members of the House when it comes to cricket. Any sport, really. It appears I lack the killer instinct.'

'Ah, lucky you.'

'Quite, sir. No, I wanted to ask you … well … do you believe in fairies, sir?'

I must have looked blank because he quickly added, 'Only that Edwin Appleby seemed to think you might be the person to ask.'

So, Edwin Appleby again. I really would have to have a word with that insightful young man …

'Well now, Daniel, why do you ask that, I wonder. It's a good question. An odd one, mind you, you were right about that, but a good one. Umm … not the sort of question you would ask of, say, Mr Bamford?'

Bruce Bamford was a housemaster and P.E. teacher of uncertain mood and a no-nonsense approach to education. He had the build and sensibilities of a bad-tempered musk ox, and any questions concerning the existence of fairies would undoubtedly have brought about a growling rant on the problem with society these days, all with a highly homophobic slant.

'No, sir. Not Mr Bamford. But what are your own thoughts on the matter?'

'Well, let me see. I love the idea, of course. Are you familiar with Brian Froud and Alan Lee's book on the subject? Let me tell you about Capel Curig—'

But it seemed that Daniel could sense a lecture and was in fact far keener to tell me something than to find out my theories on fairy-lore.

'Because, sir, I do!'

'Oh yes, well, in a sense—'

'No, sir!' Daniel's eyes were shining behind his moon spectacles, and he was almost skipping from side to side with excitement. 'Really, sir. Because last night it was Midsummer's Eve, and I couldn't sleep. And the moon was so bright and the night so warm. So I slipped out of bed and went walking across the fields – and you'll never guess!'

I thought I knew what was coming. 'Guess what, Daniel?'

He lowered his voice to a whisper and said in a trembling voice, 'I heard it, sir. Actually heard it. Coming from a hill. Fairy music. I sat under a hedge and listened for hours and hours. Real fairy music. What do you think of that, sir?'

I looked at him. A kindred spirit then. A fellow wanderer who sought after enchantment in the woods and fields.

'Daniel, how wonderful. Umm . . .'

'You don't believe me?'

'Well, I'm afraid when you get to my age . . . well, let's just say that I'd really have to hear it for myself. Hearing is believing.'

'But—'

'So, Daniel,' I said gently, 'you've really got to ask yourself, "Was I dreaming perhaps? Imagining it? Did I really hear that music?" Occam's razor and all that, yes? And only you can know the honest answer to that. Now, if you'll excuse me, I have thirty essays to mark before midnight. But thanks for sharing your … umm … hallucination with me. Good night!'

As I climbed the stairs to the North Pole, I was conscious of the boy behind me, hugging himself with the absolute certainty that no matter what any old teacher could say to the contrary, he, Daniel May, had been privileged to hear upon Midsummer the fairy music of the hollow hills.

Chapter 10

> *The fiddle made me want to dance with myself, and many did. The drum beat like my very own heart. And some little flute that looked no wider than a pencil reminded me of the Islands floating not too far from Abbeyglen.*
>
> —Jenny B. Jones

Over the next year or two, I saw a lot more of Daniel May.

He was in the Lower Sixth Form – that is, he was sixteen at the time – and it was fairy magic that had first brought him to my attention. Magic of two sorts, really – he was an accomplished conjuror and I had first watched him in admiration as during the House Singing Competition he had danced his way across the stage dressed as a cartoon bear waving a scarlet handkerchief and with a flourish turned the scrap of silk into a long and evidently solid silver cane. The student chorus of 'The Bare Necessities' went unheeded, drowned out by the applause from the delighted audience. I was determined to find out who the boy was, pin him down and cheerfully coerce the secret of the trick out of him – the main problem being that dressed as he was in a bear suit, I had no idea what he looked like.

Once I had identified Daniel as the magical dancing bear of the House Singing Competition, I shared my own interest in conjuring and soon discovered him to be out of my league in the art of stage magic. He had an impressive collection of magical paraphernalia and wonderful skills in sleight-of-hand and legerdemain and we would get together occasionally to share the secrets of some favourite trick or see if we could invent a new one altogether. More often though, Daniel would present a feat of conjuring that would leave me utterly baffled and, in response to my pleas for an explanation, primly invoke the magician's code of never revealing how a trick is done – despite all my threats to fail his next English assignment if he didn't cough up.

As I put on dramatic productions of greater complexity, I also discovered Daniel to have a natural talent for production – posters, advertising, ticket sales, front-of-house – and he became an extremely effective assistant director for many of my plays. Despite his panache on stage when doing one of his magic routines, he preferred to sit next to me in the darkness of the auditorium, quietly suggesting an improvement here, a tweak there, and taking the production to heights of theatricality I could never have achieved on my own. For all his skills and charm, he struck me as a somewhat troubled boy, never really believing that he was particularly well-liked by his peers and always feeling like a fish out of water. This was particularly puzzling because in his year group was a small but extraordinary cohort of boys who were as eccentric, independent-minded and imaginative as himself: a group of students who became the Skelligs.

Let me explain. In my earliest days at Ellesmere College, before I had really got to know other staff members well, I had decided that in the first half-term break I would set out to see if I could walk to the summit of Snowdon and back. It seemed a feasibly romantic thing to do for a young schoolteacher; I had recently read Laurie Lee's book *As I Walked Out One Midsummer Morning*, in which he describes walking to Spain with a violin on his back and he made it seem really quite easy. Snowdon would be a doddle.

At the end of the first day, I found myself footsore and utterly exhausted. I really hadn't thought this through. I had assumed that every few miles there would be some cheerful inn or hostelry where I could sit at ease and drink my fill in exchange for a florin or two. There had been nothing of the sort – just miles and miles of stifling lanes hemmed in by high nettle-bristling hedges flanked with cow parsley, swarming with summer flies and smelling of silage. And that evening, I had found myself on a wild bit of moorland road with a thunderstorm brewing in the hot summer air and no clue as to where I would find shelter that night. I cursed whatever local gods there were … and then the first flickers of lightning played over the nearby hills. I quickened my pace.

Another hour of walking, however, brought me to a tiny road winding up a steep-sided coomb and I was met with a sight to delight even the weariest of travellers. Plunging down a tall cliff at the head of the valley was a great waterfall, a shining column of white water glimmering in the cool dusk. It thundered into a deep rock basin surrounded by a wood of beech and alder trees, for all the world like Cauldron Pool in the Narnia stories. On later visits to Pistyll Rhaeadr, as this place was called, I would see it in a range of different enchanting modes – in springtime where pale yellow primroses thronged beneath the beechen trunks while snowflakes glittered down softly in a sudden snow flurry, or in winter when the white torrent of water stood out starkly against the bare black trees and roared noisily in the frost-bound silence – but that evening, it was the sight of lamplit windows in a slate house at the foot of the falls that most cheered me. It was a B&B. Before very long, I was nursing my blistered feet and aching calves in a hot bath and trying to dull the pain with a large brandy before dropping into bed utterly exhausted.

The next morning, I decided that Snowdon was quite out of reach. Resolutely, I stuck my thumb out and hitchhiked back to the College, covering in ninety minutes what it had taken me fourteen hours the day before to cover on foot. So much for Laurie Lee and his jaunt to Spain. Back at Ellesmere, I was surprised to find that the College was not, as I had expected, abandoned for the half-term break. There were strangers around and in among them a handful of senior boys and girls. Mary Du Croz, the Headmaster's wife, saw me limping across the quadrangle and hailed me cheerfully. 'Sandy, just the chap! We're all off to Colemere Woods and could do with another pair of hands. You don't mind, do you?'

And so I found myself volunteering to help out over the next five days with an organisation called Breakaway. Each year Mr and Mrs Du Croz opened the College grounds to this charitable group, who took in for a week young people with severe physical impairments, mental incapacities or behavioural problems, the idea being to give their parents a respite from their roles as full-time carers. We spent the next few days taking our young guests on houseboats on the canal or for walks along the mere to feed the geese and swans, or improvising art lessons where it didn't seem to matter if the paint got anywhere but on the canvas; and the enjoyment this produced more than made up for the times when toileting accidents had to be dealt with or young Willy Suggs had to be coaxed down out of a tree because he was terrified of waterfowl. An extra highlight was to watch in admiration the way our volunteer students engaged with our sometimes-troubled guests.

These students were, naturally, the pick of the bunch in terms of compassion and willingness to serve – oddly enough, not a single prefect or House Captain among them – but were delightful in other ways as well. They were eccentric, independent-minded, maverick – and in particular that year, musically gifted to a wonderful degree. I discovered this late one night when, after all our charges had been put to bed, I heard distant music emanating from the school hall. Intrigued, I crept along the echoing corridors and peeked into Big School. This resembled a medieval feasting hall with high hammer beams supporting a gabled roof far overhead and stained-glass windows tinting the moonlight in palest greens and silvery roses like the hues on a trout's flank. In the middle of the wooden floor, someone had lit a candle and around it sat four musicians playing a sweet folk air into the shadowy darkness. There was a tall, slender boy standing there playing a violin; he had a flop of dark hair and narrow goat-like eyes catching the candlelight with an amused gleam. I recognised him as Nick Grey from the day's toils. There was also Jonathan Jones, a gruff, shaggy-haired Labrador of a boy playing a bodhrán, or Celtic drum, tapping out a compelling rhythm to drive the tune along. Katy Parsons, a willowy girl with lake-grey eyes and a sweet smile, was singing the words to 'Down by the Sally Gardens', her voice like silver. And lastly, a lad with an unruly thatch of hair, wide eyes and a gentle smile was playing the guitar and improvising harmonies in a warm, throaty tenor. This last was Walter Thatcher, whom I would later discover was the leader of the group.

Entranced, I listened from the shadow of the hallway until the song wavered to a stop, and then hesitantly emerged. I told them how beautiful that had been and asked them how long they had been playing for. They explained that they had only got together that night, each discovering the others' love and talent for music just then. It was a pity, said Walter, that they didn't have a tin-whistle player in the group.

'Wait here,' I told them, and five minutes later had returned with my trusty instrument. This was the same whistle I had busked my way across the world with, playing on the sunny piers of New Zealand, in the streets of Darwin, the marketplaces of Penang and the forests of Laos. It had been dropped into – and recovered from – the coral seabeds of Indonesia; played to the blazing desert stars of the Egyptian Sahara; and firmly tucked away out of use as I had wandered the musical laneways of Salzburg, where even the rudest beggar busked like Bach. I was shy about introducing my playing to this group, but the rest of that evening saw us play piece after piece in one of those rare sessions where no one seems able to play a wrong note.

That was the start of the Skelligs, the name Walter chose for the band, the name drawn from a group of wild islands off the west coast of his native Ireland. The group was to become one of the factors of my life at Ellesmere that brought enchantment to my time there. As I got to know these young people better, I was astonished at their musical skill. Nick Grey had a Puckish look when he played that made his eyes crinkle and gleam with mischievous delight. He also turned out to be a superb actor and played the lead in several performances over the years with great poise. He later went on to play the lead violin in various West End musicals and became a professional actor.

Walter was especially versatile; over the next year or so, I saw him switch effortlessly from the flute to the guitar, from drums to the fiddle, and his voice had a chameleon-like character. At times, he sounded like a 65-year-old Irish trawlerman, rich and rough with decades of grog, rasping out a sea shanty; at other times he could sing with a pure countertenor like something out of the fifteenth-century Vatican, his voice as serene and golden as a candleflame in still air.

Daniel May brought all his entrepreneurial and technical skills to help us out. He would set up microphones, adjust levels, arrange publicity, organise transport. Still, however, despite his ability to wow an audience when performing his conjuring on stage, he seemed to me slightly uncertain of his welcome among the others. He remained convinced that he was tolerated rather than welcomed, in spite of all we did to include him in our warm ring of music and delight. This puzzled and saddened me, but in my experience such negative self-perceptions are difficult to shift and I accepted that not everything was in my power to change for the better.

Then one day, shortly after returning from the Easter break, Daniel came to have a cup of tea and recounted with great pride that he had spent the holiday hitchhiking up to Scotland with a friend. Remembering a story of the Well of Eternal Youth and some misadventures with Pixie Peterson, which must have somehow crept unaccountably into the curriculum sometime over the last year, Daniel and Finn had made the long pilgrimage to Iona and gone to find the Well for themselves. In fact, Daniel had told me, he had been so struck by the enchantment of the place that he had taken a silk handkerchief, patterned with irises, and thrown it into the Well as a gift for the fairies.

I had tried hard not to choke on my digestive at this news. The fact is that just a week earlier, I too had visited Iona, taking my sister Maggie to see the sights. We had climbed the hill of Dun, I to the summit, and found the Well, me recounting for her benefit my memorable visit there as a nineteen-year-old while she politely pretended not to have heard this tale seventeen times before. As we sat there in the April sunshine, I had noticed something drifting in the clear grey waters of the little pool. Wading in, I had retrieved a large silk handkerchief patterned with irises and decided to take it home as – my words to Maggie exactly – a gift from the fairies. It was currently residing in my tea-towel drawer about three feet from where Daniel was sitting telling me all about it.

The coincidence was too good to waste. Daniel would eventually know of this remarkable serendipity, but not before I had made some good mileage out of it. Over the next few weeks, my mind went to a fever-pitch of manic creativity. I was determined that Daniel would be reunited with his scarf, but only in the most magical of circumstances. The resulting folderol that arose from this seed of coincidence would, alas, take far too long to recount and was of such labyrinthine complexity that it would lose readers at the first jump; suffice to say that it involved several of the following: forging an antique and seemingly priceless volume of Yeats poetry with a lost version of *The Song of Wandering Aengus* in it – fifty stanzas rather than the better known four-stanza version – in which a golden-haired youth uses his iris-blue cloak as a net to catch a fairy fish-maiden in a sacred pool; an apparently genuine account of a visit by the poet Yeats in the 1890s to a local stately home and his vision of a ghost by the lake there, a ghostly youth with tight fair curls; the invention of a Celtic sea-witch deity called Hwinefre, who in the doctored poem pursues a fictional hero from the Hebrides to a certain sacred pool on the Welsh borders; a staged midnight glimpse by Daniel himself of the poet Yeats rowing on the local lake in misty moonlight; and a final visit to a local shrine, St Winifrede's Well, where the perplexed Daniel was to find his iris-blue scarf floating among the cresses and kingcups on a day of high summer, there to draw the only conclusion possible, namely that he, Daniel May, was somehow treading the borders of waking life and poetry; at one and the same time, an ordinary schoolboy struggling with the demands of friendships and A-Levels but also a divine figure, a golden-haired youth appearing to Yeats in a vision and inspiring the mythical figure of Wandering Aengus who searches still for those silver apples of the moon, those golden apples of the sun.

By far the loveliest part of this year-long adventure was not the manic flare of obsession on my part in contorting all these threads together but the fact that an integral part of the enterprise was the willing and loving involvement of Daniel's new friends. Each one of them had a part to play: Nick to steer Daniel in the direction of the antique shop, where the forged poetry volume had been planted, Walter to inveigle him out on an illicit midnight expedition to the shores of the mere to witness the phantasmal appearance of W.B. Yeats in a rowboat in the misty moonlight; Jonathan to invite him down to his farm on a hot summer's afternoon and allow him to discover for himself the ancient wellhouse of St Winifrede and the iris-blue scarf drifting dreamlike there.

The main intention of this whole elaborate hoax was really nothing more than making the best possible use of an incredible coincidence. Indeed, at some baser level, I suppose I rather merely hoped to reverse the status quo when it came to conjuring; that is, leave Daniel pleading for answers while I for once got to smugly invoke the magicians' code. However, the Muse that works such enchantments had nobler purposes in mind. On being presented with the extraordinary impression that he was somehow a mythical figure bestriding the two worlds of waking life and poetic myth, Daniel found a new quiet confidence in himself. Not long afterwards, he had the courage to come out to his peers as gay, the first student I ever knew to do this and, for those times, an extremely confronting step. How much of this was to do with his conviction that he straddled the two worlds of myth and reality I don't know. Perhaps once you have straddled those two worlds it becomes a simple matter to straddle other bridges as well.

Whatever the case, Daniel seemed to blossom from that point on. His friendships grew stronger – as they so often do when one shares a vulnerability – and he walked the corridors of Ellesmere with a lighter step. Years later, I caught up with him for a final time. I had heard on the grapevine that he had gone on to become a successful student at university and had continued to use his entrepreneurial spirit for good. He often did magic shows for charity in his local town, and set up a radio station that became popular within youth culture. As one of the first of his generation I knew of to become comfortable with his sexuality, a prime motivation of his radio work was to start ensuring that other young people in his situation had a voice.

It was wonderful to catch up with him again over a pint at the Black Lion and hear all his news. We chatted of this and that while Daniel showed me a new routine with a coin penetrating a beer coaster and ending up at the bottom of my glass of beer. I remained as mystified as ever. But talking of being mystified, I had tossed up whether to finally reveal the whole nature of the scarf hoax and had decided against it. If, as I suspected, his new-found confidence had come about from believing himself to be some sort of divine archetype inhabiting the dreams of poets and spanning the centuries, then I did not have the stomach to rob him of that helpful illusion. But just before we went our separate ways, I couldn't resist asking if he still had the iris-blue hanky. Smiling, he pulled it from his pocket. 'I brought it along especially,' he said.

I had last seen it four years previously when he had come to my rooms glowing with mystery and excitement, shortly after finding it in St Winifrede's Well near Jonathan's farm. He had told me the whole series of events as they happened over the course of the previous nine months – the finding of the poetry book in Mr Crabbe's Ellesmere Antiques Emporium, the discovery of the 'lost' poem and the prologue detailing Yeats' vision, his sighting of the ghostly Yeats rowing a boat on the midnight mere some six months later – and now, the final instalment, his finding of the scarf in the well of 'Hwinefre' after last casting it to the fairies in another sacred spring three hundred miles to the north of where we sat.

Now here it was again. 'It changed my life, this scarf,' he said … and I felt a twinge of guilt. Was it really healthy to allow

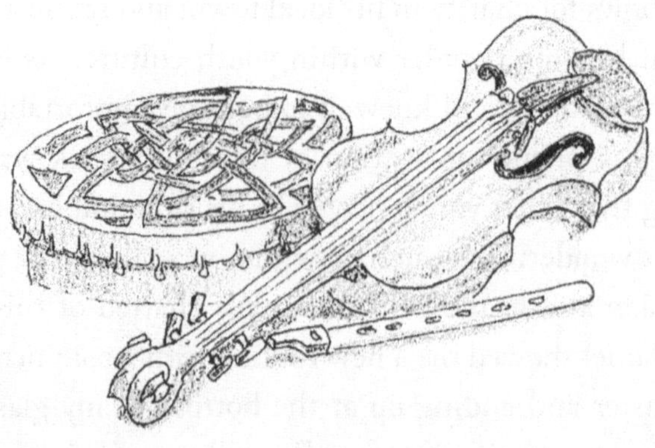

Daniel to continue in this delusion? But would the revelation of the truth deal him too severe a blow?

'You mean … you still think … um … there's magic at play?' I said hesitantly. 'That you, somehow, are Wandering Aengus?' I tailed off weakly. The whole prank now seemed rather childish, a foolish piece of showing off. But I needn't have worried.

Daniel smiled. 'Oh, not one bit of it,' he said. 'I will admit there was a moment there … a day or so at the most … when you had me convinced I was in some sort of Alan Garner book – magic and reality blurring – and it was pretty bloody awesome. But you know me, sir. The conjuror's temperament. There's always an explanation. Within a week, I'd got someone to spill the beans that it was all a clever hoax.'

Relief and foolishness and disappointment gushed over me in a warm torrent. 'Oh. Right. Well … hardly life-changing then, ha ha. Probably a good thing all round.'

'No. Seriously life-changing. I mean it.' He looked very earnest behind his wide glasses.

'I don't understand.'

'When I found out that it was a hoax – that it had taken so long to prepare, that so much thought and creativity had gone into it – and most of all, that Nick and Walter and Jonathan and

Katy – and you – had all gone to such amazing lengths to make it work ... and all to give me a sense of, a sense of ... well, purpose and meaning, well ... I'd never felt very liked up till that point. When I found out all that, I realised I was loved after all.'

As he spoke, his voice became a little croaky and his eyes reddened. I too didn't trust myself to speak. He flipped a couple of beermats to and fro between his long dextrous fingers, making one vanish into thin air and then plucking it out from behind his ear.

'There's magic right there,' he said hoarsely.

And I don't think he was talking about the beermats.

Chapter 11

> *I could not possibly hope to be a lady if I wore breeches; when I said I could do nothing in a dress, she said I wasn't supposed to be doing things that required pants ... furthermore, I should be a ray of sunshine in my father's lonely life. I suggested that one could be a ray of sunshine in pants just as well, but Aunty said that one had to behave like a sunbeam, I was born good but had grown progressively worse every year.*
>
> —Harper Lee, *To Kill a Mockingbird*

> *We shall go wild with fireworks ... and they will plunge into the sky and shatter the darkness.*
>
> —Natsuki Takaya

Despite all our shared interests and common adventures, I have somehow lost touch with Daniel May. That is the way of things. Students can become incredibly close but after leaving school vanish into oblivion. Others stick like burrs. One such ball of tenacious botanical Velcro comes to mind.

In my second year of teaching at my Adelaide school, I had taught English to a lively young girl called Nina Scarlatti. She was a clever, cheeky student and I had once made the mistake of giving her 25 out of 20 for a piece of creative writing that I thought was particularly promising – even though it referred, memorably, to 'a Scottish castle on the Yorkshire moors'. As a Year 8, she had performed in a musical I had just written; although a consummate actress, she decided that she was more than capable of holding down the role of Second Witch while also spreading her energies more widely. Two rehearsals in, she appointed herself as my Assistant Director and then proceeded to organise set construction, scenery painting, costumes, props, lighting, sound, publicity, programme printing, catering, rehearsal schedules – and would have also made me wholly redundant by taking over the directing of the actors had I not put my foot down and reserved that one last island of responsibility for myself.

After I left Australia and set off on my travels overland to Britain, young Nina continued to write to me; her letters were some of the few that seemed to manage to get to the Poste Restante offices of Singapore or Penang or Cairo without fail. She had probably by the age of sixteen already managed to shoehorn her way into some managerial position in the Australian Post Office. Her letters were lively, confident, but had a distinct hint of a schoolgirl crush about them, which worried me considerably. She addressed every one of them to 'Dear AJ', I suppose as a way of getting round that awkward transition from addressing a teacher as Mr Mackinnon to the too-familiar first name of Sandy – and this latest letter now announced that she was on her way to visit. Indeed, she would be at Shrewsbury Station the following afternoon and was quite sure I would be happy to pick up my all-time favourite student and bring her back to the College for a visit of indeterminate length. I would find, she assured me, that she was still 25 out of 20 grade material. The letter was adorned with a number of bright pink X's as kisses, and I noticed with a sinking heart that every 'i' was dotted with a smiley face. I drove to the station the next day with some trepidation.

Nina had grown into a striking young woman – not so much in height but with ample curves where there had once been the straight fall of the schoolgirls' tunic – and she was dressed in a flamingo-pink skirt and a ruffled low-cut blouse straight from the set of *Strictly Ballroom.* On the drive, she explained that she had come to do a gap year in England at St Felix in Suffolk and I could expect a visit from her on regular occasions for the rest of that year. Suffolk was very flat, she explained, and she found the Shropshire landscape more stimulating; this with a roguish wink in my direction. I found myself unaccountably having to concentrate hard on the road ahead to avoid running the car into a hedgerow.

That night Nina insisted that she accompany me to Chapel Evensong, and I still remember the echoing clack of her platform heels as she tottered up the aisle like a flamboyant but determined young tapir while the choir's rendition of 'Hear My Prayer' floundered its way to a discordant finish as every chorister's eye lost its place in the sheet music simultaneously. After the service, about five of the senior masters decided spontaneously that a post-Evensong sherry in the Common Room bar was a long-abandoned tradition that needed reviving pronto, and before I could steer her to a modest cup of tea at the North Pole, Nina found herself in the centre of a circle of bachelor masters – and some not so bachelor – holding forth in those shrill Aussie tones I remembered so well. Most of us were still in our academic gowns; I did make one feeble attempt to suggest she might want to borrow mine as protection from the night chills: by which I meant the frankly lascivious stare of Mr Jessup the Latin master, directed down the front of her blouse. This was dismissed with a hefty punch to the forearm and a laughing comment about me being just a plain old silly billy, much to the amusement of my colleagues, who were by now hanging off her every word. (Indeed, the nickname 'Silly Billy' was peculiarly hard to shake off for the following few months.) She was ghastly. She was embarrassing. She was marvellous. She was a macaw among crows and before long, had organised a drinking competition against Mr Jessup using the priceless College sherry, put down in 1876, which she won hands down.

The next few days were relatively uneventful, if you don't count that when I announced a meeting of the Skillibladnir Club one evening, the entire First XV showed up, having never evinced much of an interest in philosophy before, and Nina managed to dismiss most of my carefully thought-out ideas on consciousness as all a bit wanky. Apart from that, there was not too much damage done to my credibility. My colleagues kept asking how was charming Miss-Er-Short-Skirted-Young-Thing-You-Know, and enquiring if, being Australian, she would like to come and look at the College cricket records one evening over another sherry or two. Feeling somewhat *in loco parentis*, I managed to steer her away from such invitations and keep her occupied touring the countryside.

On a free day, I drove her out to Pistyll Rhaedr, the waterfall in Wales I had discovered on my abandoned trek to Snowdon, and we found it simply Narnian in its beauty. There were fresh yellow primroses all up the mossy banks under the beech trees and while we were there, it started snowing in big, soft flakes that glittered in the remaining beams of sunlight. 'What a place for a treasure hunt, AJ,' she said, and I couldn't help agreeing with her. I remembered then that in Year 9 she had begged leave from the last two classes of the year to set a treasure hunt for the rest of the class to do on the final day. I remember especially the last clue because this was a quote that I had passed on to the class earlier in the term. It was something like:

> Only children are low enough to the ground to see the fairies; only children know how to listen closely enough with ears still attuned to the cries of the flittering bats. Is it any wonder that when we grow up and turn into blundering giants, the world of elf-land becomes only a book … and a closed book at that … kept behind glass in a dusty library somewhere? Stay young!

Nina had bought, months earlier, from a secondhand bookshop, an old book of fairy-tales with a wonderfully evocative cover, and had hollowed it out into a box. Then she had filled the cavity with chocolate gold coins and had persuaded the school librarian to place it in the library foyer's glass display case. We had all walked past it a dozen times or more and never suspected the hidden treasure within. Even when we found that final clue, we needed some pretty intense nudging from an overexcited Nina before the light dawned and we rushed down to find the librarian and got him to unlock the display cabinet.

It was Nina's throwaway comment as we climbed among the snow and primroses of Pistyll Rhaedr that would later burgeon into something quite remarkable. Little did I know then that this was not the last visit from Nina and that she was later to become a much bigger part of my life than I suspected back then. In the meantime, however, I had to find a way of getting her back to College, packed up and driven to Shrewsbury Station, without her bumping into any of the sherry-swilling crowd from the Common Room. If she did, I wouldn't vouch for her chances of making it back to Suffolk any time soon.

During one of our evenings of reminiscence, Nina had reminded me that it had been she who was responsible for my introduction to the Rocket Club. The first I knew of this small but secretive band was when a diminutive boy in thick spectacles presented himself one morning at the staffroom door of my

Adelaide school along with two other little boys and introduced themselves as the Rocket Club. We solemnly shook hands all round. Miss Scarlatti had told them that I needed some special explosive effects for the latest production. Was this true? If so, they rather thought they could help out.

'Miss Scarlatti?' I queried.

'Well, we know she's just a year above us, sir,' said Matthew, 'but as your assistant director, she prefers to be called Miss Scarlatti. We felt it better to agree ...'

That Friday afternoon, the Rocket Club invited me to the chemistry lab to show me what they could do in the way of stage explosives. I had assumed this would be something along the lines of a few homemade sparklers or setting steel wool on fire, but I was astonished at their proficiency. Under the tuition of Doc Fenner, an ageing Chemistry teacher whose regard for health and safety regulations was even more relaxed than my own, these three miniature mad scientists had acquired the skills to make an impressive array of pyrotechnics. They demonstrated flash bombs, small devices each about the size of a cotton-reel, which when detonated set off a bright flash in an array of different colours and a mushroom cloud of white smoke. Barium for red, they explained; copper for green, and plain old cooking salt – sodium chloride – for bright yellow. The brilliance of the flash was caused, of course, by magnesium powder.

'But how do we detonate them?' I asked. 'I want them going off precisely as the witches appear, one two three.'

'Ah,' said Matthew. 'We're rather excited about a new development that Timmy here has just been working on. If you would care to step onto the oval, we can demonstrate, sir. Early stages, sir, but we're quietly hopeful.'

I followed the young Barnes Wallis and his pals onto the oval and they continued to explain. 'Timmy here is a bit of an electronics whiz, you see. He's been working on a remote-radio-controlled detonator and we're testing it for the first time today. Let's have you, young Tim.'

Timmy Dalton was a tiny tadpole of a boy with a mop of curly hair and one squiffy eye. I was amused to see him pull out a device that looked straight out of a Wile. E. Coyote cartoon, a large black box with a dial, an antenna and a big red button saying 'PUSH'.

'Now, James,' prompted President Matthew. 'Safety check, please'.

James, a lanky fair-haired boy, started handing out safety goggles as he explained the set-up.

'We've already set the explosive device. It's over there by those trees. It's quite a big one, which is why we're so far back. Goggles on please.'

'What, those trees there?' I asked, pointing at a nearby clump of salmon gums.

'Oh no, sir. Not those. Those other ones over by the railway line,' – and he pointed at a distant stand of gums some 700 metres away.

'And you're going to detonate this flash bomb all the way over there with this thing?' I indicated Timmy and his black box. He was twiddling the dial, muttering coordinates and frequencies and checking the wind direction with his one good eye.

'Well, that's the idea. But it's not a flash bomb, sir. It's a tad bigger. Ready?'

'Ready,' said Tommy.

'Ready,' said Matthew.

'How big?' said I.

'Then GO!' said James – and Timmy pushed the red button.

For a split-second, I didn't think it had worked. Then came a billowing puff of white smoke the size of a small cottage, followed two seconds later by an almighty bang and an explosion of angry white corellas from the treetops, some lightly singed. After another fifteen seconds of awed silence, broken only by the irregular patter and thud of a sizeable section of the cricket oval raining down all about us in turfy clumps, I managed to break the suspense.

'Gentlemen, you're hired.'

*

Quite apart from the brilliance they brought to my Adelaide drama productions over the next few years, my association with the Rocket Club was a fruitful one. It was they who taught me how to make gunpowder, flash powder, smoke bombs and sky-rockets, and for a while this became my favourite hobby. In fact, it allowed me to fulfil a long-cherished ambition, namely to make myself a Gandalf staff. Any aficionados of Tolkien will know that the wizard Gandalf carries with him a staff with which he can produce pyrotechnics, either flashes and whiz-bangs to amuse hobbit children or more serious firepower to ward off attacks by orcs or wolves – or simply to produce a faint bluish glow to allow him and his companions to make their way through the dark vastness of the Mines of Moria. With my newfound knowledge, I took a length of sturdy bamboo and inserted into one end a gas lighter that operated at the push of a button. This was disguised beneath a binding of leather and could produce a small flame at the top of the staff. Protruding from the top were three spiralling brass wires that looked ornamental but were in fact designed to hold in place a hollow bamboo capsule, about the height of a cigarette lighter, fitted with a fuse out the bottom and a cork in the top. This could be filled with a mixture of gunpowder and whatever other chemicals were needed for the desired effect: a brilliant white flash, a fountain of red sparks, a thick white smoke, a fierce green jet of flame. I spent many happy hours showing off my Gandalf staff to friends and students out on the playing fields at night before an unwisely generous dose of flash powder one evening resulted in an explosion so fierce that I was left dazed and blinded, clutching the remains of my splintered staff in one hand, my arm burnt to the elbow and one whole half of my face coated with a fine white ash. After that, I became a little more circumspect and limited my use of gunpowder and magnesium to the odd magic show – and in small doses.

Years later, when I was first being interviewed for the position at Ellesmere College, one of the last questions Mr Du Croz asked was whether I had any other hobbies or interests that might enhance the life of the school. 'Ooh yes,' I said, knowing I was onto a winner. 'I do conjuring and I make my own fireworks. Whiz-bang! Kids love it.'

I saw Mr Du Croz and Mr Arne exchange loaded glances. I didn't know it at the time, but that throwaway bit of enthusiasm nearly cost me the job. Only when I was fully ensconced at the College did I meet Mr Chauncy Lamont and realise why. Chauncy was one of those teachers to be found in every school in England: eccentric, unpredictable, hugely popular with the students, but whose maverick temperament make them a liability and a headache to management. It turned out that Chauncy Lamont's two hobbies happened to be conjuring and homemade fireworks; both pursuits had nearly got him sacked on a number of occasions over the past few years. Every November 5th, Chauncy would host a Guy Fawkes Night on the College croquet lawn. Every November 6th, a troop of grumbling groundskeepers would roll in to repair the damage to the turf, the surrounding shrubbery and on one memorable occasion the Headmaster's upstairs bathroom window. This was tolerated as an acceptable part of the excitement

surrounding fireworks, but when Mr Lamont started using his skills as a conjuror to terrify the students, the school felt he had perhaps overstepped the bounds of professionalism by a slight margin.

On this front, I found myself involved in a small way. I was approached one afternoon by my friend Michael Barton, fuming more than usual. It appeared that Mr Lamont had been teaching *Macbeth* to the Fifth Form when a rather boorish boy called Guy Marshall had given his smirking opinion that Shakespeare was complete rubbish because witchcraft and all that was complete tosh and everyone knew it. Mr Lamont had smiled genially and had pulled out a pack of tarot cards from his desk drawer. 'I'm sure it is, Guy. Yes, you're quite right. For example, if I asked you to choose any one of these cards at random … go on, dear boy, any card … the card would be utterly meaningless. Why, what is it, dear fellow?'

Out of the seventy-six cards in the tarot deck, Guy had pulled out one depicting a scythe-wielding skeleton. The Death card, in fact.

Guy had turned a little pale, but Mr Lamont was quick to reassure him. 'A coincidence, dear boy. I was told, mind you, that these cards once belonged to Agnes Clutterbuck, a local witch … but no, what am I thinking. Let's put that silly old card back – see, like this – and shuffle the deck – like so – and let's have another go. Go on, any card.'

Guy picked the Death card again and went the colour of feta cheese.

'No? Really?! Well, that's extraordinary. But Guy, dear chap, as you just said, it can't be magic, can it? No such thing. Load of tosh. It must be just horrible bad luck. Try again …'

And when Guy picked the Death card for a third time in a row, Guy was no longer his smug and smirking self. What Chauncy Lamont didn't know at the time was that Guy's grandma up in Lancashire had recently been quite ill. When Mr Lamont discovered this nugget of information, he saw a perfect opportunity to ram the metaphorical scythe-blade home. He persuaded a colleague to come to rugby practice that afternoon and tell Guy that he was wanted by the Headmaster. The exact words were to be, 'You're not in trouble, Guy – but I'm afraid it's serious.'

Fortunately, this message never got delivered. Michael, as Guy's housemaster, had got wind of the cruel prank and had decided to fight magic with magic. Hence, his visit to me. 'Sandy, clearly this is some conjuring trick. But if Lamont can make him choose the Death card three times in a row, surely it must be possible to make him choose … I don't know … the Love card three times in a row, just to show him it's only sleight-of-hand.'

I wasn't confident of doing that particular trick myself, but I knew someone who could – and ran off to find Daniel May. 'Good,' said Michael. 'And if there's some 'You-Are-A-Hot-Stud-Babe-Magnet' card in the bloody deck, get him to choose that three times in a row. That should take his mind off his dying granny for a bit.'

Daniel May did indeed manage the trick and restored Guy to his smug-jock self-confidence (more's the pity) and Chauncy Lamont was thwarted in his use of the Dark Arts. At the end of the year, he had moved on to wider pastures and left me as the only resident wizard-pyrotechnician in the place, a role I carried out without ever deliberately terrorising a student. Mr Du Croz seemed to breathe a little more easily with Mr Lamont several counties away, but even he agreed that Guy Fawkes Night was, smoking croquet lawn notwithstanding, never quite the same again.

*

Before we put Nina on hold for a few chapters, I should in fairness add here something I did not discover till much later, namely that Nina assures me that at no point did she ever have anything remotely resembling a crush on me. When she read about herself in these pages, she snorted so loudly with indignation that Campari came out of her Pekingese nose. The 'roguish wink' she attributes to an irritable eye caused by an over-liberal application of mascara on a bumpy train. And in case I didn't believe her, she rammed the message home with her customary physical force. My arm still bears the bruises.

Chapter 12

Boyishness – by which I mean animal life in its fullest measure, good nature and honest impulses, hatred of injustice and meanness, and thoughtlessness enough to sink a three-decker.

—Thomas Hughes, *Tom Brown's Schooldays*

In the meantime, the school year raced on. I look back on my time at Ellesmere with great nostalgia and remember it as a series of timeless delights: croquet matches and Pimms on the Headmaster's lawns; gentle rambles across the fields to the Whitemere Sailing Club on Wednesday afternoons, picking wild sloes on the way; choral practices where we brought Handel's *Messiah* fizzing to a golden climax like champagne under the expert direction of the Choral Director; evenings in the Common Room bar downing far too many pints of bitter till the wee hours with beloved colleagues. And yet my letters from that time frequently indicate that I was exhausted, frazzled, overworked and run-down. It hardly seems credible to me now, but I know that I am blessed with an incurably rosy-tinted memory and the weeks and months of drudgery have all dissolved away like so much muddy paint-dregs swilled down the plughole at the end of an art lesson, leaving only the bright impressionistic paintings behind.

For all the rigours and relentlessness of life, I found myself charmed and delighted by the likes of Walter Thatcher, Daniel

May and their friends. They were just how I imagined school students should be when I had first dreamt of being a teacher. I had read *Tom Brown's Schooldays* and *Goodbye, Mr. Chips*. I had watched the whole series of *To Serve Them All My Days* and had formed a very clear picture in my mind of how English school-mastering was meant to play out.

My first six years of boarding-school experience in Australia had signally failed to reach these ideals. As a tutor there, my job was simply to police the corridors and ensure that windows were not being broken, rules were being adhered to and everyone's movements were accounted for every fifteen minutes or so. Even on arrival at Ellesmere, I had found the Upper Sixth Formers somewhat arrogant and cool towards me. Years of lax discipline under a divided set of housemasters with very different ways of dealing with their boys had left the A-Level students running their lives as they saw fit. For example, it was the custom of the older boys to walk into their House common rooms at any time and demand that the younger boys immediately vacate their seats for their seniors. This deeply offended my egalitarian principles, and when I challenged the prefects on this matter I cast myself in their eyes as a socialist of the lowest order who clearly didn't understand the noble traditions of the English Public School system.

In vain did I point out to them that this was hardly good training for the real world – that nowhere for the rest of their lives would they find a situation in which it was acceptable to oust people from their seats or their place in a queue because of some supposed difference in rank. I was a damned Antipodean rabble-rouser in their eyes and on more than one occasion, I was taken aside by a prefect to have things explained to me in cool, patrician tones and advised not to upset the apple cart.

This came to a head one evening when I was supervising dinner in the Ellesmere Dining Hall. This was a duty much disliked by staff; in fact, just a week earlier Colonel Roland Judd, a member of staff famous for his absentmindedness, had forgotten that he was rostered on for Dinner Duty. A much younger and rather officious teacher called Bingo Todhunter had come hurrying back from the Dining Hall and burst into the Common Room, where Judd was calmly smoking his pipe and doing his beloved cryptic crossword.

'I say, Colonel,' said Todhunter gleefully. 'You'll cop it. There's a riot in the Dining Hall and the Headmaster is doing your duty for you!'

Famously, Judd had lowered his paper, puffed thoughtfully on his pipe for a second or two and replied, 'Hmm. That's uncommonly decent of him,' and resumed his perusal of Fifteen Down.

It was also the prefects' job to ensure that the tables were left clean and tidy by the departing students; that is, the students had to take their dirty crockery and cutlery to the side hatches, scrape their plates clean and stack them neatly in trays ready to be put through the dishwashers. It was the duty staff member's job in turn to ensure that this process was followed. When I first arrived at Ellesmere, this duty had fallen into disuse and the tables were often left in a disgraceful state, covered in abandoned dishes and spillages and it usually fell upon the hardworking kitchen ladies to clean up.

I remembered back to my first year teaching in Adelaide under the leadership of the Headmaster, Michael Murray. One Friday afternoon staff meeting, Mr Murray showed us three large bin bags of rubbish that he and his wife had spent the previous afternoon picking up from around the grounds. He reminded us that when on yard duty one of our jobs was to encourage the duty prefects with us to patrol the schoolyard and direct students to pick up any litter and place it in the bins. He was confident he could leave it in our capable hands.

The following week, he cut the Friday afternoon meeting short, called us all outside and handed us a bin liner each. Then he instructed us to spread out through the grounds and pick up the considerable amount of litter that strewed the area. I was a very junior teacher and would not have squeaked any sort of exception to this undignified request but some of my senior colleagues were outraged. 'Headmaster, it's not our job to go around and pick up litter!' spluttered the Head of Mathematics.

'No, Mr Hicks,' said Mr Murray drily from his great height. 'It is your job to ensure that the prefects encourage the students to pick up litter, but since it is evident that you haven't done that job as asked, it *is* now your job to pick up the litter. Starting with that chip packet there.'

That following week, there was a marked change. I witnessed a repeat of this scenario but shifted down a level, namely a staff member responding to a sniffy prefect in much the same terms. 'Yes, Shane, but I asked you to get the Year 8s to pick up their lunch litter and you didn't do it. So, if you're not prepared to do that, now it's your job to pick up their litter for them. Get on with it.'

Over the next few years, there was never another litter problem in the school.

With that in mind, I watched in frustration in the Ellesmere Dining Hall as the prefects I had just detailed to go and check that the tables were being properly cleared away lounged against a distant wall with their hands in their pockets, no doubt discussing the recent appalling decline in the quality of new staff. The junior students ate, slurped and slunk away unobserved, leaving the tables squalid with filthy plates and spilt stroganoff. Once the meal was over and the prefects had sauntered up to ask if they could go, I remembered Mr Murray all those years before.

'Not quite yet, chaps. We've got a bit of a job to do first. Every one of these tables needs clearing away, the plates need to be scraped into those buckets, stacked in those dishwasher trays and the tables wiped down with a hot cloth. Here, I'll show you.'

From the looks on the faces of the four prefects, one might assume I had just asked them to scrub out a Turkish latrine with their favourite toothbrush.

'Us, sir?' said Deverill Major, looking at me through his nostrils. 'But we are prefects, sir. We direct, sir. We point. We observe and oversee. We are trained by our breeding to do these things. But we don't *do*—'

'Well, so I imagined. But there seems to have been very little of any sort of directing or overseeing tonight. Hence the shambles. So tonight, my friends, you and I clear this mess up – and next time you're on duty, do the job you profess to be so good at. Now chop, chop.'

Half an hour later, four very surly young men stalked off to their studies and started plotting how to get rid of this tactless oik. The dinner ladies, on the other hand, had watched from the side-hatches with amused admiration and I had a devoted fan club in the school kitchens for the rest of my tenure. The next day, I was summoned to a meeting in the Head Prefect's office, where various charges were laid against me and I was advised to change my attitude. Here was the other side to English boarding. In Australia, I might not have been charmed by cherubic choirboys offering me a pre-Evensong sherry in the buttery, but there also wasn't a schoolboy in Australia who would have spoken to me as though I was an erring under-valet who had failed to get a decent shine on the family candelabra. I found it hard to keep a straight face. When they had finished, I gently explained the position as I saw it. 'Gentlemen, thank you for your feedback. The thing is, in five months' time, you'll be out of here.

You'll be making your mark at Oxford or Cambridge, and then beginning to carve out fulfilling lives in the worlds of hedge-fund management, Lloyds Insurance and overseeing the hideous slaughter of foxes from a great height like your fathers and their fathers before them. Ellesmere shall know you no more. But I'll still be here for a few years to come, and I need to start doing things my way because – sorry to say it, cobbers – I am the Ellesmere of the future. And just so we all get used to the new way of doing things, I've had Mr Marshall roster us all on for another round of Dinner Duty every day this week. See you then. Hooroo!'

I think it was because of the way they saw me deal with the old guard that Walter Thatcher, Nick Grey, Daniel May and their friends warmed to me. As senior students themselves, I never saw in them the same arrogant *droit de seigneur* of their predecessors. The same spirit of loving service that had led them to volunteer at the Breakaway holidays each summer half-term – and which had led to the formation of the Skelligs – was apparent in the way they related to the younger boys in the school, and they provided a wonderful model of free-spiritedness, creativity and compassion for the juniors to aspire to.

As any schoolteacher knows, students can be thoroughly exasperating without ever really being as obnoxious as those I encountered in the Ellesmere Dining Hall that evening. My teaching life is peppered with students who touched my life briefly, but memorably all the same. Indeed, when I recall a certain charming, wide-eyed imp called Robin, 'peppered' is a strangely apposite word; he acted upon me in the nature of an irritant, got up my nose and invariably reduced me to tears. One of the duties of a boarding house tutor is to supervise bedtime routines and act in the capacity of a nanny. It soon becomes very apparent which boys are capable of brushing their teeth unasked, attending to their toileting needs unaided and keeping their bedside areas in a seemly state of order … and which are not. Robin fell – plunged, dived, plummeted – into the latter category. Immensely amiable by day, come bedtime and the routines demanded of the boys, Robin Phipps became the anti-Christ, bringing about his own pantomime version of Armageddon each evening and reducing even the most seasoned of house staff to quivering impotent rage.

To this day, I am still unsure if it was a deliberate tactic on his part or just an inability to do the simplest tasks, but a typical bedtime for Robin would go something like this.

Me: Alright, chaps. Five minutes till lights out. Everything tidy? Good, good. Come along there, Perkins, teeth brushed? Excellent. Well done in the House Cricket today, by the way, you lot. Jolly good … er … crouching, Bryant … you know, behind the … the … um … stumps thingy. Wicket-keeping! That's it. Yes, well done on that, Bryant.

Hang on. Where's Phipps?

Oh for God's sake, where the hell is Phipps?

Phipps: (*emerging from under Throgmorton's bed*) Oh here, sir! Just checking for spiders, sir.

Me: What? What spiders? Oh, for God's sake, Phipps, you're meant to be in bed. Hang on. Why are you wearing that?

Phipps: This, sir?

Me: Yes, that! The cassock—

Phipps: Cassock, sir?

Me: Yes, cassock. And the Wellington boots?

Phipps: In case of the spiders, sir. Throgmorton's terrified of them, sir.

Throgmorton: (*trying to read a* Playboy *magazine*) No, I'm not, you tosser. If you come near my bed again, I'll deck you. Weirdo.

Me: Alright, alright, simmer down. Phipps, just get to bed for now and we'll sort things out in the morning. No, your bed is that way.

Phipps: Just got to do my teeth, sir.

Me: Right, then, hurry along and … my godfathers! What has happened to your bed?!

Phipps: It's an igloo, sir. It's for a geography assignment.

Me: This is not an igloo, boy, this is a bombsite. What on earth are … Phipps, why is your bed full of rugby boots?

Phipps: I'm doing Quardle a favour, sir. His mother died. See, he's crying, sir.

Me: It wasn't his mother, it was his father – sorry, Quardle (*this at a renewed outburst of tears from the unhappy boy in Bed 11*) – Look, just go and do your teeth and then get into bed! You have thirty seconds. One. Two. Three. Fou— What are you doing *now*?

Phipps: (*in wide-eyed surprise*) I'm getting rugged up, sir. These cassocks are very thin, I'm surprised the choirboys don't freeze to death, do you think that's why they sing so high, sir? Something to do with their balls freezing up? I've heard that—

Me: You don't *need* to get rugged up, boy, you just have to do your teeth and get into bed!

Phipps: But I've left my toothbrush in the Sports Pavilion, sir, I was doing an experiment in science, see, and … well, it's a long story but I'll need to be fetching it now. Good thing I've got the Wellington boots on already, sir? That'll shave a few seconds off the time …

… and so on.

This sort of charade went on every night. The most frustrating aspect of it was not simply that Robin Phipps himself was never in bed on time but that his tardiness and endless excuses made the other boys alternatively razzed up, entertained or infuriated by his prevarications. It was a rare night in Dormitory B which didn't end with one boy in tears, another in some murderous rage, a third wishing to launch an immediate investigation into exactly what had ended up in his shampoo bottle earlier that day, and the remainder in hoots of hilarity that took hours to dissipate.

There came a night when I had had enough. I was determined that Robin should not sabotage the whole evening routine yet again. I would put him on the shortest possible leash and hold my ground. Thirty minutes before lights out, I called him outside into the corridor.

'Phipps,' I said, trying to ignore the fact that he had what looked like a dead iguana draped over one shoulder, 'tonight is going to be different. Tonight, we are doing things by the book. Tonight, we are following very simple instructions, and the slightest deviation from them will have you sitting at the desk I have placed outside Mr Barlow's study until midnight, writing out lines.'

Phipps looked at me with limpid eyes and opened his mouth to say something.

'No, you don't need to speak. You just need to understand what I'm saying. And stop fiddling with the iguana.'

'It's a—'

'I don't care what it is. Phipps, if you don't wish to write out lines till midnight, you will go to the toilet. You will then do your teeth. You will do these in absolute silence. If you speak to anyone, you'll go to the desk. If you speak to me, you'll go to the desk. If you make eye contact with anyone else, the desk. If you touch that bloody iguana again, or attempt to correct me again on its exact species, or go anywhere or do anything that deviates so much as an inch from the normal expected routine, you will go to the desk. Is that clear? No, don't speak. Just nod your head if you understand.'

Phipps nodded and the iguana nodded with him.

'Good. Robin, I am serious about this. Understand? Right. Toilet. Teeth. Bed. Go.'

I watched him like a hawk as he headed to the bathroom. I stood in the doorway to watch him brush his teeth. He immediately turned to me as if to say, 'Wilkins swallowed my toothbrush, sir' but I silenced him with a glare and a complicated gesture that was meant to combine throat-cutting with writing-out-lines-at-a-desk-till-midnight. Robin meekly found a brush, applied toothpaste and did his teeth. I watched him walk out of the bathroom and into the dorm. His bed was right at the far end, so he had the entire gauntlet of opportunities to run before he reached his own bed. At Bed 3 he turned to say something to the occupant but a small, fierce growl from the back of my throat made him think twice. He tried this again at Beds 6 and 8 but a glance at me first told him that I was still monitoring his every move.

Once he reached his own bed, he faced his biggest challenge in compliance yet. The mattress was covered with debris: discarded gym clothes, *Mad* magazines, a Lego model of the Battlestar *Galactica*, a stuffed-toy turtle, an eighteenth-century gilded ormolu clock and what appeared to be a crossbow made out of an elephant's rib.

Robin turned to me to shrug. I was not to be moved. One eye twitching madly, I gestured fiercely that he should clear the bed. In silence. Without comment. Robin opened his mouth to say something … but thought better of it. He had never seen me in this sort of mood before. I was winning. Resolve. Preparation.

Clear communication. Non-negotiables. This is what Robin Phipps needed. This is what I needed if I was to retain my sanity and my job.

As the rest of his dorm-mates pretended to read their bedtime books in a sort of fizzling silence, their eyes glued unmoving and unreading to a random paragraph, Robin removed each item one by one and found a suitable place for it. On the shelf. Under the bed. In the wardrobe. Finally, the bed was clear. Robin pulled back the blankets, ready to hop between the covers, put his head on the pillow and sleep. I felt my shoulders relax and a sigh of deep satisfaction escaped my lips. So, too, I felt the grudging admiration of the other boys who had witnessed my triumph.

Then, just before he hopped into bed, Robin asked quickly, lightly, conversationally – too quick for me to stop him with a gesture – 'So, Mr Mackinnon, is it October or November that's Chinchilla Awareness Month, do you know?'

I am ashamed to say, even all these years on, that I cracked. Not with frustrated rage, not with righteous temper – not this time – but with sheer helpless laughter. Gone was the resolve, gone was the determination, gone any thought of desks or line-writing. And gone any illusion that I could possibly win a battle of wills against the likes of Robin Phipps.

Chapter 13

My heart aches, and a drowsy numbness pains
My sense, as though of hemlock I had drunk,
Or emptied some dull opiate to the drains
One minute past, and Lethe-wards had sunk:
'Tis not through envy of thy happy lot,
But being too happy in thine happiness,—
That thou, light-winged Dryad of the trees,
In some melodious plot
Of beechen green, and shadows numberless,
Singest of summer in full-throated ease.
—John Keats, *Ode to a Nightingale*

As summer rolled around, I found myself teaching my favourite of all the disciplines of English, namely poetry. Keats was on the curriculum, and one hot drowsy afternoon in late May I was trying to teach *Ode to a Nightingale*' to a class of sleep-drugged Sixth Formers. Walter Thatcher was there, head on his arms, practically asleep. Even Nick Grey, usually an alert and courteous student, was lolling back in his chair watching out the window the summer haze and the cool canopy of Bluebell Wood three fields away. It was hard to keep their attention. We had read through the five long dreamy stanzas – or rather, I had recited them. You're meant to get the students reading aloud but, to be honest, if it's Shakespeare or classical poetry you'll just have it mangled into an unrecognisable pulp if you get the students to do it, so I had taken upon myself the honour of reading the whole poem to my soporific charges.

In vain had I done the usual things, getting them to identify similes, metaphors, explaining the classical references: the Hippocrene spring, Bacchus and his pards and so on. We were getting nowhere. Finally I changed tack.

'You're sick of this, aren't you? Sick of school, sick of A Levels, sick of the pressure, the essays due, the assignments mounting up? Your mind's not on poetry. Scansion. Syllables. Onomatopoeia. Ogzimmeron. (Yes, Mungo, it really is pronounced like that, ask Mr Arne.) And no wonder. Your minds are on other things. Your bodies are on other things. Girls, for one. Boys, some of you, which is fine. Goats, possibly, which isn't so fine, Nick, just saying. Warm summer nights when the last thing you want to do is sleep. So, you slip out of bed, escape from the dorm and on a night when the sky is still light enough to see by even at midnight, you slip across the fields to Bluebell Wood. It's dark in there, and cool, and very still. You can smell the wild roses on the air. In fact, the whole wood smells like honey. There are tracks that wander between the trunks, badger tracks. They'll be appearing soon. But you're not interested in badgers. You want … you want … you don't know what you want. You want company, you want to be alone. You want to sleep, you want to drink in everything. You want school finished with, you want to be a twelve-year-old boy again. You definitely want a drag on that ciggy you've brought along, and a swig of that nice bottle of Chablis you hid here last week for just such a night as this. Instead, you feel as though you've been drugged with some lead-like poison that has sapped the life out of you.

'And suddenly, just as you are sitting with your back against a massive tree-trunk, wondering whether to take your shirt off and let the cool drops of wine trickle down your chest in a senseless but delicious gesture, you hear it. A bird. Singing its little heart out in some branch high above you. You can't see it but, boy, can you hear it. You've never heard anything like it. It's the loudest birdsong you've ever heard, as though it's been miked up by Daniel in one of his concerts. And it's so rich, so sweet, so powerful and abandoned and wild that it is carrying you far away from all those things that are weighing on you that night – the essays, the cranky housemaster, Dad's last letter telling you to lift your game, the obligation to play a ten-hour cricket match this weekend when you'd rather be swimming in the mere.

'That bird is carrying you away from all that. Is it magical? God, what I'd give to be that bird. Actually, no. I'm not envious. I'm just achingly happy that it seems so happy, oblivious, carefree. In fact, shoo, bird! Fly! Scarper while you can, so you're not dragged down by all this stuff. And take me with you, off to some land where there's music in the sea and the dunes and I can float effortlessly ...

'And that's what this poem is, boys. An escape to Bluebell Wood on a summer's night by a young man who was as restless and despondent as you are. But the poem ends with the fading of the enchantment. The bird has long since gone, off towards Nesscliffe perhaps, and the dawn is coming up. The bottle is empty. Was this just a dream, or something more? Even now, am I awake?

'And do I have an essay due on this on Friday? Yes, I do. Good luck. Someone wake up Thatcher for me, would you? Chairs up, classroom tidy. Thank you, gentlemen, see you next lesson.'

*

I didn't think much more of that lesson, but it had an unexpected effect. Two nights later, on a night of exquisite beauty and enchantment, Walter, Daniel, Jonathan and a number of other boys took off into Bluebell Wood at midnight, quite against school rules, and decided to try the experiment. They even took a bottle of something, though I suspect it wasn't a fine Chablis – more like a bottle of cheap vodka provided by a certain Jamie Todd, who tagged along too when he heard an illicit expedition was afoot.

I found out about all this later principally because Mr Du Croz wanted to investigate why, when caught, the boys to a man had explained that it was all part of an English assignment set by Mr Mackinnon. Horrified though I was at their misdemeanour, I was secretly glad to hear that Walter had taken his guitar along and had filled the glades with a gentle strumming that would surely have brought any fairies of good taste forth in their droves. Sadly though, Jamie, who had provided the cheap vodka, had also seen fit to provide the boys with some well-stuffed joints of marijuana which had been liberally shared around that night; another way of invoking fairyland, I suppose, though one I am vehemently opposed to. They might have all got away with it – indeed, they did for a fortnight, during which I collected some really remarkable and imaginative essay responses to '*Ode to a Nightingale*' – had Jamie not made the mistake of taking a whole lot of photos on a disposable camera of the boys smoking and drinking their cares away, and then gone and left the camera lying in the woods. It was found a week later by a passing gamekeeper and handed to our shrewd Deputy Headmaster, who had the film developed. Never has anyone been caught quite so red-handed.

The result of this foray into the perilous lands was deeply saddening for me. The school's decision to expel the boys who visited Bluebell Wood that night was entirely justified, especially considering the clear and unambiguous policies on the matter of illicit drugs. Indeed, typically, Mr Du Croz was lenient: he allowed the boys to stay on at the school for another four weeks to complete their final A-Level examinations. Their expulsion in reality simply meant they were forbidden to attend the end-of-year celebrations and the Valedictory Ball – and presumably their misdemeanours would have gone on some official record. As is so often the case, the loudest in his indignation was Jamie Todd, who had pushed the whole thing too far by introducing cannabis into the scenario; the rest of the boys were more or less resigned to the outcome. Indeed, a small number of them, after the initial shock of the decision, saw the forthcoming expulsion as a somewhat liberating thing; in those last few weeks, on the grounds that since they'd already been hanged for a lamb, there were all sorts of tempting sheep to be scored, they trebled the usual numbers of their nocturnal expeditions and tried all sorts of things they had never dared before. A glance out of any high window most nights would discover shadowy shapes flitting across the roof-tiles four storeys up or scuttling up the clocktower from the outside like vampire bats. Numerous ingenious pranks took place.

There was on the staff a certain Mr Witherspoon, a crusty gentleman who still wore his academic gown to every Maths lesson, as green with mould as an ageing sloth. As part of Ellesmere's centenary, he had recently given to the school a very imposing flagpole in spick-and-span white paint, and this was erected on the quadrangle lawn under the window where Mr Witherspoon resided high up in the gables of the main building. One morning in those last few weeks of the summer term, he woke to see below him his beautiful flagpole missing from its mount – and at a second glance, saw that it had been sawn into ten pieces and strewn about the dewy lawns. Apoplectic with rage at this wanton vandalism, he vaulted down the four flights of stairs, emerging onto the lawn like a cross between a snarling badger and a much-ruffled turkey to inspect the desecration. To his astonishment, the lawn was empty of its debris. Moreover, rising from its mounted socket was his flagpole, still pristine white, as good as new. It even had the Ellesmere flag flying from it, just beginning to shake out in the morning breeze. Needless to say, the ten sawn-up sections of timber he had seen on the lawn had been dummies, carefully painted white to give the appearance of segments of the flagpole. A simple enough trick … but it had taken split-second timing to engineer the replacement of the flagpole in its mount and the removal of the dummy sections in the ninety seconds taken by Mr Witherspoon's furious descent from the top storey. No doubt, much of this was orchestrated by Daniel with his penchant for illusion and theatrical effects.

Another prank that was artfully executed in that brief frenzied period of pre-rustification was pulled off by the bodhrán-playing Jonathan who, for all his dopey Labrador appearance, was a skilled artist. The boys took a photo of one of their cronies, Freddie, who in certain lights had a rather patrician look to him, especially when dressed in a grey suit and a borrowed academic gown, lavender silk hood and all. They had the photo blown up to full portrait size onto canvas and then, with great skill, Jonathan painted over the whole thing with oil-paints and varnish to turn the photo into a very realistic oil-painting. By the application of a hairdryer on the drying varnish, they even managed to crack the glaze into a faint honeycomb of crazing to make the portrait look ancient. Fitting it into an old heavy gilt frame acquired from Mr Crabbe the antiques proprietor, they crept into Big School one night and hung it among the portraits of all the past Headmasters, where it sat unnoticed for several years.

After the exams, by rights the boys facing expulsion should have left immediately, but Mr Du Croz allowed Walter and Jonathan and Daniel to stay on one more night as the Skelligs had been booked to play for a charity event at a local manor house. Over the course of the last two years, the band had become well-known in the district and had been in demand to play at local pubs and for the odd charity event such as this one. At each of these, we honed our skills, broadened our repertoire and thoroughly enjoyed the enchantment that came with playing the ancient jigs and reels and airs. Some of the loveliest of tunes, I found, were the lesser-known English folk songs, which rather than having the manic drive of the Irish reels or the patriotic, martial tang of the Scots marches, often had a plaintive, almost off-key cadence to them that was strangely haunting. They told stories of strange figures who lived in the fens and terrorised the lonely road at night, or lovemaking under appletrees between doomed youths. Katy's clear soprano and Walter's oboe-like tenor made the flesh shiver and the tears spring in all who heard them.

I still remember that evening with deep affection tinged with sorrow. There was a huge harvest moon, a great warm apricot in a lavender sky. The shaven lawns of the Grange were dotted with picnickers who had come to support the event, with hampers of food and bottles of champagne. Hardly a breath stirred the tops of the great elms and horse-chestnuts, and the golden scent of cut hay from the surrounding fields lay like a benison over the garden. It was our last performance together and I don't think we had ever played better. I particularly remember Walter and Katy singing 'The Blacksmith', which talks of betrayal and loss under a harvest moon, and seeing the tears on Walter's cheeks as he realised that he would be leaving Ellesmere the next morning, disgraced and outlawed.

*

After this cohort had left, I lost touch with many of these boys as they went off to various universities and other pursuits, but I thought of them often. One October evening, a night of late autumn some three years later, I was sitting in the North Pole marking a pile of essays when I heard the faintest *scritch-scratching* at the door. By the time I got to the door and opened it, there was no one there but I thought I heard the faint pad of retreating footsteps at the bottom of the staircase. Puzzled, I retreated into my flat but noticed something lying on the carpet that had evidently been shoved under the door. It was a few yellow beech leaves tied together with thread to a black crow's feather. On one of the leaves was written in what could have been dried blood but I hoped wasn't, BLAKEMERE – HOBBLEDEHOY.

I couldn't resist. Although the night was black, there was a warmish breeze blowing and I set off down the lanes on foot for Blakemere. This is one of the five meres for which the region is famed, but of all of them it is the one most shrouded in trees and inky of hue. It is this very mere that houses Jenny Greenteeth, the water-hag of local legend, so I went carefully, glancing around for a weed-plastered scalp or a grasping claw from the depths. The canal threads its way close to the shores of Blakemere and by following the towpath I soon found a narrowboat sporting the name *Hobbledehoy*. Intrigued, I tapped on a window and out popped the shaggy head of Walter Thatcher. I was delighted. He hadn't

HOBBLEDEHOY

changed a bit and his welcome was warm and sincere. Beside the pot-bellied stove, glowing with red embers, he introduced me to a girl who went by the name of Missee and filled me in on his life over the past few years. Over a glass of homemade sloe gin, he told me of a few years at Manchester University studying music and then explained that he had bought this barge and was travelling the canals and waterways of Britain. Missee lived on her own tiny barge and they travelled in convoy. Both of them had become adept at ropework, making placemats, coasters and decorations out of intricate knots, and Walter had taught himself to make didgeridoos out of hollow bits of timber found along the way. He showed me one he was working on made from an apple bough, a wonderfully polished instrument with a lip of beeswax and a tone like a deep bassoon.

In fact, in typical maverick fashion, Walter had discovered or invented something rather astonishing with this didgeridoo. In order to earn a crust in his itinerant lifestyle, Walter often busked at markets or in the streets of towns he passed through; his musical skills were such that he could charm the pennies from the local populace with ease. He had added to his repertoire conjuring, juggling and – recently – bubble-blowing, where the artist creates wondrous shapes and figures out of soap bubbles strengthened with a little glycerine. One day during a break, he had playfully dipped the end of his didgeridoo into his bowl of soap-bubble mixture and, on playing a note, had created a bubble that formed a perfect hourglass shape. When he had changed the note up a little, the hourglass took on three bulbs rather than the standard two. This in itself was not surprising; the delicate substance of the soapy film was echoing the resonating wavelengths of the note being played. However, he noticed that not only did the shape of the bubble change with each note but so did the colour. The first note had produced a bubble of rosy pink; the next note had changed the bubble to a pearly green. Playing another note had rendered the bubble a silky translucent gold and yet another change in tone had produced an iridescent blue.

Fascinated by this, Walter had read up about synaesthesia, the strange condition that allows some people to 'see' sounds or 'taste' colours. For such people, for example, Middle C might come across as green in hue, or Wednesday might be quite definitely yellow in colour. Astonishingly, he had found that most synaesthesics whose brains translated musical notes into colour reported seeing colours that were exactly predicted by his soap-bubble experiment. That is, if a synaesthesic would hear a Middle C and see it as green, sure enough, when Middle C was played on Walter's didgeridoo with its end dipped in soap-mixture, the resulting bubble would be an iridescent green.

I staggered home that night, replete with sloe gin and as happy as could be. I had urged Walter and Missee to come and visit me at the College if they were around for a few days, but Walter was curiously shy. He was convinced that having left under a cloud, he had blotted his copybook, and was quite sure that he would not be welcome to visit openly – hence the clandestine invitation left on my carpet. This saddened me but he was adamant – and when I jogged past Blakemere a few days later, the canal was empty of its two homely barges. However, when a year later at about the same time I heard a faint scratching at the door and opened onto an empty stairwell, I was not surprised to find another token on the mat – a crow's feather through a big red-and-white-spotted toadstool this time – and I knew exactly where to head for another night-time meeting.

Over the next few years, this was something I looked for when the leaves were turning and the days were shortening. I felt like Bilbo Baggins after his adventures, who would receive visits from outlandish folk or go off into the woods at certain times of the year to seek out the passing company of the grey elves, strangers to the rest of the Shire. It was a gesture of enormous privilege and I treasure those memories of clandestine evenings spent aboard *Hobbledehoy* to this day.

Chapter 14

> *Earth and sky, woods and fields, lakes and rivers, the mountain and the sea, are excellent schoolmasters, and teach of us more than we can ever learn from books.*
>
> —John Lubbock

One of the things expected of a schoolteacher is to help out with extracurricular activities. For example, one might find oneself not only employed to teach English but coaching a hockey team after school, making props for the school play, running a Tuesday night crocheting club, playing trombone in the school orchestra and editing the College yearbook – all while doing two nights of duty a week in one of the boarding houses. It is sometimes tricky to remember what subject you teach, as this minor matter tends to fade into the background with all the other stuff going on. At Ellesmere, as well, you were expected to participate in something a little more gung-ho than crochet by joining either the Cadet Corps or the Outdoor Education Programme and it was to the latter that I signed up along with my decidedly rugged colleague and friend Ross Bassenthwaite.

I had come to know Ross well over regular pints in the Common Room bar and discovered him to be a shrewd, humorous Yorkshireman with a dry wit and a low tolerance for fools. In many ways, he and I were polar opposites, but we discovered a common love of puzzles, conundrums and oddities of maths and science when, early in our acquaintance, he bowled into the Common Room bar late one night with his brother Ralph and best mate Lloyd, ready to celebrate a day of ice-climbing Snowdon with several kegs of bitter. I was thoroughly intimidated by these three rugged men, who looked as though they would feel comfortably at home manning the harpoon on a Greenland whaler – or rather, I would have been, had I not imbibed three stiff whiskies and were I not misguidedly trying to explain to the French mistress a new topological puzzle I had come across involving what happens when you try to pull a hollow doughnut inside out. To demonstrate what I meant, I had removed one sock, cut the toe off and was attempting to sticky-tape one end of the hollow woollen tube to the other.

'This is to make a doughnut, you see, Celeste,' I slurred. 'Or what we in the world of mamma … matta-mathics, MATHS!' I shouted in triumph and Mademoiselle Dubois jogged her drink. 'Ssshhh! … What we call a torus.'

I stopped, confused a little. 'Not Taurus the Bull. Bull. Bulldust. I don't, you know. Not a believer, no, sir. I'm an Aries and they're not superstitious, ha ha ha ha ha …'

Mademoiselle Dubois was trying to finish her drink so she could escape the room, and I was looking puzzled at the mutilated sock in my hand, wondering what point I had been trying to make, when the mountaineers sauntered in. The French mistress took the opportunity to flee the room.

Once settled with pints of bitter, Ross, Ralph and Lloyd took a keen interest in why I was sitting there with one bare foot trying to manipulate a damaged sock into a loop, and I found a more willing audience for my conundrum.

That was the first of many nights spent with this intelligent, good-humoured trio. I cemented a good friendship with Ross especially and we ended up spending many long hours in the

Common Room bar setting the world to rights, sometimes till dawn.

On one such occasion, Ross had staggered off to snatch two hours of sleep before the start of a busy day teaching Physics. He had started the first lesson of the day with a shocking hangover but managing to conceal the severity of his condition from the students – and more importantly, his Head of Department teaching in the next room, who had warned him about this sort of thing before.

Halfway through the lesson, however, he had begun to feel bilious and in need of a lightning dash for the toilet. The problem was that his Head of Department was by this time standing in the corridor engaged in a long conversation with the Headmaster: to dash for the bathroom would have been to risk exposure. In a flash of brilliance, Ross remembered that in the dark-room adjoining the classroom there was a sink which would meet his purposes, so, instructing his pupils to carry on copying their notes, he closeted himself in there, shut the door behind him and threw up copiously into the sink. This dark-room doubled as an equipment store, so Ross, wishing to allay any suspicions about his sudden departure, picked up a voltmeter from the shelves, re-entered the classroom and explained to the class that they were soon to do an experiment and would need this, a voltmeter. In the meantime, let us continue with taking notes off the board.

Two minutes later, Ross felt a familiar rumbling, a familiar tingling and realised that last night's curry, beer and whisky intake had not yet had its say. The Head of Department was still blocking his escape from the room, so there was nothing for it but a second visit to the dark-room. Again, the sink received a full load of Ross' stomach contents and again, to cover his tracks, Ross grabbed a piece of random equipment from the shelves and presented it to the students. 'And, we will need this … this … umm … lightbox. Yes. So where were we?'

Five more times this happened. Five more times! It really had been a very heavy night. Five more visits to the dark-room, five more upheavals and five more retrievals of a piece of laboratory equipment to justify his jack-in-the-box-like to-ing and fro-ing, until the front desk was littered with an unlikely miscellany of apparatus. Finally the bell rang to signal the end of the lesson and Ross could legitimately escape to offload the last of the toxins into the nearest lavatory. He was immensely relieved to have got away with it – or so he thought, until a week later, one of the more earnest of Ross's physics students went to the Head of Department and said, 'Sir, we're trying to work something out. The other day, Mr Bassenthwaite was going to show us an experiment which he never got around to demonstrating. But it has us puzzled. What sort of physics experiment involves a voltmeter, a lightbox, a spring balance, a metre-rule, a Bunsen burner, a gyroscope and a giant magnet?'

*

Ross and I both joined the Outdoor Education Programme, supervising a group of Sixth Formers who enjoyed the outdoors but weren't so keen on the Cadet Corps vibe of going around killing people. It was on our twice-yearly three-day expeditions that the real adventures kicked in. For these we could go off for three whole days to Snowdonia, the Peak District or even the Lakes.

As I have said, Ross shared my love for games and puzzles and we both delighted in infusing these expeditions with a sense of wonder. Thus, a straightforward hike around the gorges and hills of the White Peak became a treasure hunt contest between two teams, each following a series of riddling clues full of codes and conundrums to crack. When we planned to go to the Lake District, we decided that the whole three days should be a sort of *Swallows and Amazons* wargame between the two groups.*

To recreate their adventures, we divided the twelve students – all about sixteen years old – into two teams of six. One lot were the Swallows and the other six the Amazons, each team equipped with a flag I had made for them. They were dropped off at a particular point in the Lakes and had three days to hike to a certain spot on the flanks of the Old Man of Coniston, a place called Goat Fell, where there is a huge underground cavern – but with a very narrow entrance. That is where we would all meet up to camp – in the cave – on the third night.

---

* As many readers will know, *Swallows and Amazons* was an astonishingly popular 1930s series of children's books by Arthur Ransome and concerned a family of four children holidaying in Cumbria. It tells of their imaginative adventures as explorers sailing on the lake in their beloved *Swallow* and camping on an island and their rivalry with the Amazons, two local girls who consider themselves to be pirates. Mountain-climbing, exploring mines, sailing, treacherous mists, hostile 'natives', friendly charcoal-burners: accidents and alarums abound!

To turn it into a game, each team was provided with a list of tasks to achieve along the way. These were such things as flagging down a motorist on the Wrynose Pass, standing waist-deep in Blea Tarn, going through a slate-mine tunnel, catching a sheep on High Fell, borrowing a boat on Coniston Water, begging to use a private phone in the village of Langdale, and so on. Each team was provided with a couple of cameras to capture evidence of them doing this. However, we added this rule: if one team could successfully stalk the other team – that is, follow them without being seen – and themselves get a photo of the other team doing any of these tasks, then *they* would steal all the points for that task. So, for example, the Amazons might go to all the trouble and discomfort of standing up to their waists in the freezing waters of Blea Tarn, a mountain lake, to win fifty points, but if in doing so the Swallows suddenly popped out from behind a heathery rock and took a photo of them in the tarn, the Swallows would get those fifty points and the Amazons none!

For three days, then, the two teams were constantly engaged in pursuing each other through the valleys and over the wild fells of that spectacular landscape or trying to throw their pursuers off their track by some nifty doubling back.

One group was sabotaged from within to some extent by one of its own members. This lad, Robbie, was usually up for an adventure but on this occasion was beset by an insatiable appetite for bacon. He spent all his energy urging his group to abandon the chase so that he could cook himself up some bacon by the wayside, even forcing his companions to take a three-mile detour to a village for the sole purpose of re-provisioning his backpack with a fresh supply of bacony goodness. This obsession was later to prove a fortunate turning point in the success of his team.

Meanwhile, Ross and I spent this time driving around to various checkpoints and monitoring the progress of the groups, but on the last afternoon we walked up to the Goat Fell cave to set up camp and wait for the explorers to arrive. To my astonishment, this cave, the entrance of which was about the size of a modest sofa, opened up inside to cathedral-like dimensions and there was plenty of room for us to spend the night in there without the need to set up tents. Ross and I made ourselves comfortable, got some soup and pasta on the boil and waited for the students to arrive.

Gradually they started to drift in, and I especially enjoyed the looks on their faces as each person took in the magnitude of the cavernous space for the first time. There was a lot of excited chatter about the adventures they had shared over the last seventy-two hours and squeals of outrage as they discovered only then that their hard-won points had been stolen away by the surreptitious snapping of a photograph by their rival hidden behind a nearby tree. There were also tales of boat-theft and sheep-wrangling which Ross and I chose to expunge from our memories, making a mental note to buy the perpetrators' silence with a promise of McDonald's on the way home the next day.

After an hour or so of this, we realised that it was only Robbie's group that hadn't yet arrived. There was nothing much we could do but hope that he and his friends had sufficient navigational skills to find our location, so we returned to the depths of the cave and urged the others to get on with cooking their suppers. In the meantime, unbeknownst to us, Robbie and his group had finally arrived … but being pitch-dark outside and pouring with rain, they found themselves faced with an almost impossible task: standing on a vast pitch-black hillside looking for a miniscule pitch-black entrance to a middling-sized pitch-black cave. They had been searching fruitlessly for about forty-five minutes and the rain had strengthened to a downpour when suddenly Robbie said, 'Hang on, guys! I can smell bacon!'

Fed up with his three-day-long obsession with bacon, the group rounded on him crossly, but he said, 'No, really. I can! Frying bacon … coming from … over here! Come on!'

And sure enough, his bacon-smelling nose led them along the hillside in the dark and straight to the cave-entrance where we were indeed cooking up some bacon for supper. From that time hence, he was known back at school as Bacon Bob and never tired of telling folks the tale of how he had come by the moniker.

*

As the years went on, Ross and I racked our brains to think of ever newer novelties for the students to experience on these expeditions. At some point, one of us suggested – I cannot remember who because beer was yet again involved – providing the students not with the customary trip to the supermarket to stock up on food for the hike but instead a carrot, an onion and a dead rabbit each. When I say a dead rabbit, I do not mean a nicely skinned, jointed and filleted rabbit lying in neat chunks in a polystyrene tray. I mean a rabbit that, apart from having been killed had not been further processed in any way, shape or form by human hand.

Thinking about it, this was probably my idea. In one of the later *Swallows and Amazons* books, two of the children are faced with preparing and cooking a similarly unprocessed rabbit, and it makes a chapter of interesting, if queasy, reading. Ross was keen on the idea and arranged to pick up a bunch of dead rabbits from the local butcher and bring them along in a sack so as to reveal their identity only when the students were in too remote a place to access a phone and demand their parents fetch them forthwith.

We had organised to drop the students at one edge of Bleaklow Moor in the Peak District and they were to navigate their way across to an old shooting hut some seven miles away on the far side of the moor, where we were to camp that night. On the edge of the lonely moorland road, we waited till they had their packs on and were about to set off and then handed them their rations. One carrot each. One brown onion each. And, one between two of you, a dead rabbit. There you go.

Keeping a few bunnies for ourselves, Ross handed out the limp, furry bodies to our hikers. It would be fair to say that reactions were varied. One boy stammered out, 'But … but … how do you pluck it!' and we kindly pointed out that if he really wanted to pluck it, he would need a pair of tweezers and about five days. One particularly likeable girl called Sarah took one look at the dead rabbit, burst into tears and told us that she would never speak to either of us again. A third boy, with thick pebble glasses and acne like scarlet oatmeal, looked utterly fascinated and started muttering 'Blood! Blood! Blood!' under his breath as he set off across the moor.

Once the students were out of sight, Ross and I drove the long way round to a quiet valley where we parked and wandered a mile or so up a farm-track to the lonely shooting hut on the moor's edge. After a cup of tea on the camp-stove, Ross stretched himself out on the turf and said, 'Right. Show us how it's done then.'

'Show us how what's done?' I asked.

'How you skin that bloody thing,' he said pointing to the little limp corpse on the grass.

'Well, *I* don't know,' I said in alarm. 'I assumed *you* knew how when you agreed to the idea!'

'What?' he said. 'I assumed you'd done this dozens of times. Doesn't everybody Down Under do this sort of thing every weekend? I've watched *Crocodile Dundee*, you know.'

'Ross, have we met before? I'm Sandy. You know. Sandy who reads books. Plays chess. Talks about fairies and things. Can't catch a ball. Faints in First Aid courses. What in God's name gave you the idea that I could skin a rabbit?'

'Well, it was your idea!'

'Yes, yes, out of a book, Ross. Out of a book! A children's book! Not real life. You know I don't do real life, Ross!'

Indeed, I had assumed that Ross, with all his competent outdoor skills and gruff Yorkshire ways, had spent his boyhood running around these moors snaring rabbits by the dozen and coolly skinning them, most likely with his teeth. I told him this and his response was predictable.

'Fookin' 'ell!'

Then he rallied and said with a chuckle, 'Eh oop. We'll just have to give it a go then. Get the knife!'

There is a skill to skinning rabbits, I have since learnt, and it is not a skill that either Ross or myself even approximated to on that summer evening. We sweated and slipped our way through a process of trial and error that left us shaking and nauseous and sometimes incoherent with laughter. Slimy fluids spurted unexpectedly, scraps of bloodied fur clung tenaciously, odd organs wobbled and gleamed balefully in strange purples and off-greens and bilious yellows. At one point something unmentionable got punctured and sent wafting into the air a foetid stench that had us both retching through our tears of shared self-ridicule.

Finally we somehow managed to rid the poor rabbit of its innards, separate it from its downy coat – it truly would have been easier to pluck the damn thing – and scrape about two mouthfuls of edible flesh from its bloodied bones ready to cook. We both looked dismayed at the miniscule portion we had managed to salvage from the beast.

'Fookin' 'ell,' said Ross again. And then added, 'Good thing I brought two more, eh?'

And at that, he hauled two fresh carcases from his bag and thumped them down on the turf. 'Eh oop!'

I must confess, the second rabbit was easier to skin and disembowel and the third one was almost a doddle – though still the sort of doddle that leaves you shaky and nauseous and vowing never to foist these sorts of experiments on students again. I could almost agree with Sarah; I too never wanted to speak to Ross or myself again. But it is astonishing how soon one becomes used to things. Once the meat of all three rabbits was in the pot along with the chopped onion and carrots and beginning to turn into stew, Ross and I went to discard the rabbit skins. These were still attached to the heads and I am ashamed to say that the theatrical side of me came to the fore when I discovered that by inserting my index finger into the cavity at the base of the skull and wrapping the skin around my hand, I could re-animate the rabbit much as Sweeney Todd might have operated a Punch and Judy marionette.

Just a few yards away was a shooting croft, a wall of planks so that shooters could crouch hidden and shoot over the parapet at deer or grouse. This made an excellent improvised theatre for our grisly puppets. Ross and I crouched down behind the planks, wrapped our hands in the remains of the poor bunnies and poked them up over the parapet to enact an impromptu rendition of *Watership Down*. Our resurrected rabbits hopped. They sat up and sniffed the evening air. They danced, they kissed, they boxed. I am afraid to say that they even bonked.

So absorbed were we in our macabre puppetry – more *Medea* than *Watership Down*, now I come to think of it – that we did not hear the students approaching over the brow of the hill. The first we knew of it was when we heard Sarah's voice saying suddenly, 'Hey guys! Shhh! Look there! Just on that little hillock. It's a rabbit! And another one! Wow! They're so tame. And what are they doing?'

Other whispers drifted down the still evening air. 'Look. They're . . . they're dancing together! Isn't that cute? I didn't know rabbits did that. Perhaps it's a courting ritual. Ssshhh! Look!'

When a minute later, the group of students came closer and discovered who was behind these amorous theatrics, Sarah reaffirmed to us her vows of non-communication and stalked off to a distant spot to set up her tent. This was a pity because she missed the really spectacular thing that happened then. Johnny, the geeky boy with spectacles and acne who had never been known to willingly step outside the computer lab at school unless forcibly removed by the cleaners, proved that he had hidden talents. Taking his rabbit and holding it up by its hind legs, he made a long neat slit down the belly with his knife. Then standing a bit apart, he warned us all to stand clear and whirled the rabbit round and round his head by the hind legs, at which action the innards came clean away in one shining arc, propelled thus by centrifugal force. This, explained Johnny, was the best way to get rid of the guts without risking perforating them. He'd seen it in a video. Next, he made four neat slits around each wrist or ankle, asked me to hold the back paws and in one swift movement peeled the whole skin off the rabbit as smoothly as someone removing a cardigan from a baby. There was no blood, no slime, no sweat, no odours – just Sarah picking some flung rabbit spleen out of her hair because she'd been too far away to hear Johnny's thoughtful warning.

After that demonstration, the rest of the group went to work with a will and soon the smell of rabbit stew was rising to the primrose sky. Even Sarah rejoined the group and managed to improve her rabbit stew considerably by frying the meat first with caramelised onion before adding it to the stock. She would later confide to Ross and me that this hike had turned out to be the most memorable experience of her schooldays. In fact, when she went on to become Head Girl, it was mentioned in her valedictory speech to the school at the end of the year. But we never did try the experiment again. My blood-lust and taste for corpse puppetry is now firmly a thing of the past.

Chapter 15

There is a pleasure, sure,
In being mad, which none but madmen know!
—John Dryden, *The Spanish Friar*

This love of creating adventures for others has not always been one-way. Indeed, I have often been on the receiving end of such loving pranks, and the perpetrators have usually been students. The chief of these must surely be someone readers may have met in my earlier writings, the inimitable Newton Harris.

I first met Newton on my very first day as a tutor in the Adelaide boarding school when I was twenty-one. In fact, he has the dubious privilege of being the first student I encountered in my role as a schoolmaster. I was still several years off becoming qualified as a teacher, but as my parents had moved to Canberra I had sought alternative accommodation and someone had suggested that a very cheap alternative was to work as a house tutor in a school boarding house. For a few evening duties each week and some weekends, the school would provide accommodation and meals and, as it turned out, a first-class education in managing students that was infinitely more effective than the insipid teachings of the Diploma of Education I was undertaking at the time.

Newton had just been appointed house captain – a risky choice, as the housemaster confided to me. 'He's an odd chap,' he told me. 'You'll see.' And indeed I was to find out over the years that this was a masterly understatement. However, I did immediately take to Newton. His room was decorated with posters showing all the birds of Great Britain, the lovely RSPB illustrations with which I was intimately familiar. There was a chess set in mid-play on his desk and he was doing an experimental sort of oil-painting on a sheet of glass where you have to put all the layers on in reverse order, as he explained to me while knocking a jar of turpentine and five paint brushes onto his bedspread. In this way, I was introduced to several elements of Newton's character simultaneously: his passion for experimental creativity and his inability to make a gesture without causing some irretrievable damage to something close by.

Things tend to go spectacularly awry whenever Newton has anything to do with them. There was the time, for instance, a year after he had left school but returned to the boarding house to live and work as a tutor like myself, when he decided to play an elaborate prank on me. His idea was that I would wake from my slumbers one night with the sound of a storm brewing – distant thunder, rising wind, squalls of heavy rain – and be puzzled by the fact that out the window the night seemed fine and dry. My puzzlement would grow, however, when mixed in with the storm would be heard chimes, church bells far off, tolling a solemn peal. Then would come distant howling as of wolves under an icy moon, then the creaking of dungeon doors, the rattling of chains, the wailing of banshees and the hideous cries of a woman in torment.

To this end, Newton purchased a cassette of horror movie effects and set to work with his usual manic genius. I rarely locked my school apartment, so Newton had plenty of opportunity to set things up when I was absent. He decided that he wanted the sound to be both very subtle but all-pervasive and to this end he bought six state-of-the-art speakers and a spool of wire.

Over the course of a week or so, he sneaked into my bedroom and managed to conceal all six speakers about the room in such a way that I had no idea of their presence. Several were screwed under the baseboard of my bed. Others were affixed to the top and underside of my wardrobe, out of sight to the casual eye. One was even inserted into a panel behind the wall just above my head where I would be sleeping. Even the wires were somehow hidden and led by secret ways through the wall cavities to the boarding house study down the corridor.

This was where, in the wee hours of a Saturday night when I was deep in slumber, Newton was poised to put his plan into action. He popped the sound effects tape into the cassette player. Clicked the flap shut. Turned the master volume down to its lowest setting so that he could achieve the desired slow crescendo – just so. Sound check. All good. Volume set to low. Excellent. And now, let the haunting begin …

(I must add here that, typical of Newton's tendency to have bizarre technical failures dog his every move, it dawned on him during this pre-test that even for a horror movie sound effects tape, the cassette sounded awfully odd. The chiming of church bells started off as a faint vibration and then grew to a reverberating *DWOP!* Wolves howled in strangely rising crescendos. It took a few minutes for Newton to realise that after his weeks of careful set up, he had somehow purchased the one tape in the world that had been inadvertently recorded backwards. In just such a frame of mind, I imagine, would Wile E. Coyote realise he had just been handed a stick of dynamite instead of the expected candy cane. Undaunted by this spanner in the works, his manic genius had soon made good use of a screwdriver and a rubber band artfully deployed to force the cassette player to play in reverse, thus giving off the sounds as intended. One more test and he was ready to go.)

Now Newton had decided that he wanted to monitor my reactions: the faint stirring, the slow awakening, the puzzled looks as I tried to reconcile the sounds of a violent storm with a clear starry sky, and then the increasing bewilderment at the chimes, the thrill of fear at the howling of the wolves and so on. To this end, he had rigged up an angled mirror on a stick, a bit like an enlarged dentist's mirror, and planned to use this to stand concealed beneath my ground-floor bedroom and peek through the window. So having set the cassette in motion, he dashed out of the study and used the mirror to see how I was reacting. Hmmm. Fast asleep still. Back to the study to edge up the volume a bit. Back to the window. Odd. Still fast asleep. Back again to the study to crank up the volume to a level that was sure to wake me. Ah, the bells, the bells! This should rouse the slumbering Quasimodo.

Nup. Still I was lying blissfully dormant, eyes closed in deep slumber. Five more times, Newton upped the volume and five more times he tiptoed back to peek in my window to see me still unconscious, even when the volume was such that the whole bed was vibrating and the sound of howling, screaming and thrashing chains had set half the dogs in the neighbourhood barking in frenzied unison. The next morning, in fact, the groundsman and his wife, who lived the length of four playing fields away, came to complain about the thunderous racket that had woken them in the middle of the night, a fact that Newton found hard to explain to the disgruntled housemaster on the receiving end of the complaint.

And I slept through it all. Eventually ... eventually ... but only when one of the throbbing speakers had vibrated its screws loose and toppled from the wardrobe with a crash – did I come awake with a start. I am not particularly quick on the uptake under normal circumstances, let alone when emerging from the throes of sleep, but somehow on this occasion my synapses went through the following steps – *werewolves howling, bed vibrating, must be bloody Newton, bet he's in the study.* Seconds later, I had stormed out of my flat, down the corridor, and flung open the study door to find Newton crouching like a startled ferret with an enormous set of headphones in front of a device that looked like the flight deck of a Boeing 747. Once there, I snarled, 'For God's sake, Newton. Go to bed!', slammed the door shut and stomped back to my room.

I really don't like being woken.

Poor Newton. Had he caught me at any other point in history, he would have found me delighted by the trick, flattered by the effort, amused by the concept – but by the time morning had come and I was prepared to be a little more gracious, he had packed up his contraptions, left the boarding house and didn't dare approach me for another six months.

*

Newton continued in his somewhat manic vein to provide colour and interest to my life, but his schemes were characterised by an almost supernatural tendency to go spectacularly wrong. There was, for example, the time he set an elaborate nocturnal treasure hunt for me up Brownhill Creek. The anonymous instructions to send me on this quest were that I should go on a certain date at sunset and – very specific, this – that I had to wear a cloak and take my trusty cavalry sabre with me. (Yes, dear reader, I possessed both these arcane items, left over from my days of playing Dungeons & Dragons and taking Tolkien far too seriously.) The resulting treasure hunt was particularly memorable because of one minor fact that had eluded Newton's notice, namely that the previous day a corpse had been found savagely hacked to death with an edged weapon not ten yards from where Newton had airily decided I should find the prize – nothing less than a broadsword of considerable dimensions stuck into the altar of a ruined chapel. Needless to say, my stumbling from clue to clue in the summer dusk was made somewhat more nerveracking than Newton ever intended by the need to avoid a number of police patrols, tracking dogs and search parties who were combing the area that evening for any signs of the discarded murder weapon. Fortunately, my cloak must have been woven of elvish *hithlain* (concealment points 5+) whose enchantment hid me from the eyes of the law. Otherwise, I am not sure I could have given them a plausible reason for my presence at the crime scene, dressed outlandishly and bearing not only a cavalry sabre but a newly acquired broadsword to boot. This was the hand of Coincidence yet again being woken to life by the treasure-hunt phenomenon, but playing a considerably more macabre game than she had been wont to play in the past.

I must tell one final tale to redeem Newton, though yet again it shows him in the light of hapless genius. Moreover, it goes some way to explaining why Newton absolutely refuses to have candles on his birthday cake. Some think this is to do with vanity associated with ageing, but the real reason is quite different.

When I announced that I was leaving the Adelaide school after six years to travel overseas, Newton decided to arrange a farewell gift. Typically, this was not going to be a travel diary and card. Something more elaborate was in order. His idea was to gather as many candles as he could and, on my final night, while I was sleeping, to arrange them in a galaxy of flickering lights out on the cricket oval just beyond my front door. When he discovered how expensive new candles were, he spent months going to every church in Adelaide asking if he could take their almost-spent candles off their hands. In this way, he managed to amass hundreds and hundreds, in every shape and size, from waxy misshapen lumps to barely used Paschal candles adorned with the Chi-Rho in blue and scarlet. Once they were all lit, he would yet again use his superb sound engineering skills to have one of Albinoni's oboe concertoes playing through the still summer night, and then he would come and wake me.

Knowing from bitter experience just how hard this might be to do, he had decided to dispense with subtlety this time. He would just stride into my bedroom, lob a boot at my head and then run like blazes to leave me to follow the unearthly strain of oboe music and find outside the ethereal galaxy of candles spreading away into the distance.

That, at least, was the idea.

The night in question was perfect for his scheme, one of those still, dead nights of an Adelaide summer, hot and breathless under a dome of hazy stars. There was nothing stirring within a hundred miles. He set to his task efficiently and quietly, unloading his car of hundreds and hundreds of candles and placing them strategically in the turning circle at my door and then out on the playing fields that spread away in every direction. Those closest to my door were clustered thickly; as they got further-away, they diminished in size and were spaced further apart to give a heightened sense of perspective. Then in the still, hot air, he went around and lit every one of them – a longish job – and stood back to admire the effect.

Just then, a stiff little breeze sprang out of nowhere and extinguished every single one. Having done its work, it died to nothing again.

With a patient sigh, Newton set to work again. He'd lit just over two-thirds of the candles this time – some four hundred or so – when the breeze sprang up again with a capricious twinkle and – *pht, pphht, phht* – blew out every candle again.

Not to be defeated, Newton decided that a similar effect could be achieved by setting up the candles in my living room. It would not be as ethereal, of course, but still spectacular in a more modest way. The next half-hour was spent moving every one of the candles inside, along with the sound system. When Newton had finished, the candles occupied every level surface: windowsills, bookshelves, the top of the dresser, the dining room table, encircling my newly acquired harp like a wreath. Out came the matches again, and Newton circled the room, bringing each wick to golden life.

It was only when he'd lit about a hundred of them that Newton noticed several alarming things. The room's temperature had shot up to a level at which you could have slow-roasted a Christmas turkey, and most of the candles were melting at an astonishing rate. Already the ones on the windowsill were dripping off it like molten lard. There was a distinct smell of scorching from the bookshelf as several of the books started curling and turning brown, and when a couple of my harp strings snapped with a resounding twang as the timbers of the harp warped in the fierce heat, Newton realised he might have misjudged the joules of candlepower involved. It was when one of my sitting room windows cracked that Newton realised he would have to extinguish them all, starting with the ones that had melted into a liquid pool of wax all over my carpet and were threatening to set it alight.

This he did, and then staggered out into the night air, his hair charring and his skin beginning to blister. Outside it was once again as still as the tomb with not a breath stirring. Newton is nothing if not persistent, and once again he thought it might be worthwhile to attempt the original design. This he finally successfully achieved, several hours after he had hoped to get it done and with dawn not far off. Setting Albinoni in motion, he somewhat wearily made his way to my bedroom, where I had slept through all this, shook me roughly awake and shouted, 'Get up! Get up! Get up!' in my ear – he was done with subtlety – and sprinted out the door while I came blearily awake.

And from that point, it was a piece of cake. All went as planned. I hopped out of bed, still unsure what or who had woken me, and became gradually aware of the strains of oboe music drifting from outside. In wonderment, I followed my ears and when I opened the front door there was the sight as Newton had intended – hundreds and hundreds of golden flames spangling the darkness, each pure and straight in the still air. The music drifted, soared and wound its way up in spiralling flights of sound, punctuated only by the distant *twang! p-tung* as a few last harp strings succumbed inside. As a farewell gift, it could not have been more touching, more beautiful, and I carry the memory of it to this day.

As, I'm sure, does Newton, as evidenced by his slight flinching at the sight of even a single candleflame – and now you know why.

Chapter 16

Old Tom Bombadil was a merry fellow;
Bright blue his jacket was, and his boots were yellow!
—J.R.R. Tolkien, *The Fellowship of the Ring*

Shortly after I arrived at Ellesmere, I realised that I needed wheels. I am not a car person in the least. If asked what model of car I own, I tend to answer something like 'white' or 'yellow', as the case may be. Nevertheless, I needed some form of transport, and I was pushed in the direction of a rundown caryard in the back lanes of Shropshire by the kindly bursar – and there discovered the existence of the Citroën 2CV.

I was smitten at first sight. For those of you who are not familiar with this classic model, picture a VW Beetle with French sass. It has been described as an upside-down pram, a sardine can on wheels and a tin snail. It was used in one of the classic James Bond chase sequences, where it outsmarted the ten black Ford Falcons pursuing it by lurching down through olive groves on a steep Sicilian hillside, bouncing along on its extraordinary suspension and occasionally rolling over to land on its springy wheels once more, ready to putter onwards while the villainous but inflexible Falcons came to grief one by one in the rugged terrain.

I have since been told that the original design brief included a requirement that a French peasant farmer could drive across a ploughed field without breaking a basket of eggs in the front

seat, and that one could comfortably fit a fully grown sheep in the back seat. I also suspect that another design brief element was that if it broke down it could always be fixed by even a rank amateur using a paperclip, a length of stocking or a wine cork, or a clever combination of all three.

I fell in love at first sight with a model in bright blue, the clear azure of a deep summer sky or a piece of Lego. I bought it immediately and once the mechanic had shown me the workings of the eccentric gearstick and handbrake – both of which are terribly easily confused with one another in moments of stress, as I was to discover – I was on my way, the proud owner of my very own Citroën 2CV, or Betty Bombadil as I christened her on a whim.

My first outing was that evening. Colonel Roland Judd, that magnificently calm and kindly colleague, had offered to take me badger-watching, and I rang him proudly to say that I could give him a lift rather than the other way round as we had originally planned. I picked him up from his lovely house on St John's Hill and then realised that I would need fuel, so I pulled into the petrol station at the bottom of the hill. Once I had parked by the pump, carefully applying the eccentric handbrake rod because of the slight slope of the forecourt, I went to get out of the car to use the bowser. My first attempt to open the door resulted in the window flapping open; these cars have an antiquated system whereby each window is hinged horizontally in the middle and flaps open like Dumbo's ears to allow fresh air to enter. I had inadvertently pushed the window so hard it had swung up and was now locked in place by a catch designed to keep it in the upright open position. I was not aware of the operation of this catch at the time. As it was a chilly evening and the somewhat elderly Colonel was already showing signs of mild hypothermia, I struggled in vain to get the window to flap closed again. In scrabbling around, however, I somehow managed to release the door catch accidentally and was spent spilling onto the concrete of the forecourt in a rolling somersault. All this, Colonel Judd watched with the air of courteous, impassive calm for which he was famous.

Springing to my feet, I went to find the cap of the petrol tank and discovered it to be on the passenger's side of the car rather than the driver's. I would have to move the car. After a brief tussle – no more than a minute at most – I worked out how to open the driver's door and started the car up. Carefully manoeuvring the eccentric gear rod as I had been taught how, I put the car into first gear and prepared to inch forwards to make my three-point turn. I released the clutch slowly and nothing happened. The engine was revving madly but the car wasn't going anywhere. Or rather it was: it was slowly rolling backwards towards the bonnet of an expensive Range Rover that had unwisely pulled in behind me. In a swift movement, I pulled on what I thought was the handbrake to stop the backward glide. The device clutched in my hand was, however, the gearstick – and I had just knocked it from neutral to fifth gear while the engine was revving hard.

The car leapt off all four wheels at once as the engine attempted to jump clear of the bonnet, and the whole car lurched forwards sickeningly a good three yards before the engine stalled and the car mercifully stopped dead, rocking on its baby-pram suspension for a soothing thirty seconds after coming to an abrupt standstill. Sweating, I managed to calm myself sufficiently to identify which was the gearstick and which the handbrake, and tentatively restarted the motor. I used the gearstick this time to put the car in first – up, in and to the left – released the handbrake gently – and reversed majestically into a row of rubbish bins. Up, in and to the left now having declared itself as *reverse* gear, I finally managed to get the car parallel with the pumps ready to fill the car with petrol.

Extricating myself from the car this time was easier, though it did take me two attempts to locate the correct door handle. The first lever I pulled sent the back of my car seat collapsing back with a thump onto the back seat, where it would have undoubtedly concussed any sheep I was carrying at the time. As I had now pulled up at the diesel pump instead of the petrol one, it was a matter of mere minutes before I had manoeuvred the car – via another brief mix-up between the gearstick, the handbrake and what turned out to be the windscreen wiper control rod – into a position where I could fill it.

Then it was only a matter of locating the lever to release the petrol cap – *under here? No, there goes the bonnet, it must be on a spring of sorts – How about this one? Oh, sorry Roland, let me get you upright again – What about this little lever? Ah, so that's how the squirters work, sorry Roland, you won't get that wet again once I work out how to shut the window-flap thingy* – and the car was at last full.

As we bunny-hopped away and onto the main road, Roland Judd gave one of his famous ruminant hums. 'Have you driven cars much before, I wonder? You do *have* them, I suppose, in Australia?' He sounded perfectly serious.

*

After this shaky start, Betty Bombadil and I got on like a house on fire. Mind you, I soon discovered that she didn't much like cold weather. Any morning lower than five degrees Celsius resulted in her starter motor refusing to turn over. However, to my great delight, I discovered in her boot a crank – a real-old fashioned crank – which could be inserted into a hole in her nose and used to start her up like some old vintage car from *Wacky Races*. In actual fact, the crank was difficult to use; its real effectiveness lay in its ability to attract a small crowd of astonished and admiring boys into the quadrangle who could then be dragooned into giving me a push to get the car roaring into life.

Once the warmer weather came along, I discovered the simple mechanism that allowed the canvas top to be rolled back like the lid of a sardine can and so turn the car into a convertible. My mother sent me a leather flying cap and a pair of goggles such as Spitfire pilots used to wear and I looked like Toad of Toad Hall as I flew along the country lanes, occasionally murmuring 'Poop, poop!' to myself in sheer delight.

Over the years I spent at Ellesmere College, I travelled enormous distances in Betty Bombadil. In the long holidays – one of the undoubted boons of a teacher's life – I drove her to the West Coast of Ireland, the very north of Scotland, down to the wilds of Cornwall and along the coast of East Anglia. On three separate occasions, I took her to Europe, each time discovering her to be the prime target of customs inspectors, one of whom revealed to me that they were classic smuggler's cars, equipped as they often were with all sorts of hidden compartments beneath the floorboards. Once across the Channel, I drove her as far afield as Norway, Spain, Italy and even a brief foray into Greece on one occasion. There were frequent breakdowns, but to my delight

I found that even my unmechanical eye could often see what was adrift and put it right with a bit of wire, a spare bolt or, in one desperate case in the wilds of Czechoslovakia, a length of peppermint-flavoured dental floss that had to be renewed every hundred miles almost to the inch.

On one occasion, stopping for some reason on the edge of a Scottish motorway with traffic thundering past, I opened the door a little and the wind from a passing truck blew the door right off its hinges and deposited it on the verge some ten yards ahead. No matter. I was able to wind back the roof, shove the errant door into the car through the ceiling space and drive to a more tranquil spot to reattach the door upon hinges that were as pliable as liquorice.

On another occasion, crossing some mighty Alpine pass in Switzerland, I stopped to pick up three burly Serbian hitchhikers with enormous backpacks. Betty Bombadil was not used to the extra weight and once over the pass and on the downward run the brakes began to emit an ominous squeal and a stench of burning rubber. I was a bit slow on the uptake, but when the foot brakes failed altogether and the car gathered momentum down a long winding descent with extraordinary rapidity, there was a quickfire burst of anxious Serbian dialogue before the chap in the passenger seat next to me had the foresight to pull on the handbrake and bring the car to a rocking stop in a gravel pit. Very politely but very firmly, my three passengers bade me farewell and good luck and left me to continue the descent on my own.

As instructed by my Serbian friend, I kept the car in second gear and with my hand on the handbrake, as the main brakes were now completely defunct. Even so, I was roaring along far quicker than I was comfortable with, and soon even the handbrake seemed to give up the ghost. Down and down I swooped and curved, totally unable to check my speed, even when I saw looming ahead of me the Italian border crossing and a boom gate with an armed guard standing there to stop traffic. I knew I would be unable to stop. My only hope was to keep rolling onwards until the road flattened out and I lost momentum; from the look of the valley spreading out far below me, that was not going to be for another ten miles of winding mountain descent. With a hundred yards to go before the checkpoint, I stuck my head out of the window and bellowed, 'Sorry!! Terribly sorry! Can't stop! No brakes! Would you mind awfully opening up?!! So sorry!! English!'

At the last moment, the border guard seemed to get the picture and swung the boom gate high as I whisked through with inches to spare. I must have been going at least fifty miles an hour and there was nothing I could do about it. For the next ten minutes, I hurtled round bends, swayed to and fro across the road, soared in and out of shadows cast by pine trees and jutting outcrops of silvery rock and could find nothing more useful to do than hum the James Bond theme music furiously to myself as I plummeted down the mountain road.

Finally, at the bottom of the valley, the road flattened and the car slowed – to forty, to thirty, fifteen, ten miles per hour – as I entered a small Italian village with a mercifully empty high street. In fact, in an inspired case of sheer serendipity, I rolled to a stop on the very forecourt of a small garage that doubled as a car mechanic's workshop. Shaking like a leaf and uttering the faintest of *poop-poops*, I climbed out of the car and went to find someone who could restore the various braking systems of my car. I didn't quite trust my proven ingenuity with peppermint-flavoured dental floss enough to do the job myself.

A few years later, Betty Bombadil became even more eccentric in appearance. I had been driving back from the sailing club at Whitemere one afternoon when I had run headlong around a blind corner into a tractor the size of the Albert Hall. My vehicle's bright blue bonnet and front wheel arches were crumpled like a used napkin; the tractor sustained a faint smudge of blue paint on its huge steel counterweight that protruded from its nose like a medieval battering ram. The farmer laconically climbed down from a great height, inspected the damage and said, 'Knock for a knock?'

Now I had never been involved in an accident before, so I failed to understand that this is motorist-speak for 'Shall we regard this as mutually caused damage, no blame to either party, you fix your damage and I'll fix mine, agreed?' In fact, I thought he was making some strange Shropshire version of a knock-knock joke. 'Yes, indeed, ha ha. Knock knock. Who's there? Bloody big tractor, ha ha.'

The farmer took this wittering attempt at jocularity for the legal disclaimer he was after, fixed his own damage with one swipe of a grubby hanky, and backed off into a field to let me limp homewards, scraping large parts of the chassis along the tarmac. Back at the College, I surveyed the damage with considerable despair. I was just off to ring a scrapyard to take the crumpled corpse away when my friend Ross Bassenthwaite came sauntering around the corner. 'Eeeh oop,' he exclaimed cheerfully. 'Good thing it's a 2CV, eh?'

When I asked him to elaborate, he explained. 'They're just one big crumple zone really,' he said. 'The motor won't be damaged, I imagine. And the good thing is that all those panels just screw off with a Meccano spanner and you can replace them with new ones.'

And sure enough, that's what we did. The only problem was that the local scrapyard only had a left-hand wheel arch in bright yellow and a bonnet in bright red, so that when the replacements were made Betty Bombadil took on the jaunty air of a harlequin. In fact, a few days later, I found that the Design and Tech

Department had fashioned a large tin key and attached it to the boot to make the whole thing look like a wind-up Noddy car from Toyland. Over the next few years, I found out that this new jester's coat had a surprisingly beneficial quality. When I parked inadvertently in the middle of London on some double yellow lines not far from Harrods and then got distracted for three days – a long story for another time – I returned to the abandoned car fully expecting a parking fine ticking up into the thousands of pounds. Bizarrely, Betty Bombadil's eccentric piebald look seemed to render her invisible to the authorities. Perhaps they thought she was an art installation, or some sort of clown car that might douse them with whitewash if they approached her. Whatever the case, she seemed immune to the predations of traffic wardens no matter how brazenly I flouted parking regulations, and I continued to drive her with renewed pride and confidence over the next few years.

This fond relationship finally came to an end in a way that is somewhat bizarre. I was approaching my last few weeks at Ellesmere and already had plans to sail away in a little rowboat – literally. I'd managed to rid myself of all my goods and chattels by means I shall explain later, but I was puzzled about what to do with the car. It seemed very unlikely that any respectable salesyard would want to purchase her, and I wasn't quite sure how one went about disposing of a collection of brightly painted tin enclosing a failing motor and some badly frayed lengths of dental floss. I should have trusted to my usual luck in these matters. It was on a final trip to Whitemere that it happened. I was there to check out the report that there was an abandoned Mirror dinghy lying in the lakeside grass that might be suitable for my burgeoning daydream of a riparian departure. I parked Betty under the chestnut trees and went to examine the boat in question. Even as I did so, I could sense Betty's somewhat reproachful glance from her headlamp eyes as I investigated the dinghy with growing excitement. Had I found a new love? A new wingéd chariot? A new mistress to bear me away whithersoever I desired?

It seemed I had, at least in Betty Bombadil's eyes. When I went to drive off in her, bumping over the roots of the old chestnut trees, something beneath my feet went *CRACK!* and the car rocked to a stop, never to move again. It seemed that, sensing my imminent abandonment, Betty had died of a broken crankshaft and given up the ghost for good.

Chapter 17

Theatre is a series of insurmountable obstacles on the road to imminent disaster.

—Tom Stoppard, *Shakespeare in Love*

Directing school plays became a large part of my Ellesmere life and although I write of some of them with glowing pride in these pages, not all of them were a breeze to stage. The head of Junior School, an imperious lady called Mrs Hilary Wainwright, asked me to direct the Junior School musical in terms that brooked no denial. She had already chosen the production, she informed me, and a key ingredient was that it had to involve every child in the Junior School. She had chosen *Oh! What a Lovely War.*

This musical, dear reader, is a satirical attack on the First World War, largely delivered in the form of a circus, and demands a level of sophistication well beyond school-age students, let alone the seven-to-eleven-year-old sons of Shropshire farmers, grocers and bank clerks. Nevertheless, Mrs Wainwright was breezily confident that I could pull it off and left me entirely in charge of the forty-seven hamster-like children three times a week for an entire term, aided only by my upstairs neighbour, the nervous Welsh organist who was more used to playing Sumsion settings for Evensong than bashing out the saucy cancan rhythms of the Moulin Rouge that the play demanded.

From the very first rehearsal, the process was a trainwreck;

I privately christened it *Oh! What a Ghastly Mess*. The lead actors, being all of eleven, could barely pronounce the plethora of Belgian and French names that peppered the script – Ypres, Verdun, Lesdins – and the little chap playing the Ringmaster could not be dissuaded from referring to the Supreme Commander of the Allied Forces as 'Fieldmouse Haig' time and time again. Only after I had picked him up by the collar and said very clearly an inch from his nose, 'Jamie, it is Field*marshal*, Field*marshal*, repeat after me, *marshal*, *marshal*, Field*marshal* Haig!' did he get it. For a while at least; then he erred in a different direction by changing the name to 'Marshmallow Haig', which is where it stuck for the rest of the production. As for the choreography needed for the songs, the poor little boys had the terpsichorean coordination of baby hamsters, frequently falling over each other as they attempted to distinguish their lefts from their rights.

I am ashamed to admit that I became so despairing of ever getting the production into shape that I fell into a rare depression, not helped one little bit by Mrs Wainwright's breezy confidence that I would pull it out of the bag as I always did. There were many other pressures at the time; exams to be marked, lessons to be planned, the sudden realisation that the Drama course I had been teaching for the last eight months actually had a National Curriculum I was meant to follow and wasn't just counted as part of the school's hobby programme as I had fondly believed. In fact, with two weeks to go before opening night, I had only directed a fifth of the sodding play. There was only one thing for it. I decided to hop in Betty Bombadil that very evening and drive as fast as I could around the narrow lanes of North Shropshire in the hope that I might plough headlong into another tractor and this time break a leg or worse. That might be the only excuse that would get the relentlessly optimistic Mrs Wainwright to let me off directing this hideous shambles.

To that end, I set off in the late afternoon under a sky that was lurid with summer thunder. The air seemed almost greenish, an aquarium tint that made the hedgerows and ash trees look nightmarish enough to match my feverish mood. I hurtled along the lanes, diving down ways I had never taken before, but the countryside was frustratingly empty of other vehicles under that apocalyptic sky. Soon I was hopelessly lost. The lanes between their high hedges kept running to muddy dead ends at the banks of a large river – the Severn, I guessed – or came to a halt in abandoned farmyards where huge pigs squealed savagely behind rusting gates. By that time, the air was glowing an unnatural gold and I could see across the fields the tall mass of hills I later came to know as the Breiddens, standing up like atomic mushroom clouds from the radioactive plains. In my wild mood, I decided to ditch my plan of staging a head-on collision and head for the summit of these precipitous heights instead. There I could go for a walk along the clifftops and accidentally come to grief: a broken leg, a snapped spine, anything to get me out of having to take responsibility for the debacle of the Junior Play.

Getting to the damn hills proved to be quite enough of a challenge. As the River Severn lay between me and the foot of the Breiddens, and the only bridge for miles was at the one little village of Melverley, it took me another hour to navigate my way to this spot and make the crossing. Under normal circumstances, I would have found Melverley, with its magpie church of black and white beams set on the reedy banks of the river, charming, but nothing that evening was going to distract me from my fell purpose. Eventually I got to the foot of the hills and started roaring up the narrow winding road that led to the summit. It wound up through pinewoods seamed with cliffs, occasionally shooting out onto banks of turf and russet bracken glowing like copper in the strange light. Far below me the plain dropped away into a green haze. Above me, thunderclouds gathered like curdled cream and the air crackled. It was a perfect evening for a dramatic accident.

Suddenly, something happened that brought all my instinct for self-preservation flooding back. On a bend of the steep road, a huge stag leapt out in front of the car, bronze-antlered, tagged with dark sweat, looming above the car. I jammed on the brake, something went *ping!*, the engine slipped into neutral and the car started gently reversing back down the tiny wriggle of a road I had just ascended. In vain did I grope for the handbrake. In vain did I try to shove the car into first gear. Nothing seemed to slow the backward rolling of Betty Bombadil. It seemed she had read my mind and was only too happy to oblige in bringing about my tragic demise. In fact, in order to expedite the process, she was now rocketing backwards at a steady thirty miles per hour, looking for a handy cliff to plunge over.

'I've changed my mind!' I shouted to whichever gods were listening and, craning my head over my shoulder like a demented owl, tried to focus fiercely on steering the backwards-plummeting car down the torturous road. Somehow, God knows how, I made it – a two-mile winding descent in reverse with no brakes. I rolled to a halt at the base of the Breiddens, hopped out and started shaking uncontrollably. A minute later, the heavens opened and the rain came down in golden sheets, still lit by that fantastical chlorinous light. Apologising to my parents, my Maker and any other deities present, I drove very slowly, very carefully, very thoughtfully home.

The next day, I announced to the cast that for artistic reasons I had cut half of Act One, the parade scene, the cancan number, all that bit in the middle with the horseys, five scenes in Act Two and most of Act Three – and had thus at one stroke of a pen,

changed things such that instead of having only directed a measly fifth of the play, I had achieved the very respectable goal of having directed a chunky seven-eighths. And still with two weeks to go. Very impressive, Mackinnon.

In the end, the whole thing pulled together in that miraculous way plays have. The appalling choreography was assumed by the parent body to be a masterful bit of comic satire; the fact that the little chaps kept toppling over mid-dance was taken to represent the tragic falling of troops in battle, a subtlety I was congratulated on more than once. Even the continual reference to Marshmallow Haig was thought by many to be an ironic comment on the character of High Command. Most parents, however, just thanked me for the merciful shortness of the whole thing.

'Thank God,' they'd say conspiratorially, keeping a weather eye out in case Mrs Wainwright was about. 'These things usually last hours. Amazing you got this to under twenty minutes, old chap. Well done, you!'

But the best part was not my doing at all. Unbeknownst to me, Hilary Wainwright had not been as hands-off as she had appeared. Without my knowledge, she had arranged for a body of devoted mums to cut out hundreds – no, thousands – of red poppy petals from vast swathes of scarlet crêpe paper and had had them concealed in a huge net in the ceiling above the stage. As the last piece played – 'And When They Ask Us' – the only song the boys really got right with their childishly sweet and shaky voices – down came the poppy petals in a fluttering scarlet shower, gently, inexorably, endlessly – and there was not, as they say, a dry eye in the house.

And Mrs Wainwright never knew how dangerous it had been, her breezy confidence in my directing abilities, and I never told her. But when she asked me (and she was certainly going to ask me) if I would do next year's Junior Musical, the answer was inevitable.

'Of course, Hilary. Of course I will.'

Chapter 18

The world is grey, the mountains old,
The forge's fire is ashen-cold;
No harp is wrung, no hammer falls:
The darkness dwells in Durin's halls;
The shadow lies upon his tomb
In Moria, in Khazad-dûm.

—J.R.R. Tolkien, *The Fellowship of the Ring*

As an Australian, I was not always as cluey as I might have been about the dearly cherished cultural practices of my adopted county and outlying regions. Who would have thought, for example, that Welsh love spoons could play such an important part in the local economy of the Welsh region of Snowdonia? Or rather, to be more accurate, *once* played an important part in the life of the valleys – right up until the day when Ross and I made a fateful visit to the remote village of Cwm Penmachno.

This was the location of the College's Outdoor Education base, an old converted chapel in a tiny hamlet right at the end of a winding Snowdonian valley, surrounded by bleak hills scarred with slate quarries. Ross and I were keen to take some students there for a weekend of mountain-climbing and exploration and were given directions and the keys to the chapel by Colonel Judd. The Colonel, as has been previously noted, was an amiable chap but noted for his vagueness of manner so it was no surprise when we arrived one dark and rainy afternoon at Cwm Penmachno to find that none of the keys worked on the chapel doors. Ross eventually had to shimmy up a drainpipe and squeeze through a half-open window on the second floor to gain access.

The place was somewhat unprepossessing at first sight. The main room was a large draughty space – the original chapel, in fact – with old wooden pews arranged around the walls and a cavernous fireplace containing nothing but a ton of soot and a dead jackdaw. Nevertheless, the Colonel had told us that out the back we would find a supply of firewood in a lean-to shed of sorts. He had added that we'd have to go easy on the wood because, from memory, supply had run pretty low and he hadn't been able to organise another delivery. A quick scout around the back of the chapel in the late afternoon gloom took us through a gate to a locked shed. Of course, none of the keys worked on the padlock here either, but Ross soon managed to jemmy the lock away and access the firewood within. Despite the Colonel's misgivings, there was plenty of firewood here, all beautifully cut into short lengths and as dry and flammable as one could wish for: on this occasion his muddle-headedness was working in our favour. In a matter of minutes, we had organised the lads to transport a barrowload inside and soon had a merry fire crackling on the hearth. It is amazing what a difference a fire makes to a place. Soon the dampness seemed to have dissipated, the air grew warm and cosy and we were eating a hot supper of macaroni cheese around the fireplace, our faces ruddy in the bright glow. Indeed, I have never seen a fire burn so brightly and cleanly. It seemed to give off a sweet smell as well, a fragrant wood-smoke quite unlike the sullen acrid smoke that would have emanated from the damp, fungi-rotten logs I had been expecting.

So cheering was the fire that we dragged the mattresses down from the upstairs dormitories and laid them out on the floor of the chapel so we could fall asleep by the flickering glow of the firelight, made sleepy by the wine we had all enjoyed together.

Yes, wine. It seems incredible to me now, but the rules governing alcohol and students back then were considerably more relaxed than they are now. Not only was it permissible for Ross and me to enjoy a few pints of beer or a bottle of red in the presence of students under our care, but it was even acceptable to allow the students to drink as well. Because the College had some senior students who were over eighteen, it ran a student bar – The Ring and Raven – as did most similar schools in those days. Even for students not yet over the legal drinking age, it was almost expected that a housemaster or tutor would judiciously introduce his young charges to the joys of drinking alcohol. There were certain guidelines: younger boys, those fourteen or under, might be offered nothing stronger than a shandy, for example. Spirits and hard liquor were discouraged. But for students fifteen to seventeen years of age, it was perfectly acceptable to offer them a glass of wine or two, or a couple of pints of beer.

The next day, we set off to explore the mountains at the head of the valley. Ross had heard that there were some slate mines nearby and rumour had it that it was possible to find your way right through the mountains by way of these mines and pop out on the other side. Sure enough, we soon found the entrance to a cavern and decided to explore. We were well equipped with head torches and spare batteries and had each brought some ham sandwiches and an apple in case our exploration took us through to lunchtime. There were just three boys with us on that first expedition; Huw Davies, whom we have met earlier in these pages, and two others, Archie Hobbs and Sam Evans. For some reason, all three boys had decided that the expedition would be considerably enhanced by the donning of black balaclavas, which they thought gave them a suitably dangerous SAS vibe, but which Ross and I personally thought made them look like mentally deficient seal-cubs. Our opinion to that effect was cheerfully ignored.

The entrance tunnel was wide and high and made easy walking at first. Two rusted railway tracks led straight into the hillside, once used for the slate carts. Occasionally a side tunnel would curve off to either side, but we kept to the main tunnel until we were deep inside the mountain. Eventually the tunnel split into three directions and I felt the thrill I always get in a maze or labyrinth – the dividing of the ways, the frisson of the choice. It was very tempting to split our group and send each party down a different tunnel, but Ross's cooler sense prevailed and we opted for one tunnel to explore together. I remember vividly the sights we saw over the next few hours. At one point we came across a vast cavern that dropped away into an echoing darkness below us. On the other side of the cavern was a continuation of our tunnel, just visible in the probing torchlight. Linking the two was a great wooden beam, as big as a mighty tree trunk though roughly squared, making a bridge across the chasm. The only problem was that there was nothing by way of a handrail; nothing to prevent you plunging into the depths below. A dropped pebble descended in complete silence for three whole seconds before sending up a series of ever-fainter echoes as it ricocheted off the walls of some cavern unimaginably far below us. You might be relieved to know that even I, optimistic risk-taker that I am, reluctantly resisted the temptation posed by the potential of the far tunnel and recognised that this was for us a dead end.

On exploring the second of the tunnels, we found within a hundred yards a different sort of challenge. This time the tunnel came to another cavern, but it was flooded right up to the lip of the tunnel by inky dark water. Again, a continuation of the tunnel could be seen across this subterranean lake but twenty yards of deep and icy water lay between us and the way onwards. Again, it seemed we were to be thwarted. Archie Hobbs had other ideas though. Before we knew it, he had stripped down to his underwear and slipped, Gollum-like, into the water. 'Permission to explore, sir?' At our reluctant nod, he dog paddled across the flooded chasm and hauled himself out into the tunnel on the other side. Beginning to shiver already, he grinned broadly and gave us a thumbs up. Explaining that he would go and see where the tunnel led, he padded off barefoot out of sight. I don't know how long he was actually gone, but to my strained nerves it seemed at least an hour or two before the faint glimmer of his torch showed across the lake once more. He called out something that echoed indistinctly and when it was clear we couldn't hear him, he clambered into the water and swam back to our side. In the torchlight, he was distinctly bluish in colour and looked more like Gollum than ever with his hair plastered to his scalp and his eyes bulging.

It seemed that he had encountered another similar flooded cavern further on … and so swum that as well. Then another one … and another … and always with a further tunnel enticing his adventurous spirit on. Finally, however, the tunnel had become so sharp and stony underfoot that his bare feet could no longer handle the damage and he had had no recourse but to make the return trip, swimming in icy water another four times to make it back here. I have never seen a boy so cold. I have never seen a boy so glowing with pride, as Huw and Sam towelled him dry with his flannelette shirt and got him back into warm clothes and his beloved balaclava.

Now there was only left the third of the three tunnels if we were to find our way through the mountain.

On exploring the last of the passages, we found ourselves in a honeycomb of branching passages that looped back on themselves, linked up and redivided, wriggled and wound and split, so that we were constantly finding ourselves inexplicably back where we had been a few minutes before. To try to keep track of which passages we had explored, we made little cairns of stones at each new entrance, but even so we soon became bewildered and disorientated. It was only after enjoying the comic absurdity of getting lost so easily – as one does in a hall of mirrors or a funfair maze – that we realised we didn't actually know how to get out of here; we certainly didn't know the way to the rumoured exit on the far side of the mountain, nor did we have a clue as to which tunnel led back to the main entrance. And there wasn't going to be some sideshow operator along any minute with a torch and a key to open the emergency escape route. In plain truth, we were getting seriously worried.

This was when I realised I had the mathematical skills to get us out of trouble. I have long been interested in the science of topology; that is, the mathematical principles behind shapes and lines and pathways. I carefully explained to my fellow explorers that anyone lost in a labyrinth need only put their right hand on one of the walls and, without taking it off that wall for any reason, walk their way out of the maze. Simple. To that end, I rallied the troops, suggested Ross bring up the rear, placed my right hand on a tunnel wall and marched into the darkness.

In less than a minute, I saw something ahead that jolted me with fear. There was another figure in the tunnel; like us it wore a head torch and a red backpack and whoever it might be was striding purposefully away from us around a curve in the tunnel ahead. It seemed very odd that there was another person here; we had been underground for about three hours and seen no signs of a stranger. Perhaps he had been stalking us all this while. Then again, a stranger might be able to point us in the right direction. Should I call out? Or wait for Ross to catch up?

I waited and within a minute everyone had caught up, Ross last of all. I told them in whispers what I had seen.

'A backpack, you say? A red backpack?' Ross asked.

'Yes, that's right. Tall chap – about your height, actually.'

'With a red backpack? Like this one?' Ross turned to show me the pack on his back.

'Yes, just like that. What are the chances?'

The realisation hit me. 'So that was you ... and we've—'

'—been going in a circle, yes. So much for fookin' topology! Come on, it's this way, I can feel a breeze.'

And after a few more minutes of determined marching, Ross led us through the labyrinth and into a new tunnel unmarked by one of our cairns. This led straight as a die and, sure enough, after another fifteen minutes of walking, daylight glimmered ahead, ghostly and blue as it always appears to one who has been a long time underground. Hurrying on, we found ourselves at the bottom of a great funnel-shaped quarry, open to the sky above, but whose steep sides were a mass of mighty jagged slates, some of them as big as elephants but as sharp as blades. It was like emerging into some titanic pit of Mordor, a cruel wasteland of stone and rusted iron.

We had found the way through the mountain, but it was not at all clear to us that we would be able to safely climb up to the lip of this gigantic quarry. Every step was precarious; rocks shifted and tilted under our feet. A careless move would bring a small avalanche of smaller slates sliding down, threatening to cut our boots to shreds. It had started to rain, a thin cold drizzle that made every stone treacherously slick beneath our feet. On the other hand, the thought of trying to make our way back through the bewildering labyrinth of dark tunnels was disheartening in the extreme.

Eventually, with extreme caution, we managed to stumble our way to the top of the scree and out onto more solid ground. We were on a great mountainside of short grass and heather, seamed with rocky screes and outcrops. Below us the valley swept in a desolate, slate-strewn wilderness into the grey distance, bare slate fields as far as the eye could see, like hard grey filo pastry on a gigantic scale. Above us, the heights of the mountain disappeared into fog and cold drizzle – but there was a path, a sheep track winding that way, and we guessed this to be the route home. It was exquisite to be out under the open sky, even such a damp and drizzly one – to feel rain on our lips, cool air on our brows, to see a horizon, to hear the soughing of wind across the sheep-nibbled turf. And oh, the smells, sharp and earthy and aromatic – heather and peat and the wild mountain thyme. There is an intensity about all the senses after having been in the scentless, sightless, stifling darkness of a mine, and none more so than the sense of smell, which is heightened to that of a fox. Why, we could pick up the lanolin and dung smell of a sheep on a hillside half a mile away. But for now, there was a two-hour trek up over the great whaleback of the mountain and down into the pine forests beyond which lay the chapel and our beds.

That night back at Cwm Penmachno, we cooked up sausages and mash, grilled tomatoes and bacon and peas. We got the fire roaring again, crackling merrily and bright, and Archie regained his ruddy colour once more – even more so as a bottle of shiraz did the rounds and set our eyes sparkling. We spoke of plans to come back and make further explorations – to bring ropes to make crossing the great beam bridge a possibility, and a small inflatable dinghy to get across the flooded caverns without risking hypothermia.

Thirty years on, I shudder at the risks we took with these young people in the outdoors. A couple of years later, a kayaking tragedy in Lyme Bay, Dorset, cost the lives of four students; the aftermath saw the whole world of outdoor education in the UK overhauled and regulated – and no doubt many lives were saved because of this. I thoroughly approve of these changes, not least

because it has rid the outdoor education world of a certain type of trainer who was characterised by macho bullying and a military style of coaching that verged on the sadistic. But there is a small part of me that deeply appreciates the fact that Ross and I were able to operate in ways that provided some true adventures in the wild places of the world.

*

One other memory of the trip is less fortunate. On arrival back at College and having dispatched the boys off to their Houses and hot showers and dinner, Ross and I convened in the Common Room bar for a congratulatory debrief. This was interrupted a few minutes later by the appearance of the Colonel, looking more distraught than ever and running his hands wildly through his thinning hair. He was less than pleased to see us and didn't even seem terribly interested in the theories of maze topology that I attempted to explain while pulling him a pint from the beer pump.

'I've just had a call from Mrs Pritchard,' he said. 'She's not happy! Not happy at all.'

'Who's Mrs Pritchard?' we asked in unison.

'Mrs Pritchard is the lady who lives next door to the Chapel at Cwm Penmachno. She also happens to be the champion Welsh love spoon carver for the whole of North Wales.'

'What's a Welsh love spoon?' I asked.

'A Welsh love spoon?! *What's a Welsh love spoon?* How can you not know what a Welsh love spoon is?' cried the Colonel in anguish.

I felt this to be a little unfair. As a recent newcomer to this part of the world, I didn't feel obliged to become familiar with the folk customs of the rural Welsh community.

'The Welsh love spoon industry,' said the Colonel in clipped terms, 'is the sole driver of the economy for that part of Wales. That, and making things out of slate.'

'Oh yes, I've seen those slate things. Owls and dragons and little clocks. Not my cup of tea, really.'

'That is irrelevant. The salient fact is that it's the Welsh love spoon industry that really puts the leeks and rarebit on the table for the people of Cwm Penmachno and outlying areas. And let me ask you this,' I still didn't quite see where this was going, but I think Ross had cottoned on by the way he was pouring himself a particularly stiff whisky, 'did you have a fire during your stay at Cwm Penmachno, by any chance?'

'Er, yes. A lovely one, actually. You were wrong about the firewood supply, by the way. There was plenty. In fact, we used it all. Nothing like a good fire, is there?'

'And where did you find this firewood, may I ask?'

'Out the back. Like you said. Well, in a locked shed actually – I think you'd given us the wrong keys. But we soon got the padlock off. Good old Ross here—'

The Colonel groaned and Ross shot me a killing look.

'That,' said the Colonel in wearily patient tones, 'wasn't the Cwm Penmachno firewood. That was the entire supply of highest-grade cherrywood that Mrs Pritchard has been seasoning for ten years to carve Welsh love spoons from. *Ten years*. And you burnt the lot!'

Shaking his head in despair, the Colonel left his pint unfinished and stormed out.

There was a long silence.

'I wonder if Mrs Pritchard also makes those things out of slate, owls and suchlike,' said Ross at last.

'Possibly. I wouldn't know. Why?'

'Oh, just that we could tell her where she could get a heck of a lot of slate. Replace the woodcarving, perhaps.'

It was certainly an idea – but I think we both suspected that a better strategy would be to postpone a visit to Cwm Penmachno for some while yet. And when we did visit, ensure we wore a couple of balaclavas of our own.

Chapter 19

I want to leave behind me the name of a fellow who never bullied a little boy, or turned his back on a big one.
—Thomas Hughes, *Tom Brown's School Days*

Archie Hobbs, the intrepid cave diver, was one of the more extraordinary boys I came across at Ellesmere. I first encountered him in my Third Form English class, a small stocky figure with a face like a bulldog puppy. He was exceptionally earnest in his work ethic but suffered from perhaps the most serious case of dyslexia I had ever encountered. This made his writing almost indecipherable and stretched my code-cracking skills to their limit. I soon learnt that the best way to decipher something like this – *Thur solja unssad the foan and korl dout twiz fren ditz fyoo* – was to read it quickly to a colleague exactly as it was written and then ask him to repeat back what I had just said: '*The soldier answered the phone and called out to his friend, "It's for you."*' Simple.

This disability had forged in Archie's young spirit an unquenchable desire to overcome all obstacles, and he brought to his schoolwork and his life in general an astonishing maturity and determination to succeed. He joined the School Cadet Corps and hero-worshipped Michael Barton, who was by that time in charge of the Cadets. Archie had decided at an early age that he was going to join the military, and he became a model soldier under Michael's care. He revelled in going out on night patrols, smothered in camouflage paint, a sizeable shrub tucked into his helmet, planning campaign after brilliant campaign to rout the enemy or capture the foe. On parade he was always meticulously turned out, his boots gleaming, his uniform spotless, his eyes on the far horizon as the troops were inspected, his hand ready to give a smart salute to the inspecting officer.

I had little to do with him in this military role, but I still remember him in one of my classes demonstrating that dyslexia was no handicap when it came to some skills. On occasions, when the joys of correct apostrophe usage had begun to lose its lustre or the dramatic irony in *Macbeth* had begun to pall, I would take the class out onto the playing fields and engage them with a game I had invented years ago. It is a sort of trading game, played with a couple of decks of playing cards. Four students are appointed to be 'Kings' and are dispatched with some cards to four different corners of the playing field, which will become their 'Kingdoms'. The rest of the players are 'Traders'. As such, they can run freely to and fro between the four Kings, facilitating the swapping of cards between the Kings. All are told to accumulate as much wealth in the way of cards as they can. As this occurs, I circulate with a bag full of spare playing cards, visiting each King in turn to facilitate the progress of the game.

On this basis, alliances are forged, treacheries enacted. Economies rise and fall. The supply of spades all but dries up, and everyone realises that they are all doomed unless the Spade King can be encouraged to produce more spades to keep the wheels of commerce spinning smoothly. This game, played in many different schools where I have worked, has always proven to be an enormous success. Its relevance to the teaching of English has, admittedly, not always been immediately clear to the reigning Director of Learning or Head of English, so it has usually been played in the remotest fringes of the school campus, well out of sight of the main office block windows – and this particular game I played with Archie Hobbs was no exception. From the beginning, dyslexia notwithstanding, Archie quickly assumed complete control. As one of the Kings, he had a queue of Traders eager to do business with him, but Archie was not to be hustled.

'Jasper, sorry, you'll need to wait. I need to deal with Mungo first, and then Bruno. Now, Mungo, I can give you three clubs for those diamonds but not a club more. No? Then off you go, we can't do business, I'm afraid. Ah, Simon, you're back. Good. Take these three cards and get over to Liam as quick as you can. He's the Spade King but my spies tell me he's going under and if he goes, we all go. Off you go. Right then, gentlemen, sorry to keep you waiting but I can see you now. Jasper, you first. What can you offer me?'

In the space of ten minutes, Archie had divined the whole nature of the game; before long, whether they knew it or not, every player in the game was actually working for Archie, and everyone was thriving. In fact, all the Kingdoms were making such a steady profit and amassing such a fortune in cards that soon the bank was completely broke. After that, I had to invent a new rule that involved taxing every player two cards every few minutes – at which point, the buggers just disappeared behind the bike sheds and invented a form of offshore trading. It may not have been much help in passing the Literature examination, but the game did wonders for the acuity of these future stock market aficionados and hedge fund traders.

By the time Archie had reached Fifth Form, he had filled out to become a very impressive young man. He was nuggetty and tough, well-muscled and strong; an asset to the First XV rugby side and a tireless cross-country runner. In all this time, he was still absolutely set on joining the army and often spoke passionately about his dreams of rising through the ranks to one day lead others.

His ambition was by no means fuelled by a lust for bloodshed or glory. In fact, he often spoke with sadness of the worst aspects of the military: rogue soldiers committing atrocities, bastardisation in the training programmes, a misogynistic and homophobic attitude among recruits. His main desire was to change these things from within, and I could hardly think of a better person for the job. It was therefore with great interest that I saw him off from the College gates one afternoon to go and attend a three-day entry test down at Exeter. This, I gathered, was where hundreds of Fifth Formers from around the country got to prove their dedication and skills as the first step towards military recruitment once their school studies were concluded. Archie departed on a cloud of shining aspiration, determined to prove his fitness as one of the top cadets in the country.

A busy weekend drove Archie from my mind until after Evensong two boys came to me in considerable distress. Archie had returned from Exeter, they said, and something was terribly wrong with him. He was crying and incoherent and couldn't be coaxed from his bed. His housemaster was on days off, and though I had nothing officially to do with Archie the boys had sought me out for help.

When I reached his room, it was as his friends had said. Archie was curled into a tight foetal ball, moaning and weeping softly. Every now and then he would uncurl sufficiently to smack a clenched fist into the mattress. His bulldog face was red and puffy with tears and his eyes were dazed and unfocused.

'What's wrong, Archie?' I asked.

'I killed them,' he sobbed, snuffling on great gobs of snot and tears. 'I killed them all.'

My God! My thoughts went immediately to the school armoury, where the live rounds were kept – supposedly under lock and key but in the care of the absentminded Colonel Judd.

I frantically thought back to Evensong to see if I could recall any gaps in the ranks.

'Archie, listen,' I said gently. 'It's all right. Who did you kill?'

'My own men! All my own men! All blown up' – and he collapsed on the floor.

Blown up? Were there grenades in the Cadet Armoury? Mortars? Surely we would have heard something.

'Okay,' I said, trying to inject a soothing tone into my voice. 'Where was this, Archie? Here at Ellesmere? Just this evening?'

'What? No!' Archie looked more dazed than ever. 'Down at Exeter. I got the coordinates wrong. Bloody dyslexia. I blew up all my own men. And I failed the entry test. I can never join the army' – and once again, he collapsed into sobs.

So relieved was I to realise that there hadn't been a massacre of my colleagues or students out on Parry's Field or in the Quad that my next words were not as sympathetic as they might have been. 'Oh, thank God for that! Oh, that is good news. This was a map exercise, was it? Just troops on paper. Well, that's alright then. Call off the cavalry. There, there ...'

At this point, even in his misery, Archie must have realised he was dealing with an idiot and came and gave me a huge hug. We stood there for what seemed an eternity while Archie hiccupped out apology after apology for having frightened me. A dozen whispers of caution went through my head – *inappropriate physical contact with a student – jeopardising your career – school guidelines insist – ensure others are present and doors are open* – but in the moment I could no more have extricated myself from Archie's hug than I could have pushed him down a well. The boy was in distress, physically, emotionally and mentally, and needed just to be held. No words. No advice. No judgement. Just stillness.

Afterwards, Archie explained more coherently what had happened. The whole weekend had gone superbly and Archie had excelled in every quarter, winning golden opinions from all the instructors there. But the final exercise had indeed been a map exercise where recruits were asked to plot some coordinates to enable the shelling of a wood where the enemy were hidden. Here, Archie's dyslexia tripped him up horribly. The coordinates he entered had sent the shells to a completely different part of the wood where, Archie had been informed – cruelly it seems to me – he had just wiped out his own platoon. His chances of joining the army were now nil.

Numbed and shocked by the disappointment, Archie had trudged into the Station Bar at Bristol while waiting for a change of train and ordered a triple whisky. This was the first time he had ever done anything out of the Boy Scout mould in his life, and the first time he had tasted hard liquor. Having downed the first glass, he had promptly ordered another one and had then descended into a drunken mess all the way back to College. Throwing up three times in the taxi from Shrewsbury had done little to lessen the effects of the alcohol and had served only to deepen the shame. All this I gathered while Archie sat on his bed clutching his pounding head and spilling the beans – and spilling the last of his stomach contents onto my well-polished shoes, before bringing forth a final wail of anguished shame.

After he got cleaned up and into bed, I sat for a while watching him drift into exhausted sleep. My heart ached for him; I knew how much his strong will was set upon a military career. I also reflected how much the army would be missing out on by rejecting this young man; his passion for the job, his ability to motivate people, his astonishing grasp of logistics as shown in my trading game – indeed, his sheer integrity. I also worried about how Archie would cope with the disappointment going into the future.

Over the next week, I saw nothing of him. A few disturbing reports came my way – a missed Chemistry class, an absence from rugby training, his room left uncharacteristically dishevelled – but this period didn't last. One day after school, Archie vanished, no one knew where. He had missed yet another sports practice and wasn't there for six o'clock rollcall and dinner. When he didn't appear for evening rollcall either, his housemaster was beginning to think about sending out search parties. Personally, I was wondering if dragging the nearby canal might not be a step too far. But just before we were able to galvanise into action, Archie appeared on his housemaster's doorstep. He was muddy, grinning, apologetic – and the sparkle was back in his eye. He had just taken himself off for a twenty-five-mile run and that, he assured us, had done the trick. The army door had closed. Another would open. Now it was time to get back to studies, sport, friendships, duties – and being the best possible version of himself he could be.

And he did. As far as I know, there was never another lapse, never another dip into despair, never the slightest wavering of that bright flame again. Indeed, he went on to be the School Captain two years later and, to my great delight, ended up becoming a teacher. He came and visited me some years ago at my current school and asked if he could teach a practice lesson on the biology of plants. He did so, and I was thrilled to observe – though hardly surprised – to see that he had all his notes and presentation slides colour-coded for those people who might have learning difficulties; red for must-know information, blue for important vocabulary, green for interesting sidelines that were fascinating but not part of the overall assessment. It hardly mattered that the first introductory slide was 'The Blodgy of Pants'. We all knew what he meant, and the kids loved it.

Chapter 20

Light thickens;
and the crow makes wing to the rooky wood:
Good things of day begin to droop and drowse;
While night's black agents to their preys do rouse.
Look like the innocent flower, but be the serpent under't.
—William Shakespeare, *Macbeth*

I would never claim to be actually magical – well, not more than twice a month – but it is an odd fact that on no less than five occasions, I have wished for an animal and within a marvellously short period of time, that very animal has popped into my life. The arrival of Jack de Crow is one example of this but there are others, stretching back to my childhood. I remember when I lived in the grounds of Shrewsbury School at the age of nine and reading Gerald Durrell's account of finding tortoises roaming the hills of his childhood Corfu. I fervently wished to find a tortoise I could bring home to keep as a pet, went for a walk down through the Ridgemount Wood and forty minutes later tripped over a tortoise crackling through the leaf litter. I wasn't terribly surprised at the time, I must confess. I assumed that if this sort of thing could happen to Durrell in Greece, then it was likely to be a reasonably commonplace occurrence in the woods of Shropshire. I christened the reptile Herbert and for five happy days devoted all my attention to my new treasure, unwilling to admit that a tortoise is not

the most rewarding of pets in the ball-fetching or cuddling categories of pet adorability, before Dad arrived home to announce that the Ridgemount housemaster had put an irate note on the Common Room noticeboard asking if anyone had seen Ridgie the House Tortoise on their travels.

On another occasion after we had moved to Adelaide, while staying with some friends I watched a nature documentary in which one of the presenters was hand-feeding a joey. 'I'd love to have a baby kangaroo to pet,' I sighed – and about ten minutes later, the grown-up son of the family arrived home and plonked a gangly joey in my arms. He had found it abandoned next to its dead mother on the highway and had brought it home to be nursed; even I was struck this time by the coincidence.

A few months later, on the last day of primary school, some minor competition had resulted in me winning a mouse cage – just the cage, no occupant – to take home with me. All the way home in the car, I chatted excitedly to Mum about the possibility of having a pet mouse, only gradually picking up that this would happen over her dead body. Two minutes after we got home, my sister Maggie arrived home on the bus from her school looking a little fraught and irritable. And well she might. Her own teachers had held an end-of-year competition of some sort which Maggie had won without realising that the prize was a white mouse. Somewhat bizarrely, the prize hadn't included any sort of cage or receptacle for said mouse, but someone had obviously heard that goldfish were often dispatched into the care of customers in a clear plastic bag and this is what they had sent Maggie home with; a plastic lunch-bag with an asphyxiating mouse scrabbling

around in it. Maggie has always been a somewhat shy and retiring person, shunning the limelight when in public, and the twenty-minute journey home on the bus holding a frantically pop-eyed white mouse in plain sight, with outraged citizens commenting on the cruelty of little girls nowadays, had rendered Maggie pink with indignant embarrassment. The sheer coincidence of me standing there with a fully equipped mouse cage – sawdust, running wheel, feeder bottle and all – had Maggie convinced that I had somehow engineered this synchronicity.

With this history, I was hardly surprised when Jack de Crow arrived so promptly on the scene within a day of me wishing out loud to my vet friend for a tame member of the *corvidae* family. I made a mental note to myself not to inadvertently wish for a snow leopard or a giant squid. However, it was to happen one more time, and the coincidence staggers me to this day.

As I have mentioned before, one of my roles in the school was to help out with the College drama productions. In fact, after the departure of the Head of Drama, I became wholly responsible for producing the various plays expected each year. After my production of *A Midsummer Night's Dream*, the following year I wanted to try my hand at *Macbeth.* I had a good potential cast of actors for the main parts and, most important of all, a stunning Lady Macbeth. This was a sixteen-year-old girl called Lilian Reeves. She had raven black hair, skin the colour of new milk and flashing dark eyes and had already proven her skills as a leading lady in previous productions.

I decided to stage the production in Big School. Many traditional independent schools have a Big School: generally an old school hall where assemblies are held and examinations take place. They are often the oldest parts of a school's architecture, and Ellesmere's Big School was no exception; it was a baronial hall with the dimensions of a medium-sized church and a magnificent hammer-beam roof, high diamond-paned windows, an organ loft at one end and a high wooden stage at the other. It had all the appearance of a medieval feasting hall and was perfect for the sombre desolation of the play.

I had a scaffolding tower built in one corner of the huge stage with a platform at the top – the watchtower – and another larger acting platform halfway up. This would act as the Macbeths' bedchamber. The main stage would become the feasting hall and the focus of the action. On the floor of Big School itself, where an orchestra pit would sit in a musical, I filled a space with straw, out of which the witches would appear at the beginning of the play. In fact, the play proper started before any of Shakespeare's dialogue began. To the clashing, atonal music of Janáček, I had twenty or so soldiers stage a battle in slow motion, waving long poles from which silken pennants rippled and billowed, while smoke from a fog machine drifted across the battlefield. Once the battle had passed and there were corpses strewn on the scattered straw, the audience watched in astonishment as the straw rustled and humped, heaved and parted, and the three witches appeared from beneath it – 'the earth hath bubbles, as the water has, And these are of them' – and began their grisly stripping and looting of the corpses, cutting out a tongue here, gouging out an eye there, to store them away for later devilry in their cauldron.

An image used again and again throughout *Macbeth* is that of the raven or crow: indeed, any birds associated with darkness, death and evil. A gamekeeper friend had two crows as part of his business; he lent me these two crows in their big portable cage for the duration of the performance season. I placed this cage such that, at moments in the play where Macbeth is tortured by dark and tempestuous thoughts a bright spotlight shining through the cage would agitate the birds slightly and cause them to hop and flap from perch to perch, throwing their shadows as vast winged figures on the scarlet drapes that comprised the backdrop. It appeared as if giant demonic shadows were thronging about Macbeth's tortured figure; a small microphone near the cage picked up and amplified the feverish rustling of the straw, the flap and scrape of feathers, the rattle of stabbing bills as an unsettling counterpoint to Macbeth's sonorous madness.

A final touch was that all the great draped panels, huge banners in scarlet with heraldic ravens or serpents upon them, were hung in such a way that they could be moved imperceptibly in, inch by inch, so that as the play progressed, the acting space shrank and shrank, reflecting Macbeth's feelings of claustrophobia and confinement. At his final downfall, slain by Macduff, the tops of the five great banners were released from their scaffolding. These came toppling down in a billowing cloud of tumbling scarlet fabric and revealed the three witches sitting perched up high, as though on gibbets, hailing the newly crowned Malcolm in hoarse tones of malice and mischief. The intended impression was that they had been behind the wainscoting of Macbeth's ambition all along, as it were, controlling his destiny with whispers and sly words, prophecies and hinted predictions, and were now there to control the new monarch in like fashion.

For me, directing a play is a high-octane activity. It is one of the few spheres of activity where I show the same sort of misplaced zeal that I so disparage in my colleagues when they bellow like enraged mastodons up and down the sidelines at intercollegiate rugby matches. The witches-from-straw idea, for example, was no exception.

The poor girls playing the three Weird Sisters had to hide buried beneath the battlefield straw for a full half hour before the audience took their seats. It was pure misfortune that one of the girls suffered considerably from hayfever and would emerge each night with streaming eyes and a suitably hoarse voice for a witch. I assumed this was just particularly good work on the part of the make-up team and the voice coach. It was also unfortunate that on one occasion, the trampling of soldierly feet during the battle resulted in a sprained wrist and a badly bruised cheekbone, something I yet again attributed to a welcome initiative from the ladies in make-up. These were not the only indignities my three hapless witches had to endure. I had unwisely decided that in the cauldron scene, the play could achieve an air of verisimilitude if the ingredients I provided – the eye of newt and toe of bat et cetera. – were actual slabs of raw kidney, liver, lungs and gizzards obtained from the local butcher. Papier-maché props would not, I felt, glisten in the correct manner. What I failed to take into account was the fact that over the ten-day season of the play, these props, left unrefrigerated, soon took on a malodorous air that could apparently be smelt right to the back of the hall. I had at the time a terrible head cold and no sense of smell so the querulous complaints of the three girls went unheeded; they were just told to stop making a fuss, get into character and take their places under the sea of straw for the half-hour curtain call. (It may be a related fact that these particular girls chose to make this production their swan song on the stage.)

That aside, the play was shaping up to be rather splendid, but it had one problem: namely that there was nothing yet in my

vision that focused the spotlight on the role of Lady Macbeth. She is such a key figure in the play and my young actress Lilian had such potential to play the part powerfully, but I needed something in the way of a visual effect to lift her role towards something memorable. Then a few days before opening night, I was out in the hills doing some rock climbing with Ross and our Outdoor Education group when one of the boys suddenly pounced into a clump of grass and came up holding a slender, wriggling, serpentine creature in his hand. Having grown up in Australia, where most snakes are deadly, I very nearly beat this creature to death with a wildly thrashing stick, but Ross quickly restrained me and explained that this was a slow worm, a legless lizard that closely resembles a snake but is completely harmless.

As it slithered gracefully between the boy's cupped hands like a shining thread of molten bronze, I thought how wonderful it would look sliding between Lady Macbeth's fingers as she gave her famous speech inviting evil to enter her soul. 'Come, you spirits, That tend on mortal thoughts! Unsex me here, And fill me from the crown to the toe top-full Of direst cruelty!'

On further thought, however, I realised that the slow worm was far too small to be seen in the vast space of Big School. If only I had something bigger, I mused – a python, perhaps. Then common sense prevailed. The chances of finding a pet python in this remote corner of Shropshire were almost non-existent; I should forget the idea with all speed.

I had entirely forgotten about my strange magical gift. Just then, Ross said, 'Hang on. There's a boy in the Junior School who has a pet python. He was talking about it to someone on the bus the other day. Richie, I think his name is. He's in Miss Bloom's class. You could chat to him.'

I still had my doubts. Even if I tracked this Richie down, it was highly unlikely that anyone would be prepared to lend me such a valuable and unusual pet for the ten performances required.

And what were the chances that any student, let alone the ethereal Lilian Reeves, could be persuaded to handle a large snake at short notice merely to satisfy a director's whim? It was bad enough with the three witches whining about sprained wrists and hay allergies and the rotting intestines. Actors could be so difficult.

Nevertheless, a nagging thought sent me off the next day to find this nascent herpetologist and I found Richie in the Junior School playground. I approached him, introduced myself and explained why I was there.

'I believe you have a pet python at home, Richie. How interesting!'

'Oh no, sir. Not me sir.'

'Oh. Is there another Richie here then? I was told that a boy called Richie had a pet python at home.'

'Oh, that would be me, sir. We do have one at home, a whopper, sir. But it's not my pet really. It's my sister's. I'm just allowed to feed it live mice occasionally, sir.'

'So, this sister of yours? Could you point her out?'

'Oh no, sir. She's not here, sir.'

'Oh. Never mind.' It had been a long shot, but at least I'd tried.

'She's in Senior School, sir. Lilian's her name. Lilian Reeves, sir. It's her python. And it's a whopper, sir!'

Well, I ask you. Out there on the hills, I had a vision of my Lady Macbeth handling a giant python and blow me down, my lead actress happened to have just such a python as a pet. When I broached the idea with Lilian, she took it perfectly in her stride. She was completely comfortable handling the beast – its name was Oswald – and for the dress rehearsal the next evening, she brought it in to show us.

We decided that at the beginning of her famous speech, she should start halfway up the tower, lit by a spotlight that made her white gown shimmer like the moon. Then she would move slowly

down the winding staircase, while Oswald moved sinuously to coil about her breast and along her outstretched arm. I still recall with a shuddering delight peeking each night from behind the curtains and watching the faces of the audience during this scene. It was always the same; there would be a slight gasp when Oswald first appeared and then a look of amused complacency on the faces of the audience, who were clearly thinking, 'Goodness me. How realistic. Nice work, props team.' Then, as she spiralled slowly down the stairs, you could see those same expressions tinged with admiration and just a tiny shred of doubt. 'Goodness, clever lass to make it move like that. I wonder how she does it.' And finally, as she reached the front row of the audience and held the great python's head within an inch of the mesmerised eyes of the audience, the sudden realisation: 'Oh my God, it's real, it's a real snake, it's enormous and we're all going to die.'

Oswald played his part well but had one last trick which proved useful. The Director of Mathematics, no friend of the Drama Department, for some reason insisted that every one of the three hundred chairs set out for the audience should be packed away into their store cupboards at the end of each performance. There was no good reason for this. I suspect this edict was just to let the Drama Department know they'd be better off sticking to their ready-made theatre in future and not imposing their subversive theatrics on the sober, hardworking and highly academic portion of the school, who were engaged in the legitimate business of inducting students into the mysteries of quadratic equations, trigonometry and set theory.

The packing away was made all the more difficult by the fact that each night, the parents seemed loath to leave the hall after the performance. Despite my nightly pleas from the stage for them to gather outside in the quadrangle to continue the social chitchat common on such occasions – *I knew the python was real of course, I've shot a dozen such beasts during my time in Burma, ma'am – Is it just me or is there a funny odour in here? Something dead perhaps?* – the parents lingered among the chairs, making it impossible to get them packed away. On the final night, I had had enough. I decided I was in no mood for yet another forty minutes of futile circulating among limpet-like parents. After I had accepted the gift and the thanks of the cast, I gave the customary reply – well done to all the cast and crew; thanks of course to the wonderful team of mothers helping behind the scenes, thank you, thank you – but this time I added, 'Sorry, just one more thing, ladies and gentlemen. Umm, we appear to have mislaid the python. Could you check under your chairs?'

I have never seen a space vacated so quickly. In about thirty seconds flat, the parents were stampeding out to the Quad, and the cast and I had the place to ourselves to get the seats stacked away, the room swept and Big School ready to hand back to the Mathematics Department in the morning – and still time for a double whisky before the Common Room bar closed for the night.

Oswald got an extra mouse that night as a reward for his part in the evening's success.

Chapter 21

> *Annual income twenty pounds, annual expenditure nineteen and six, result happiness. Annual income twenty pounds, annual expenditure twenty pounds nought and six, result misery.*
>
> —Charles Dickens, *David Copperfield*

One of the more eccentric individuals at the College was a lady called Miss Pike. She was the school accountant and lived in a cottage in the grounds where she nursed, apparently, an impressive collection of cacti. I have heard it said that pet owners gradually come to resemble their pets, but in this case it seemed that the same was true of Miss Pike and her horticultural collection; on first acquaintance at least, she appeared desiccated, prickly and forbidding, a spinsterish lady with a greying bun scraped back on her hair, a shrew-like nose, weak eyes behind small spectacles and a humourless mouth turned down in constant disapproval. I spent the first couple of years being thoroughly intimidated by her presence and her habit – not a word of exaggeration here – of leaving curt notes in my pigeonhole informing me that I had four pence owing on my school account.

The first time I realised that there was a twinkle of wry humanity behind her cactus persona was shortly after the production of *Macbeth.* I had very little idea how the budgeting of these school productions worked. I'd ask Stanley Pinkerton, now the Head of

Maintenance, for a scaffolding tower and for all the lighting to be moved from the theatre to Big School and it would be done, albeit grumpily. I'd have a word with the housekeeper about running up half a dozen giant banners in scarlet, enough material to cover a tennis court, and they'd appear three days later, suitably appliquéd with heraldic ravens and serpents as per my designs. I'd even ask Brian the Iron, the monosyllabic and gloomy-visaged Welsh metalworker who operated out of some subterranean forge below floors, for eight authentic-looking broadswords and never stop to ask if these might be pushing the budget up a tad too high.

So when I was called to the Administration Office one day, I was ill-prepared for the righteous indignation of the new bursar. An ex-military man called Captain Powlett-Pryce had recently been brought in to try to tighten the sloppy budgeting practices that had been the norm for the last fifty years. To judge from the glassy look in his eye, I was clearly an excellent candidate to be made an example of.

'Now look here, Mackinnon. I've just received the account sheet for this latest production of yours, this *Macbeth* farrago. It's a disgrace. Eight hundred and fifty-three pounds owing! And sixty pence! What do you say to that, eh? Eh?'

Miss Pike, hovering in the background, tried to say something, but Captain Powlett-Pryce was having none of it.

'Thank you, Miss Pike, but there's no need to defend the man. I want to hear what he has to say, what! Out with it!'

I didn't really know what to say. I hadn't ever been told there was a budget for school plays. One just got on and did them; asked for things – costumes, make-up, paint for the sets – sold tickets, printed programmes on the ancient photocopier to save some money and never saw the balance sheet again. This didn't stop me feeling thoroughly guilty. My Scottish blood has taught me to be thrifty and economical in most things and I certainly don't like the idea of extravagant wastage.

'Well, gosh, eight-hundred and fifty-three pounds? That does sound a lot.'

'And sixty pence!' barked the Captain. 'I would remind you that we are not the West End here, Mackinnon. Nor is the College's remit to fund your private ambitions to recreate the Stratford-upon-Avon Shakespeare Festival at a whim.'

Again, Miss Pike attempted to interject, but was once more overridden by the Captain's increasing apoplexy.

'As for health and safety, I believe there was a live anaconda loose on stage. Well? Well?'

'A carpet python, actually. Rather a jolly thing. Affectionate even—'

'I am talking about the budget, man. Really! I've a good mind to take it out of your salary, do you hear? Eight-hundred and fifty-three pounds. That'll teach you to be quite so cavalier with the College funds. In fact, it seems only fair. Take this, Miss Pike,' he said and thrust the account into her waiting hand, 'and add it as a debit to Mr Mackinnon's account. Hmm, what!'

'Sir.' Finally Miss Pike was able to get a word in. She thrust the paper back under the Captain's nose. 'Sir, that's eight-hundred and fifty-three pounds *profit*, sir. Not loss. From the ticket sales. The production itself was remarkably low-budget, and well-attended considering it was Shakespeare.'

I slumped with relief. I didn't think I could have bungled the finances quite that badly. Captain Powlett-Pryce looked for a few seconds as though he'd sat down on a chair that wasn't there, and then recovered himself sufficiently to mutter, 'Profit, eh? Let me see that thing. Ah yes, profit, quite so, quite so. Hhhrmphh. Well, well, let this be a lesson to us all, hrmmph, hrrrmph' – and he turned to seek the sanctuary of his office.

Before he could close the door, Miss Pike asked sweetly, 'And shall we *add* this amount to Mr Mackinnon's school account as a credit, sir? It seems only fair.'

The only reply was a closing door, which we both took as a firm no, but I saw Miss Pike in a new light from that moment. I had seen the brief twinkle in her grey eyes and the twitch of those lips and knew I had an ally there. Not in everything, of course. Her last words were to remind me that I still had four pence owing and that if it wasn't paid by the end of the week, interest would have bumped it up to five pence. And I knew that in this, at least, she wasn't joking.

Before we leave Miss Pike to retire into the background with her cacti family, there is one more anecdote to relate. The following year, I did a production of Alan Bennett's brilliant play *The Madness of George III.* A new staff member called Arthur Beagle had arrived at the College. He had a rather Eeyore-ish disposition, smoked a pipe and referred to the students as God's lambs in an ironic tone; despite the fact that he was relatively young, he seemed to have dropped straight out of *Goodbye, Mr. Chips,* and affected a weary impatience for the teaching life. He had been told that as part of his extracurricular load, he should offer to make himself useful for the upcoming drama production and as I needed someone to gather props for the play, I asked him if he would do this. He agreed with a feigned reluctance that I think was meant to be humorous, but he made it quite clear that he would only do it if I wrote a list with everything on it, gave him a due date and then let him be. He had done this job before at a previous school, he told me, and had not appreciated being asked to come up with some new item – an ormolu clock, a sherry decanter, a Japanese folding screen – at short notice every three hours on the day before opening night. So, a definitive list please, and no last-minute requests. Harrumph.

The next morning I popped the list of required props in his pigeonhole – two china bedpans, a dozen powdered wigs, a leather notebook, four quills, a dressing mirror and so on – but playfully added at the bottom 'One stuffed elk'. This was designed to jolly him out of his pernickety reluctance and make the bugger smile. I felt sure that under that cranky exterior there was a good sense of irony and a playful wit if only one could bring it bubbling to the surface.

Life got busy, as it so often did, and I didn't get a chance to catch up with Arthur for some time. A quick nod across a crowded Common Room was enough to assure me that he'd got the list, was working on it and I'd have the props I needed well before opening night. So it took me by surprise one bright Tuesday morning to receive a few weeks later a note from Miss Pike, curter than ever, demanding my presence in her office. On presenting myself there, my cheery compliment on the shape and style of her bun did nothing to sweeten the sour look on her face. 'Can you explain this?' she snapped, and held out a letter for me to read.

Dear Mr Beagle,

*Thank you for your enquiry about the possibility of having on loan from our museum a specimen of an elk (*Alcis alcis*) for your school's upcoming production. By a fortunate chance, a recent rearrangement of our large mammal display has meant that the elk has gone into temporary storage and is available for hire. I have arranged for it to* *arrive next Tuesday. As you will no doubt appreciate, there are considerable costs involved in the transportation and handling of such a valuable specimen and of course insurance is an important consideration. I am therefore enclosing an invoice for the total amount, which* I hope *you will be able to settle at your earliest convenience.*

I wish you and your students all best wishes for the performance.

Yours faithfully,

Miss Clarissa Lyon,

Chester Zoo and Natural History Museum

The attached invoice showed a staggering three thousand pounds for the delivery and insurance of *Alcis alcis* – and today was the day it was due to arrive.

I must have gone white as a sheet. I can't recall what exactly I spluttered but I know that the bottom of my stomach appeared to have dropped out and seemed now to be flopping its way around the floor like an injured dugong. The door to Captain Powlett-Pryce's office was ajar and I could hear him on the telephone, so my spluttering was perforce *pianissimo.* Despite the kudos gained over the *Macbeth* budget, this was enough to put me well below the bottom line in his estimation. Perhaps I should just leave the country in a hurry. Cuba was nice at this time of year, I recalled.

Then there was Arthur Beagle in the room, looking grumpier than usual, asking if I could come and sign for a delivery. I looked from Miss Pike to Mr Beagle and back again.

'Umm, can we cancel the elk?' I asked in a hoarse squawk.

Now Miss Pike was an excellent accountant but no poker player. After a few seconds of my discomfit, I saw that mouth twitch and a gleam of mirth steal into those frosty eyes. Arthur's impatient look melted away and he spoke wryly.

'Clarissa Lyon. C. Lyon. Sea lion. I thought for you of all

people, that would have been a dead giveaway. Don't mess with me, Mackinnon. Stuffed elk indeed.'

The props for *The Madness of George III* were excellent – well-organised, authentic, provided in plenty of time for rehearsals – but I never did ask Arthur Beagle to help me out with props again. And pranks were strictly off-limits between us.

Chapter 22

I've got a friend who is a lion tamer. He used to be a schoolteacher till he lost his nerve.

—Les Dawson

Your reality, sir, is lies and balderdash and I'm delighted to say that I have no grasp of it whatsoever.

—*The Adventures of Baron Munchausen* (1988)

Hanging over the mantlepiece on one wall of the staff Common Room, there was a large and ancient mirror. It had an ornate gilded frame and was speckled with age, a sort of grey freckling not dissimilar to the leprous mottling on the faces of some of our more elderly and gout-ridden colleagues. I found this mirror a great comfort at times, because I had discovered I could use it to do a sort of mental escape trick when Common Room life became a bit much. At morning tea, we were all expected to gather in this room to imbibe tea from a vast cauldron and nibble on Fig Newtons while various people made announcements pertaining to the daily routines. As a consequence, the room was crowded and noisy, a barrage of querulous conversation being bawled across the teacups. Over there would be Mr Hickinbotham, turning his usual shade of puce and fulminating against the cricket umpire's latest misguided decision in the House cricket competition. Beyond him would be Mr Olsen, explaining in no uncertain terms to Miss Thripp that choir practice, even if it was down on the term calendar, would only take priority over the badminton tournament over his – or preferably her – dead body. From further afield, someone would have buttonholed the bursar and be pointing out the varied deficiencies of the school photocopier, which was so old as to be practically steam-driven. Felix Arne and Bruce Bamford would be having their usual contretemps about the behaviour of young Teddy Bigalow in the Fifth Form; Arne thought he was a free spirit; Bamford thought him a thug. To see them in combat, the one so verbally dextrous and the other so lumberingly apoplectic, was like watching a mongoose pitted against a musk ox.

All very entertaining – but after several years, the drama had begun to pall. This is where the mirror became useful. I discovered one morning that if I took my cup of tea and biscuit and stood over by the mirror, so close I could practically lean my forehead against it, then by gazing into it I could magically distance myself from the fever and the fret behind me in the room. The mirror somehow made my colleagues seem as though they were imprisoned behind the glass, in another room altogether, and strangely remote. Indeed, I came to see them as the denizens of some large aquarium of exotic creatures, swimming in a greenish, silver-mottled light; bloated blowfish or cephalopods, puce-coloured squid or prickly seadragons, pouting groupers or sinuous conger eels. Oddly enough, this view of them seemed to tune out the clamour as well. I felt that I was standing alone, the Common Room empty behind me, heavy with solitude and tranquillity, allowing me to gaze dispassionately at a world of marine creatures leading busy mute lives that had nothing to do with me.

Until, that is, Bingo Todhunter would jog my elbow and remind me that I was meant to be on yard duty these last twenty minutes and deftly remove the remaining Fig Newton from my saucer for his own enjoyment.

But now, five years into my time at Ellesmere, I realised that the illusion of escape provided by the mirror was not enough. I had begun to find it all a bit unbearable, especially in the dark and sodden months of November and December, and in the Christmas holiday of my fifth year I departed on an exotic holiday with a strong sense that I might not find it in me to return.

My oldest friend Rupert, he who had provided me with the original Jack de Crow and later my beloved pith helmet, had moved to Zimbabwe to continue his equine veterinary career and had invited me out to spend Christmas on a homestead outside Harare. Africa! I could write an entire novel in praise of my short sojourn there. Every aspect of the place smote me like a blast furnace of colour, vibrancy, drenching sunlight, cicada shrillness and raw splendour. A highlight was a visit to the Ngorongoro Conservation Area, a vast protected area lying in the bowl of a giant extinct volcanic crater, some twelve miles across. From the rim of this crater, the view is breathtaking. Down there, tiny as ants, a family of elephants drifts minutely across the tawny plain. Over there a plume of dust is freckled with glinting barcoded silver, a herd of zebra galloping in the afternoon light. In one corner of this vast crater is a shimmer of silk blue dusted with pink: a salt lake blooming with flamingos in their thousands. In another corner, a lazy river winds between mud banks where miniscule hippos gleam wet like tiny pebbles. Over there, rocky hills rise clothed in the topaz of savannah grass, as gold velvet as the rough fur of the lions that lounge concealed there.

The place was not without its hidden perils. At one stage, we were being driven along a dusty road by the bed of a dried-up stream in the safari jeep. I had opened the window to allow some fresh air in. Very politely, our African guide had asked me in a soft voice to wind the window up again.

'Really?' I had remonstrated. 'All that lovely fresh air?'

'Really, sah,' he had said, and leant over me to wind the window up for himself.

Two seconds later, there was a savage thud on the window pane about an inch from my ear. I had a split second to register the lightning strike of a fanged head lashing at the glass from the outside. There was a fan of viscous liquid sprayed right across the window and streaming down the glass.

'Spitting cobra, sah. So sorry. Always just there. You can open the window now, sah.'

But for all the fresh air, the exciting scents of grass and dust and dung, and the fact that I could now see almost nothing through a film of deadly venom, the window remained firmly closed.

One of Rupert's horsey clients was a young woman called Annabel who had married a Swiss nobleman going by the resounding title of Baron Siegfried von Himmelhof. Rupert had insisted that we visit this couple on their remote paprika farm, quoting as a reason that I would be mightily impressed with the house. In that regard, he was certainly correct. I cannot, alas, say the same for Annabel, a somewhat difficult woman to warm to; she had a hard set to her jawline and a glint in her eye which gave the impression that she was customarily surrounded by fools and knaves and that my arrival on the scene had not in any way altered the situation. The eccentric Baron von Himmelhof turned out, on the other hand, to be a gangling, enthusiastic young man with arms that spun like windmills when he was trying to explain anything – which was most of the time, and with breathless rapidity. While we sat on the broad verandah over a few gin and tonics in the late afternoon light, a thunderstorm brewing on the horizon and their infant child crawling at our feet (looking strangely leprous in the lurid light, I couldn't help thinking), the Baron – or Ziggy, as he insisted on being called – explained in a strong French accent just how the house had come into being. He had bought the land three years previously and on a whim had decided that he wouldn't do anything as tame as hire a building contractor to construct a dwelling for his new bride; no, he would build the whole thing himself. How hard could it be? A complete lack of experience in the building trade had not put him off in the slightest. Moreover, he decided to really start from scratch and, to that end, kicked off the whole process by constructing a sawmill on the property to turn large sections of the native forest into sawn beams, boards and planks. In a similar vein, he dug a quarry out of red-anthill earth and taught himself the art of brickmaking, following that venture up with learning how to chisel slate slabs from a nearby riverbed in order to create tiles for the house's three bathrooms.

Nothing, it seemed, was too hard for the Baron to master. The house did indeed take my breath away. Although only a few years old, the house looked as ancient and snug in the landscape as the House of Beorn. Great timber beams supported by sturdy wooden posts held up a broad roof thatched by Ziggy himself – and no doubt by his sizeable staff of African farmhands – from reeds cut in the local river. The bathrooms were not only floored with the blue slate cut in neat slabs but walled with beautifully decorated ceramic tiles of white clay found on the property; the tiles had been fired in a kiln of his own making. Rugs and carpets glowed on every floor as a testament to his weaving skills, along with the odd zebra-skin rug cured, of course, by Ziggy in a spare moment. As a final medieval touch, in every room were curly iron candelabras and elaborate sconces on the walls, all forged by the seemingly unstoppable Baron himself, who had decided to add blacksmithing to his skillset. These were more than merely decorative because, as Ziggy confessed sheepishly, the one thing he had forgotten to do was install electric power. (This might have gone some way towards explaining his wife's look of weary impatience with her lot.) As a result of this omission, dozens of candles – made (inevitably) by Ziggy as a result of a beekeeping craze – decorated every room and dripped wax in molten globules onto every surface, including at times Ziggy's infant child, who seemed to have grown immune to the experience of having scalding wax splashing from above onto his tender skin, though the experience did explain his scabrous flaking appearance.

Over dinner, Ziggy started enthusing about a recent project. A few years previously, he had invented a sort of fold-up set of wings which he could strap to his back in a compact bundle while skiing the slopes of his native Swiss Alps. In the middle of a jump, he explained, he could spread his elbows in a certain way and the bundle would transform instantly into a rigid set of hang-glider wings, allowing him to glide an enormous distance before landing again. Another flick of the elbows would collapse the whole contraption again to allow him to go on skiing unencumbered by air resistance.

This sounded somewhat unlikely to me, but Ziggy whipped out a glossy Patagonia catalogue and showed me a photo of himself in full flight, spread-eagled against a dazzling blue sky and his skis dangling from his feet. 'Zat,' he beamed proudly, 'was ze longest flight I did. Six hundred metres, *mon ami*! Six hundred metres!'

I murmured some appreciation for the feat.

'And you know, zirty zeconds after zat photo was taken,' he continued with unabated enthusiasm, 'I broke both my legs!'

Shortly after this, I was to discover one of Ziggy's more prominent traits and possibly another reason for his wife's customary air of barely suppressed irritation. The fact is that Ziggy had a habit of asking for advice with great enthusiasm and cordiality from all and sundry and then utterly failing to heed it. This he proceeded to do in regard to an improved version of his flying contraption. Despite Annabel's pleas that he concentrate on serving the newly prepared dinner to the guests, he bounced out of the dining room and returned with a new prototype of the device, an arrangement of poles, rods and sails seemingly made from a couple of disused windsurfing kits. He showed how it strapped on and how, with a flourish of his elbows, it sprang into an outspread span like a rainbow pterodactyl, thereby knocking half a dozen lit candles off an overhead candelabra into the soup tureen.

'I 'ave improved ze design, I zink,' he said, 'but, you know, I 'ave no way of testing zis out. In Switzerland, *c'est simple*, I make ze ski-ing, but 'ere, you know, zere is not ze snow, ze *montagnes*. So I 'ave an idea. Tell me what you zink, eh?'

The Baron's idea was simple. He would attach a very long upright pole to the side of his open-tray ute and tie a long elastic bungy cord to the very top of it. Then he would get a trampoline and place it in the vehicle's tray. He would strap on his new wings, attach himself to the lower end of the elastic cord and start bouncing up and down on the trampoline while his African farm manager Tommy would drive at seventy-five miles an hour along the straightest stretch of road they could find. At some point in this process, *phffttt!*, out would pop the wings and the Baron would be airborne.

Simple, as I say – simple and deadly. Rupert and I glanced at one another in horror and then proceeded to explain to the Baron in earnest detail all the manifold things that could go very badly wrong with this plan. Ziggy listened with rapt attention, nodding in comprehension as we painted a picture of just what would happen when the cord wrapped itself inevitably and lethally around a roadside telegraph pole.

'I zink zis will not be a problem,' he concluded. 'What do you zink?' His boyish eagerness was unabated.

Rupert and I looked at one another again. 'We think you'll die, Ziggy. A hundred per cent certainty. Horribly. Please don't try this.'

'Really? I don't zink so. What do you zink, tell me?' It was as though we had said nothing at all.

I opened my mouth several times like a bemused goldfish wondering how to frame the asked-for advice in a way that would be more compelling to the optimistic Baron. Across the table, Rupert and I could see Annabel, stony-faced and fishing candle stubs out of the bouillabaisse while wiping soup globules off her yet-again-scalded infant son. I suspected, from her tight-lipped expression, that this was a path she had been down many a time before, and we decided that any more efforts at dissuasion on our part would be fruitless.

'Good idea,' we chorused, 'and bravo!'

The Baron von Himmelhof beamed like a schoolboy. '*Oui*, zis is what I am thinking. I agree!' he enthused and went to fetch another bottle of wine.

*

The next morning, Rupert was due to depart and start a busy period of work, but when I let slip that I had four days before I was due to fly out from Harare and head back to England for the start of the Lent term Ziggy lit up like a Catherine wheel with renewed enthusiasm. There was another project he had in mind, and I would be the very person to help him make it a reality.

'Oh yes,' Rupert asked. 'And what is that exactly?'

Yet again, the Baron launched into an excitable explanation. He wanted to set up a safari company with a difference; instead of all those passé jeeps and four-wheel-drive vehicles – all so '60s and *Daktari*, he scoffed – Ziggy was proposing that the punters would tour the conservation reserves on bicycles. What did we zink?

'Ziggy, dear chap,' said Rupert as he packed his bags into his vehicle, 'You are stark raving mad. Bicycles? In a wildlife reserve?

In among the lions and leopards and cheetahs and whatnot?'

'Yes, ees great, no?'

'No,' said Rupert firmly. 'Ziggy, to your average lion, a chap on a bicycle is about the same height, speed and shape as a passing gazelle. Trust me, I'm a vet.'

'I know!' burbled Ziggy. 'Isn't it great? I zink zis is not a problem. What do you zink? In fact,' he added, 'I 'ave already made up a brochure. Look!'

He whipped out a mock-up of a glossy brochure for Ziggy's Zany Bike Safaris. It showed the Baron himself mounted on a snazzy-looking bike in front of a sign depicting a skull and crossbones with the words MINEFIELD: DANGER, DO NOT ENTER emblazoned in blood-red across it. A coil of razor wire sat just behind him. The slogan at the top was 'We Go Anywhere!!'

'And, you know, San-dee, I need someone to help, how you say, do ze reconnaissance for ze trips. You come wiz me, *oui*? What do you zink?'

'Umm, no, thanks and all that, but it's a definite no from me. Wouldn't you say, Rupert?'

I turned to my friend for support just in time to see his vehicle disappearing out the front gate. There was a distant cry of 'See you back in England next year—' and he was gone.

Ziggy beamed at me. 'Zis is great, *oui*? Let's go straightaway. What do you zink?'

My jaw hardened in a silent rictus of exasperation, much like that customarily worn by Annabel. It had taken me less than twelve bours to realise that where Ziggy was concerned, any request for a second opinion was entirely rhetorical.

*

Five hours later, I tumbled out of a jeep, stiff and dusty and jolted half to death by the road journey. We had stopped by a wide river winding through grasslands and reedbeds. The water looked invitingly blue in the late afternoon light, until one realised that the pinkish brown boulders that lay midstream or in the shallows each sported a pair of ears that flicked to and fro and occasionally broke into the widest yawn in the animal kingdom, that of a soporific hippopotamus at peace with the world. Beyond a thin fringe of forest trees behind us, low hills dotted with scrub rose to a distant horizon. Tommy the farm manager and I managed to put up a khaki tent on a flat lawn of grass while Ziggy lifted two bicycles out of the back of the jeep. Leaving Tommy to prepare a meal, Ziggy insisted we mount the bikes and set off to explore the nearby veldt. My cautious enquiry about the likelihood of encountering a lion was met with a rueful and very Gallic shrug of the shoulders from the Baron. No, zis was very unlikely. Lions had not been seen here in decades. But wouldn't it be great, *oui*?!

For an hour or so, we zigzagged our way along little dirt paths that wound their way through thorn scrub and baobabs that rose up a gentle hillside to an outcrop of rock surrounded by acacias. From there we could see back down to the river but in the other direction we gazed across a wide stretch of hillocky hummocky country, the westering sun throwing rounded bluish shadows on each mound. Far off in the distance, herds of antelope grazed peacefully, and in a nearby tree a pair of hornbills clowned noisily. Perhaps this whole bike safari thing wasn't such a bad idea after all. After a few minutes admiring the scenery, Ziggy suggested we get back to the campsite before nightfall. For once, we seemed to be on the same page. This was not to last.

On our descent, we came to a fork in the path. Both left and right wound away out of sight between thorn trees and long tawny grass. 'Hmm,' said Ziggy. 'Which way eez it, do you zink? Eez confusing, no?'

'Er, no, not at all,' I replied with some puzzlement. The left-hand track was quite clearly the one leading back to the campsite. It led downhill, as opposed to the right-hand track, which wound upwards to a further ridge; besides, the left-hand was quite definitely in the direction of the river we had been able to see from the outcrop just minutes before. 'It's this way, Ziggy.'

Maddeningly, the Baron was inclined to disagree. 'You zink so? No, I zink it is zis way, ze right-hand path. What do you zink, eh?'

Here we go again, I thought. 'Ziggy, I'm telling you, it's this way. Look. Downhill, see?'

'Hmmm.' He was not convinced. 'You know, I'm zinking zis path looks better, *oui*? What do you zink?'

Just as I was resigning myself to another hour of this baffling intercourse, I heard a sound from nearby. This was a sound I had first come across as described by Gerald Durrell, a favourite author of my childhood, who likened it to someone sawing a large sonorous barrel in half. And this was it exactly: a deep, rasping vibrato as the saw teeth bit into the timber, then another and another in quicker and quicker succession, the whole thing amplified by the hollow echo chamber of the barrel's interior. As it drew to a close, he had written, one almost expected to hear the wooden clunk as the sawn-off end hit the workshop floor.

Except I didn't wait around for the end of the sawing process because I knew exactly what Durrell had been describing. It wasn't carpentry; it was the sound of a fully grown lion warming up for the evening hunt – and this one seemed to be about thirty yards away in the thick thorn scrub. Notwithstanding Rupert's advice on the semblance between a chap on a bike and your average antelope, I did not wait around to continue the fruitless debate with the Baron. I turned my bicycle leftwards and hurtled off down the winding path, expecting at any moment to be snatched from the saddle by a lunging paw.

*

That evening, I had one more occasion to curse the Baron for his cavalier attitude to the safety of his travelling companions. We were sharing a tent and lying there on our fold-up canvas camp beds by the light of a kerosene lantern, listening to the noises of the tropical African night. A billion tree frogs croaked all around, mosquitoes whined, some nocturnal bird hooted mournfully in the distance ... and then there came a strange sound within a dozen yards of the tent that I could not recognise. It sounded like somebody riffling through a giant pack of cards again and again while grunting softly to themselves. At the same time there was the sound of something like mud being splattered around, flung by a naughty child. To my enquiry, Ziggy explained that there were hippos grazing on the grass around the tents. The riffling sound was made by their tails, windmilling rapidly as they defecated, a habit that spread their rich and pungent dung across a wide area in a fine shower rather than depositing it all in one solid pile.

'Hippos?' I whispered. 'Aren't they meant to be the most dangerous animals in Africa?'

'No, no, no, not at all,' Ziggy reassured me. 'Zey are ze peaceful giants of ze animal kingdom, you know. Zey would only crush you by accident. And zis zey will not do while we have ze lantern lit. Zat is why we must have it lit ze whole night long, *oui*?'

And right on cue, with a timing that Laurence Olivier would envy, the lantern went out. Ziggy had neglected to replenish the kerosene.

'Oh, zis is not good,' conceded the Baron. 'And you know, I zink ze kerosene is in ze jeep. One of us must fetch it. What do you zink?' The jeep was thirty yards away across a pitch-black expanse of hippo-studded grass.

'I think we're going to die,' was the answer on my lips, but I was interrupted by another bout of phlegmatic gurgling that was definitely now nearer.

'I think we go together,' I said, 'and we go now.'

I must have been using my schoolmaster's voice at last because for once Ziggy didn't stop to suggest alternative courses of action. We emerged from the tent and stared out into the night, taking a moment to let our eyes become accustomed to the darkness. After a little while, in the faint starlight, we could see several mammoth silhouettes grazing nearby, drawing ever nearer to the tent. Moving as slowly and silently as drifting ghosts, we glided across the grass between the massive shapes towards the truck, freezing every now and then when one of the hippos raised its head warily to assess the situation. It was like a somewhat terrifying version of Grandmother's Footsteps. At last, we reached the safety of the jeep. 'Okay, Sandy, here is ze kerosene. Hand me ze lantern.'

'What?'

'Ze lantern. You have ze lantern, no?'

'I don't have the lantern! I thought we were fetching the kerosene to the tent!'

'But Sandy, as you can see, zis kerosene drum is too 'eavy to lift,' Ziggy explained patiently as though to a wayward child. 'It is simpler to bring ze lantern, *oui*?'

In the end, I persuaded Ziggy to pour some kerosene into a couple of shallow bowls – the only receptacles we could find in the jeep – and we tiptoed our way back to the tent though the grazing hippos, adding an element of egg-and-spoon race to the challenge as we tried to keep the kerosene from slopping out of the bowls. We moved at a snail's pace though the pitch dark – until the last ten yards when the telltale riffling sound started up close by and we found ourselves being well-manured by a fine mist of fresh dung out of the blackness. At this, we both accelerated rapidly to the tent's shelter, heedless of whether there were any hippos in our way. Shakily we got the lantern filled and lit, and surveyed each other in the soft lamplight. We were both trembling with sweat, slick with kerosene and hippo-dung. I was harbouring some pretty murderous thoughts towards the Baron as I fell into an exhausted sleep. My only satisfaction came the next morning when I was informed by Ziggy that my snoring had been so stertorous and resonant that it had not only kept all the hippos at bay more effectively than any lantern but had kept him wide awake all night long.

The last day of our adventure turned out to be more satisfying, mainly because I spent it largely on my own. Ziggy informed me the next morning that he intended to swim across the river with Tommy, somehow hauling the bikes along as well. As there was no river crossing for the jeep, my job was to take the jeep and drive off into the landscape and search for a place to cross the river and then pick them up on the other side. 'How does zat sound, eh?'

Hastily I explained that I had never driven a four-wheel drive before, let alone anything as rugged and massive as this jeep, but Ziggy waved his hand in the direction of the gearstick and said, 'Oh zis is easy. Just don't let ze transmission torque build up too much, you know, or *twang, kaput!* What do you zink?'

As he may as well have just told me not to let the porpoise-snorkels bifurcate in the quantum box, I started to protest – but, as ever, to no avail. He and Tommy were already striding towards the hippo-ridden, croc-infested river with a bike each on their heads.

Once they had vanished, I sat in the cabin of the jeep and taught myself how to use a four-wheel-drive mechanism from scratch, discovering the delightful mysteries of low-range, high-range, axle torque and power gears. I mut say that despite some agonising moments of gear-crunching and clutch-burring, with worrying smells of burning metal emanating from the bonnet, I enjoyed myself immensely. There was something wonderfully liberating about being on my own in the vast African wilderness with a mighty throbbing engine beneath my legs that seemed capable of tackling the steepest and rockiest of bush tracks. I understood for the first time the attraction felt by so many men for the virile power of a V8 engine, and could have happily gone straight home and decorated my bedroom with posters of semitrailers, motorbikes and monster trucks.

I had no idea where I was going. The landscape was free of anything resembling a road, so I found myself jolting across grassy plains, winding my way between giant baobabs, crunching down into dried gullies and splashing through river shallows with delightful abandon. Wildlife was everywhere: finches in scarlets and purples flew up from beneath my tyres; giant flying grasshoppers with primrose-yellow wings sprang into the air as I passed; lizards in emerald green scuttled off the track and launched themselves up the red-earth banks on either side of the track. Sometimes I would pass through a tiny village where children played in the dust or ran laughing after the jeep and old men in crimson robes sat in the shade of an acacia tree playing games with bright red seed pods in shallow wooden bowls.

My route had taken me far from the river, but I tried to keep an idea of the direction in which it lay. Eventually, I ended up driving some 150 miles southwards though a superb variety of landscapes before I could find a road that took me to a bridge. From here it was another three hours of driving northwards until

I found the bush track that brought me down to the river opposite the campsite of the night before. There I found the Baron and Tommy stretched out on the grass in the shade of an enormous tree. Each, I was relieved to see, with their limbs intact and unmolested by crocodiles or passing hyenas. Mind you, if they had lost a limb or two neither would have been in a fit state to care very much, as both were stupendously high on marijuana. When I arrived, they were giggling away and attempting a love duet together, sharing a fat stuffed joint between them. My heart sank when I saw them. The plan was to get back to Ziggy's house that night; I had a plane to catch from Harare the next day. Neither Ziggy nor Tommy was in any fit state to drive, and I didn't know the way. Yet another night of camping with the hippos was out of the question.

Ziggy seemed pleased to see me, his irritation at my snoring having dispersed in plumes of cannabis smoke. He waved away my offers to drive and told me dreamily, and with a big amiable hug, that he was perfectly capable of operating the jeep. Indeed, he assured me, he found that marijuana tended to improve his driving performance – this as he attempted to mount the steps to the driver's seat, missed his footing by a mile and sprawled back on the grass giggling manically.

By this time, he had the keys and nothing could dissuade him from relinquishing the role of driver. So it was that I found myself being chauffeured the two hundred miles or so via rough roads along which we swooped and swerved like demented swallows, dicing with death and imminent collision the whole way. Ziggy kept up a continual babble, asking me at ten-second intervals what I thought of his driving, didn't I agree that the cannabis made it a smoother and more enjoyable ride, and whether I thought this was the way home, what do you zink? For my part, I clung to the bucking dashboard, clenched my teeth and blenched furiously at every near miss of the numerous roadside trees, fence posts and deep potholes that dotted the way.

By the time we ground to a halt back at the paprika farm, I was a shaking wreck. I could barely bring myself to spend another minute in the Baron von Himmelhof's exhausting company and even my newfound sympathy for the long-suffering Annabel did not render her granite-like demeanour any more engaging. But one thing the whole experience had done for me: the grey skies and damp days of an English Michaelmas term, the late-night drama rehearsals, the lumpish pudding-faces of the Fourth Form, and yes, even the clamour and rancour of the Common Room seen through a mottled glass darkly, seemed in contrast to be soothing, sane and thoroughly desirable. I couldn't wait to get back to Ellesmere College and pick up the baton of learning once more.

Chapter 23

A labyrinth is a symbolic journey . . . but it is a map we can really walk on, blurring the difference between map and world.

—Rebecca Solnit, *Wanderlust: A History of Walking*

But the monotonous life led by invalids often makes them like children, inasmuch as they have neither of them any sense of proportion in events, and seem each to believe that the walls and curtains which shut in their world, and shut out everything else, must of necessity be larger than anything hidden beyond.

—Elizabeth Gaskell, *North and South*

It will come as no surprise to the reader that I am rather fond of mazes, so I was quite pleased to find when I first arrived at Ellesmere College that some like-minded soul had decided to create a maze on the shores of Ellesmere, just down from the Boathouse Tearooms. This was a medieval-style pavement labyrinth, a single spiralling path switch-backing its way to the centre but, having no choice of ways, not to the modern mind a true maze at all. An idea had been growing in my mind for many years that it should be possible to design a maze with an ingenious paradoxical property, namely that if one single-mindedly took only the paths that led inwards to the centre one would find oneself coming at last out into the world again, having missed the centre altogether. On the other hand, by turning one's back on the desired goal and taking only those paths that run outwards and away from the spiral's heart, then one would come in the shortest time to the secret heart of the maze.

This was my aim and I had gone through an awful lot of pencil lead in my pursuit of this elusive possibility. In fact, I had finally come to shelve it as downright impossible without somehow accessing a fifth dimension and decided this would be a project for the afterlife perhaps. Then in my fifth year at Ellesmere one afternoon in early February, it started snowing.

It snowed and snowed all that evening and all through the night. The entire College woke up to a blank canvas of whiteness stretching to the Berwyn Hills ten miles to the west. Even the hedgerows had become muffled walls of rounded snow. And still it kept snowing, great hypnotic flakes falling softly from a blank white sky, silencing the world under a cold blanket of enchantment.

Unheeding of the cold, I went outside. Behind me, the myriad windows of the main building were lit up like an Advent calendar, each window showing a separate picture: here a head bent in study over a lamplit desk, there a boy practising his flute; in this window a bare-chested, balaclavaed young man flexing his muscles in front of a mirror; in that window yonder, an enraged Mr Pebmarsh trying to swipe a playful jackdaw from his windowsill.

As my boots swished through the snow, they made a thick furrow and I was struck with a preposterous idea. I started by stamping out a circle about five yards wide. Then I left the circle heading north, swishing a furrow as I went. I soon turned westwards in an arc … and then southwards and then eastwards … and half an hour later, I had carved into the snowy canvas a giant triple spiral, a pattern beloved of the Celts to represent the seasons, the ebb and flow of tides and the warrior's journey. Such a spiral seems to promise a smooth and effortless way to the heart of the pattern. It is only when you are within sight of your goal that the path turns and sweeps you outwards again … and it is only when you are on the verge of being thrust into the outer darkness that the path turns once more and takes you on a final spiralling journey to the desired destination.

However, like the pavement labyrinth at the mere, this pattern still lacked any choice of ways. Short cross-sections linking the spiral loops were needed, so on I shuffled, eventually placing four pairs of cross pieces at the cardinal points of the compass. With the addition of these, something rather remarkable happened. Pursuing an outwards course had led me – how is this possible – inwards to the maze's heart, just as I had dreamed. The paradox worked.

But then, the opposite was true. As soon as I left the centre and took every possible inwards-turning pathway to return there, I found myself orbiting relentlessly outwards until I was free of the labyrinth altogether.

Inside a maze, they say, compasses fail to work and the ordinary laws of Nature are suspended. North, South, East and West become meaningless. Time itself ceases its own relentless march to the End of All Things and instead sloshes to and fro like a tide. The spirit wanders freely from the body and the World stops its spinning. So it began to feel like in the fading light of that February afternoon while the falling flakes made of the cosmos a cold, limitless netherworld and the maze was the only thing to exist in it, stretching to the borders of the known. The endless spiralling – in, then out, then in again like some slow-motion hokey-cokey – made me dreamy, disoriented, almost hallucinotory. I had the strangest feeling that I was truly trapped in this maze; something compelled me to follow the curves beneath my feet. To override them would break more than my mother's back. I felt like some character in an as-yet-unwritten Alan Garner novel, mesmerised by snow magic.

Two hours later, nearing exhaustion from cold and exertion, my mind lost in an Arctic waste, I realised it was nearly dark. The snowfall had stopped and the spell was broken by the lights of the College building shining in fuzzy haloes of gold from every window. And at every window was a face, pressed against the glass, each one bearing a puzzled or scornful expression. Prep was forgotten, the flute abandoned; even the building of babe-magnet pecs had been put on hold for the last hour. The same thought was perhaps in every young mind. Why had this young teacher, this Australian, just spent the last two hours walking round and round . . . and *round* and *round* . . . in the snow for no apparent reason? This man might need careful looking after when the next cold snap was due.

After that wintry afternoon, I became obsessed. As time has gone by, the original design has developed in my mind to something of rare beauty. In its most complete form, the maze will consist not just of dreary passages between high yew-hedges but nine walled gardens – one at the very heart of the maze with a single door to its cool and fragrant bower, and the other eight each with its own enchantment. One is a rose garden where a thousand crimson and white roses bloom. Another is a formal walled Elizabethan garden where espaliered pear trees stand crucified knee-deep in clumps of silver sage and borage. A third contains a wide pond where waterlilies dream and a frog plops at the approach of a walker, and a fourth will be a quiet stretch of shaven grass and white benches and the croquet hoops set out ready for play.

The pattern of the maze I had devised has since been drawn in the sand of wild, lonely beaches on the West Coast of Ireland, scratched into the pine needles and soft forest earth on wooded

Shropshire hills and doodled onto countless scraps of paper in idle meetings or railway cafés. It has, at times, come close to engulfing me in its folds forever.

In fact, I realised shortly afterwards that it came close to being the death of me. A few days after my creation of the snow maze, still feeling chilled and shaky from my prolonged exposure to the cold, I headed off on a half-term break to some Yorkshire friends – Jill and Mike – and broke down on the motorway in a snowstorm. Betty Bombadil was towed off somewhere for repairs and Mike came and rescued me from near hypothermia by taking me back to their comfortable farmhouse on the moors. I showed my gratitude by immediately succumbing to a fever with alarming rapidity. Jill whisked me off to a doctor who examined me and then tutted alarmingly. I had, he said, a quinsy. To me, this sounded like something rather charming and old-fashioned – a thing you might find growing in a herbaceous border perhaps, or the Edwardian name for a pipe-cleaner made from the tail of a junior squirrel – but the doctor explained that it was in fact a swollen ulcer in my throat that was pumping toxins into my bloodstream; hence the high fever. (Hence, possibly, I thought to myself, my recent dreamy spirals of snow delirium, but I did not feel the need to share this with the doctor.) What was that? He was saying something. It what? It needed lancing immediately. Then I would need to take three weeks off work – three weeks and not a day less. This was serious.

I tried to protest but the fiery hedgehog in my throat prevented me from making anything but a whimpering sound, and soon I found myself in the ward of the Bradford and Leeds General Hospital awaiting an operation. Even in my sorry state, I couldn't help wondering why the whole ward was lit by a series of fluorescent tubes that gave off a dead, soulless light that made all the occupants of the beds look already like corpses. The one above my bed was faulty; it flickered and buzzed constantly in a way reminiscent of torture rooms in the gulag. When the doctor arrived three days later, I was alarmed to see that he appeared to be about fourteen. He assured me he was fully qualified – showed me his scout badge for scalpel proficiency on his sleeve, in fact – squirted some anaesthetic spray down my throat and jabbed something down there with what looked like a roasting skewer. There was an audible pop, a gush of something slimy and putrid down my throat and the young man was off to skateboard practice with barely a backward glance.

Jill nursed me back to health for the next few days while the snow fell in endless curtains of white gauze outside the window. I set about composing a letter to my Headmaster as to why I couldn't possibly take three weeks off work. The exams were coming up. I was in the middle of directing *The Madness of George III.* Ross and I had a snow-camping expedition planned for the Sixth Formers. I was perfectly fine to resume duties, with the only handicap being an inability to talk louder than a laryngitic dormouse in a box of cottonwool. But, might I remind the Head, being a Drama teacher and a performer *par excellence*, I would be able to carry out all my duties through the time-honoured medium of mime.

In the meanwhile, I had totally forgotten the whereabouts of the garage where I had abandoned my Citroën 2CV. All I remembered was that it was somewhere in a grimy village somewhere north of Hebden Bridge. No matter. The indefatigable Mike put his multi-million-dollar business on hold for a few days, somehow tracked down the garage and retrieved the now mended Betty Bombadil in a snowstorm. As a guest, I could not have posed a greater nuisance to the entire family, but they kept reassuring me that my charming company and witty puns were worth every minor inconvenience. In the last dregs of my delirium, I believed them. A few days later I drove shakily back to Ellesmere.

*

When I arrived back at the College, I was all prepared to fight it out, albeit in a hoarse whisper. I had never taken a day sick in my life and wasn't going to take three whole weeks off, for goodness' sake. Headmaster David Du Croz, meeting me in the quadrangle as I climbed out of my car, told me quite firmly that I would indeed be following doctor's orders – besides, he had already found someone to fill my position. An old friend, in fact … and here she comes now.

There was a clack-clack-clack of platform shoes across the quadrangle and a familiar voice calling out a cheery bit of abuse. 'Slacking off again, AJ? Don't worry. Nina to the rescue. Ta-daaa!'

Shaking my head to dislodge what I thought was a last miasma of delirium, I watched slack-jawed as Nina Scarlatti, my old student from Adelaide days, gave me a wave. 'Can't stop now. I've got a play rehearsal in five minutes. Oh, I sacked that guy playing King George. He wouldn't learn the lines, so I've got Oliver Whatshisname to do the part instead. Much better. *Ciao!*'

David beamed after her. 'She's marvellous, isn't she? She turned up looking for you at the beginning of half-term and when we found out you were sick, she seemed the obvious replacement. She's taking all your classes, running the play and has the Outdoor Venture group heading off to Albania next week. Now off you go, enjoy your bed rest and I'll send Mary along with a lamb casserole she's made for you. I don't want to see you for three weeks. Shoo!'

So it was that Nina managed to turn a flying visit into a career move. I was relieved to discover that over the last three years she had toned down her searchlight personality to a certain degree; she no longer sported a hip-hugging flamingo mini-skirt, for instance, and she'd learnt not to call me a wanker – at least, not in public. Moreover, she had attained a first-class degree in education and was more than qualified for the job. It was largely due to the bursar, Captain Powlett-Pryce, that she had ended up being employed on a temporary basis to cover my workload; another sherry party in my absence had seen Nina at her most vivacious and the good Captain at his most susceptible to her charms; indeed, he was already working hard to retain her once my convalescence was over.

*

That period of convalescence, much resisted though it was, became an important turning point for me. After a few days of dozing in bed, supping on soothing jellies and lamb-shank soup provided by the saintly Mrs Du Croz, I realised just how run-down I had become. It is odd that although I look back on my time at Ellesmere with unalloyed delight, my letters from that period often told another story: exhaustion, frustration, ricocheting from lessons to play rehearsals, from sports practices to staff meetings, with the marking piling up and the House duties never-ending, and a constant chafing against the crankiness of dinosaur-like colleagues or the boorishness of ill-mannered students. Because I filled every holiday or half-term with extensive travels, driving off around Ireland or up to Scotland, I rarely made time to simply sit and doze, read, daydream … and I had little idea just how undernourished I was in these important things. Over those three weeks, while the angry red lump in my throat subsided, I sat in the bright March sunshine of my room, high above the world, taking time to realise a few things.

One of those things was that the Common Room mirror escape-trick was wearing thin yet again. Another realisation was that I was, after all, thoroughly dispensable. My English and

Drama classes were taken smoothly and efficiently; *The Madness of George III* was brought to a highly successful conclusion, much improved by all sorts of ideas that Nina brought to it; my Outdoor Ed. troop – a surly lot that year with a contempt for treasure-hunts, skinning rabbits and all that nonsense – were taken gently out of my hands and given trips to theme parks and Blackpool and not asked to identify five different hedgerow birds on every outing, much to their satisfaction. And the realisation came upon me, as slowly but surely as a flower opening to the warming sun, that it was time to move on.

From my high windows, I could see right across the Shropshire plain to the Berwyn Hills on the edge of Wales. Down south I could see the massive bulk of the Breiddens, blue and sun-crowned. Over yonder were the pine-wood heights of Nesscliffe Hill with its highwayman's cave in its red sandstone cliff; across those fields was the ruin of Whittington Castle, where I had been with young Huw in my first few weeks of teaching here. And somewhere hidden in those winding valleys was the waterfall of Pistyll Rhaedr. Nina's presence at the College reminded me of something she had said years ago when we visited the waterfall. 'It's a great place for a treasure-hunt, AJ …'

It was a truly enchanted landscape and already I think I saw in my mind's eye a little dinghy toiling along the silver thread of the canal that wound under the Faery Hill where I had sat playing airs to the Midsummer moon one night. But there was something I wanted to do first, something to bring a greater enchantment to those shining plains and blue-shadowed hills. Something to leave as a gift for this place I had so come to love but which was now beginning to kill me.

Chapter 24

'Contrariwise,' continued Tweedledee, 'if it was so, it might be; and if it were so, it would be; but as it isn't, it ain't. That's logic.'
—Lewis Carroll, *Alice's Adventures in Wonderland*

From ghoulies and ghoosties, long-leggety beasties, and things that go bump in the night, Good Lord, deliver us!
—Quaint Old Litany

Unconnected with all that, but part of my convalescence, was my reading of an old book plucked from some dusty shelf somewhere, excitingly called *Boolean Algebra and Circuitry: A Guide.* This had been published in the '30s and was dry as dust but with my newfound leisure, I devoured it with interest. While doing a short stint of philosophy at university, one subject that had fascinated me was the world of logic and truth tables, and such conundrums as this sort of thing:

Abelard claims that there is a pigeon in this bag. Beatrice claims that if there is not a pigeon in the bag, there must be a quail. Clotilde claims that, ignorant as she is of the status of pigeons, there is definitely not a quail in the bag. Only one of these three is lying. What can you tell me about the contents of this bag?

If you found this easy, then further complications can be added, such as claiming that if Abelard is lying, then Clotilde is telling the truth – but that if the bag is empty, then Beatrice is the liar.

Or whatever . . .

Boolean Logic – invented by George Boole in the nineteenth century – provides a very clean and mechanical way to cut through the tangle and come up with conclusions. I had found it fascinating that an almost mathematical approach could be applied to something as seemingly fuzzy as language; for instance, a statement claiming that a bag contained both a pigeon and a quail could be represented by the code TFFF. A different statement – such that there was at least one type of bird in the bag – would be represented by TTTF. The Ts and Fs stand for 'true' and 'false', by the way. These codes can be manipulated mathematically to produce a final result: let us say, FTTF, which is the code for 'Either a pigeon OR a quail but not both.'

I had played around a lot with Boolean Logic, but my knowledge was always limited to manipulating just two items – a pigeon and a quail, say. I had no idea how to deal with problems that involved, say, a raven as well – or a seagull or turtle dove. Nor did I have any idea how Boolean Logic applied to basic circuitry. This little green book tackled both and I found myself in seventh heaven, learning about these things from scratch. Warm sun through the windows, the life of the school going on frantically – but successfully – without me, a steaming bowl of casserole for lunch and a ream of paper gradually filling up with truth tables, Boolean algebra, circuit diagrams and newly devised puzzles involving a bag and as many hypothetical birds as I wanted.

I mention this because it allows me to introduce one of the last of the students from my days at Ellesmere. Ned Marlow was a newcomer into the Shell – Third Form – and somewhat a fish out of water. He had carroty red hair, owlish spectacles, a somewhat camelious nose – and a brain the size of a small planet, to quote

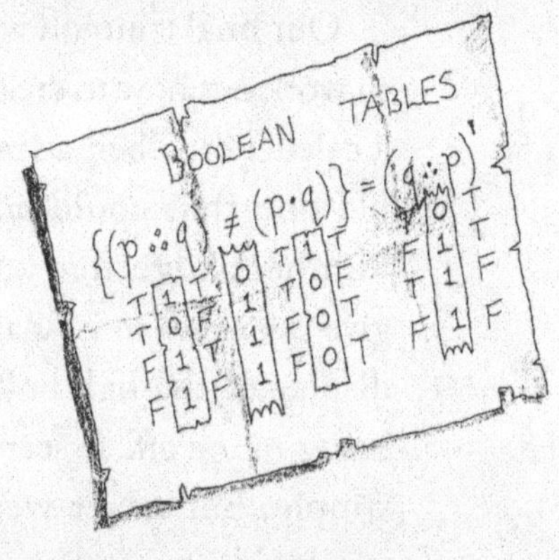

the late Douglas Adams. His slight frame meant he came off rather worse for wear on the rugby pitch, and he had taken to knocking on my door for a cup of tea and a chat when he discovered that I was about as enthusiastic for the benefits of being regularly pummelled into the mud as he was.

During my convalescence, he discovered me one day surrounded by reams of paper covered with a peculiar sort of algebra: $(p'q + pq')' = (p+q')(p'+q) = (p=q)$. It wasn't long before I found myself explaining the mysteries of formal logic and the Boolean method. When he discovered that this was all connected with electric circuitry, his eyes widened even more behind his glasses.

On the next visit, he brought along a contraption hoisted out of a store cupboard by Mr Pettigrew, one of the more ancient Mathematics teachers. This was a trapezoid wooden box with a series of metal-rimmed holes drilled into it in rows and five small electric lightbulbs along the top. With dozens of wires that could be plugged into these holes, it looked like a primitive telephone exchange. This, Ned explained, was a circuitry box, and with it we could put some of the Boolean circuitry into practice. There followed weeks and weeks of visits from Ned in which we fathomed out how to create circuits in series (*p AND q*) or circuits in parallel (*p OR q*), and more importantly how to link them in such ways that they would solve problems for us. How did we arrange things such that lightbulb A lit up if and only if switches P and Q were both on? What did we do to make it such that lightbulb C would only turn on if either bulb A or bulb B was lit, but not both?

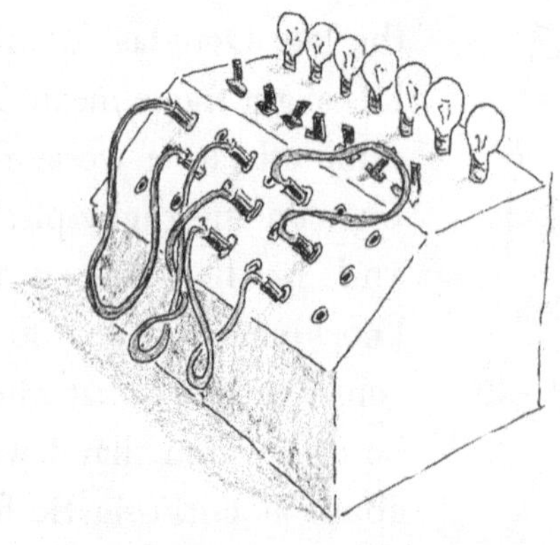

Our final triumph was to work out how to create a calculator, albeit a simple one that could add numbers together and give the result in a binary display of the lightbulbs being on or off. It seems simple, but never were two budding scientists so pleased to be able to reliably add 3 and 8 and get the bulbs reading off the right answer from left to right.

Ned became a frequent visitor over the next few months and when he learnt that I knew a bit about homemade fireworks but nothing about the electronic detonation of them, he set himself the challenge to combine the two skills and provide the pyrotechnic displays for my next production. This happened to be the very play in which Nina had performed as Second Witch all those years ago, and now the three witches were able to appear in puffs of coloured smoke and sparks with precision timing, thanks to Ned and his ingenuity.

On one of his many visits, Ned arrived with a tin tube of Pringles, explaining that he had just come from the school tuckshop. We ignored those, as I had some chocolate biscuits to share with him over the inevitable cup of tea, and Ned explained that he was working on a way of representing an *if/therefore* statement to a simple bit of circuitry involving an off-switch and a parallel alignment – or some such piece of wizardry.

Out of nowhere, Ned turned a little red and asked if I believed in ghosts. I was somewhat astonished. Cautiously I gave my opinion on the subject, namely that although I couldn't dispute their existence on logical grounds I would have to see one personally to believe they really did exist. As we have seen, the College did in fact have one or two resident phantoms if one could believe the stories. The hard-bitten and cynical Physics teacher, for example, marking some papers one quiet Sunday afternoon in the labs, had seen a boy dressed in clothes of yesteryear so plainly that he had assumed the school was putting on some sort of historical pageant for the upcoming Open Day. He had grunted a cursory greeting and then watched the boy turn and walk straight through a solid wall. My cleaning lady, Mrs Ralphs, a stolid, motherly figure if ever there was one, came down from hoovering an upper dormitory one ordinary Wednesday morning as white as a sheet and told me what she had just seen – a boy standing over by one of the beds just under a window. She had said something typically comforting – 'Don't mind me, dear, I'll be finished in a jiffy' – when the boy faded before her eyes. A second later, the hoover's hum died to nothing and she saw that the switch on the wall, not three feet from where she stood, had been turned off. She had gone straight down to share her experience with Beryl, the housekeeper, who had said, placidly enough, 'Don't tell me, dear. Third window along on the right? I thought as much. I've seen the poor mite a dozen or so times since I started working here twenty years ago.' 'Lawks-a-mussy,' had been Mrs Ralphs' only comment, but I observed that she tended from then on to trot through that section of the house cleaning rather more quickly than before. I later found out that a wild prank in the 1940s had resulted in a schoolboy falling to his death from some high window in that very wing, though accounts differed as to where exactly it had taken place. There were a dozen other similar stories of sightings like these: the white lady who could be observed at times haunting the cavernous space of the ante-chapel on moonlit nights; a phantom black cat that melted through doors and walls on the top floor of Maynard House.

I shared some of these stories with Ned and tried to elicit from him why he had brought up this subject. Was there something troubling him? Had he seen anything untoward? But Ned was evasive, and I decided not to push him further on the subject. Besides, before we knew it, it was Prep time and I had to hurry him out the door. A few minutes after Ned left, I was washing the teacups in the kitchenette when I heard a strange noise emanating from the sitting room. It was a sort of clattering and clanking as though a large hamster had got his head stuck in a condensed milk tin and was blundering about the room trying to dislodge it. With the recent talk of ghosts still in mind, I cautiously approached the sitting room door and flung it open. There was the Pringles tin lying in the middle of the carpet; Ned had forgotten in his haste to take it with him. But how had it ended up on the floor? Then as I watched, the tin started rolling across the floor towards me. My hair stood on end. Halfway across the carpet, the tin stopped – and reversed. It shot backwards as though kicked by a poltergeist forward-centre until it hit a table leg, whereupon it began to spin and dance like a dervish.

I checked my brow for any signs of feverish sweating. My malady had mostly cleared up by now, but I wondered if I was having a relapse into febrile hallucinations.

For a full two minutes I watched the tin as it clattered about the room, propelled by an invisible hand. At times, its agitation was so intense that it would spin itself upright and execute a smart jitterbug around the room, colliding with the coffee table, the standard lamp and the wastepaper basket before coming to rest against my armchair. If this was one of Ellesmere's regular phantoms, it was a new one to me.

There came a knock at the door. Eyeing the tin closely to watch for further sign of movement, I sidled to the door to open it. There stood Ned.

'Do you believe in ghosts now?' he asked ... and grinned from ear to ear. In his hand was a device remarkably like the one I had seen in Timmy Dalton's hands all those years ago on the Adelaide school oval blowing up the local galah population: a box with an antenna and a couple of dials. As he stood there and twiddled the dials, the Pringles tin behind me leapt into life again, did a brief jig and then rolled across the floor to us, where it lay tamely for Ned to pick up.

'Just something I've been working on,' he explained, and opened it up.

Inside was a small motor attached to a heavy lead weight. When the device was activated by remote control, the weight swung rapidly round and round, causing the relatively light Pringles tin to leap and roll and judder, just as I had witnessed. For a fourteen-year-old, it was pretty impressive and brilliantly executed; I had an idea even back then that this young man would go far.

*

Ned was in Fifth Form when I left, just at the time when the internet was beginning its rise to ubiquity. He had a knack of seeing the future way of things and quietly went and registered the name EllesmereCollege.co.uk under his name, for the princely sum of ten pounds. Six months later, when the school decided to join the digital age and went to set up its own domain, it found the name already taken – and worse, by the rather weedy redheaded Fifth Former who had a reputation, according to his Housemaster, for showing a lack of House spirit and refusing to muck in on the rugby field when it came to the Inter-House Trophy match.

Mr Briggs, the new Headmaster – Mr and Mrs Du Croz had sadly departed the previous year for a new life at Marlborough

College down south – called Ned in to his office, congratulated him on his prank and then made the mistake of suggesting that the joke was now over and it was time to hand the domain rights over to where they belonged. And promptly.

'Sorry,' said Ned. 'I don't quite understand. You'd like to buy the rights from me?'

Mr Briggs boggled and spluttered and told him that a joke was a joke, very clever and all that, but now it was time to be reasonable.

'And what would you regard as a reasonable price, sir?'

Ned had done his homework. In the six months since he had registered the domain rights, the cost had soared astronomically. A thousand pounds would not have been an unreasonable asking price, and this fact he shared with Mr Briggs. After watching another bout of indignant spluttering with cool detachment, Ned informed the Headmaster that he was, of course, open to negotiation, and that remuneration need not necessarily be entirely financial. There was the matter of compulsory rugby practice, for example, something Ned found conducive to neither his studies nor his mental wellbeing. There was also the fact that the hours he spent as technician for the various school productions seemed currently to count for nothing when it came to accruing merit points in the House points system. Perhaps a refocusing of priorities was in order, especially as we were now clearly eager to embrace a digital age. 'As you say, Headmaster, I'm sure we all want to be reasonable . . .'

I have no idea what was eventually settled between them – Ned was coy on the details – but he assured me that he never found himself being ground into the mud again by the Sixth Form rugger types – and this left him more time for his studies and his tinkering. These served him well. He is currently the founder and owner of a multi-million-pound app development company, which aims to allow electric cars all over Britain to be conveniently recharged by a fleet of mobile charging vans during the wee hours. I hope when it is fully launched, its logo turns out to be a dancing Pringles tin.

Chapter 25

I flamed amazement: sometime I'd divide,
And burn in many places; on the topmast,
The yards and bowsprit, would I flame distinctly,
Then meet and join. Jove's lightnings, the precursors
O' the dreadful thunder-claps, more momentary
And sight-outrunning were not; the fire and cracks
Of sulphurous roaring the most mighty Neptune
Seem to besiege and make his bold waves tremble,
Yea, his dread trident shake.

—William Shakespeare, *The Tempest*

Despite the distractions provided by the impish and ingenious Ned and his poltergeist Pringles tin, once I was fully recovered, I found myself getting back into the swing of Ellesmere College life. The long summer holidays came and went. September rolled around and I began my sixth and final year at the College. The year is now in my memory a blur. Apart from Ned, I remember very few of the younger students who arrived that year. Nina Scarlatti was now a fully fledged colleague and was a wonderful asset to the school; she and I found ourselves collaborating on a number of murder mystery games played with staff, a shared interest since that school-student essay she had written all those years ago, entitled 'The Mystery of the Salmon Dinner', the one set in 'a Scottish castle on the Yorkshire Moors'. She had also fallen deeply in love with a young teacher from New Zealand called Tim – though the entire staff with cruel wit called him 'Turm', due to his Kiwi accent. Indeed, the ingenious Felix Arne, who prided himself on writing limericks using supposedly unrhymable words such as *orange*, *month* and *purple*, composed a limerick in Tim's honour that went as follows:

> There was a young Kiwi called Turm
> Who liked his sex saucy but firm.
> He would tweak his own nurple
> Until it turned purple
> And squiggle and squeal and squirm.

Needless to say, it only works if read in a broad Kiwi accent where all the vowels slither around like oysters on a bed of kelp. Whether it was the sadomasochistic suggestions as to Tim's predilections in bed that attracted Nina or not, she threw herself into wooing the gentle Aucklander with her customary determination, and before long he and Nina were inseparable – as they are to this day.

*

Despite all the busyness of the school year, my letters show that my time seemed to be spent in a frenzy of activity. I think I was unconsciously making the most of my time there. One weekend, I took a couple of students caving in the Ceiriog Valley. The tunnel system was a series of natural, water-carved caverns. A senior colleague told me where to find the entrance and added that he had been reliably informed that these caverns wound right through the hill and emerged at the far end. I took with me the ever-adventurous Toby Larkin and a slim red-haired lass called Ginny, who for all her frail appearance was up for any exploit.

The perils of this sort of caving – pot-holing, as it is sometimes called – are different from the ones associated with the human-engineered caverns of the slate mines. Rockfalls are less likely, but to make up for that the tunnels are often tortuously narrow and branch off in unexpected directions. Water, too, is a hazard. In our exploration, we sometimes found ourselves wriggling along in fissures whose rock walls fitted us like a second skin, pulling ourselves along on our bellies by the tips of our fingers outstretched in front of us and propelling ourselves by our toes stretched backwards behind us. At one point, just such a tunnel descended slightly, and I found myself confronted by the tunnel half-flooded with water. The water was so close to the ceiling that we had to inch ourselves along with our heads turned sideways to be able to breathe out of the top half of our mouths.

Mercifully, this stretch didn't last too long – fifty yards perhaps, though it seemed like several miles – before the tunnel turned abruptly upwards into a vertical chimney of slick red rock. Climbing up this, we found ourselves in a much larger cavern with many cracks and fissures winding away into darkness. Having experienced the ordeal of the flooded tunnel, we were more determined than ever to find the far exit. For hours we explored, sometimes wriggling through upright slits that popped the buttons off my shirt, sometimes scaling slippery cliffs to reach a promising tunnel high above us. Eventually we had exhausted all possibilities but one – the tunnels we had explored had either ended in dead ends or looped around on themselves and returned to the main passage. Only one was left … and sure enough, as Toby suddenly pointed out, there was a faint but distinct breeze flowing from it. For another hour or so we pursued this passage, wriggling through the tight bits, marvelling at the streaks of colour in the flowstone of the walls – ambers, saffrons, copper greens, honeycomb golds, lying in wavy bands and stripes down every wall.

Alas, eventually the tunnel narrowed and narrowed; the ceiling dropped and dropped until we could go no further. But there in the silence, we suddenly heard something, faint but unmistakable. The sound of a car passing along a road. The bleat of a sheep. We had found it, the far exit! The problem was that it was through a hole not much larger than a sizeable rabbit hole. Toby dropped to the ground, and with sudden determination wiggled as far as he could into this hole until we could only see his feet, thrashing and kicking with the exertion. A muffled call came back, something about seeing daylight ... and something about being stuck. Then his feet went limp.

Ginny and I grabbed a boot each and hauled with all our might and Toby slithered back into our laps. Daylight. He had seen daylight – but the tunnel was impassable. It was tiny. There was no way through. But look, he had grabbed something. In his hands were a bunch of wilting leaves, glossy and green, and smelling of garlic. I recognised them as the wild garlic that grows all through the woods of Wales. It seemed that we had come to the back of some sort of animal's burrow, some creature that lined its nest with fresh leaves. As we speculated about this over the aroma of crushed garlic, we slowly became aware of an appalling stench of a different sort. Toby examined his hands more closely and found them smeared with a mustardy paste that stank to high heaven – and we all simultaneously identified it as something like dog faeces. Nesting burrow or improvised toilet, we never found out. The salient fact was that as a means of egress it was useless, and our way out lay back the way we had come.

The trickiest part of our retreat was the red chimney and the flooded tunnel. As we stood at the top of the chimney, we realised that if we were to climb down it in the usual fashion, feet first like someone descending a ladder, we would be forced to enter the narrow, flooded passage feet first as well, which would mean a backward tummy-crawl along the fifty yards or so of tight-fitting tunnel. This was unthinkable. We had to be able to enter the tunnel head first – but this meant descending the slippery red-rock chimney head first too. A terrifying thought but it had to be done. One by one we edged over the lip of the shaft and slithered our way down head first like a trio of greased geckos sliding down a drainpipe, trying to slow our descent by jamming our hands and knees into any crevice we could find. But this at least allowed us to slither into the tunnel heading in the right direction and making our way to the outside world.

We were underground for six hours on that occasion. I still remember the utter joy of emerging from the cave's entrance into the wooded valley and finding the afternoon light filtering through the tall beech trees; the gleeful slither and slide down through drifts of dead leaves and clumps of wild garlic to the chattering stream below; the plunging in heedlessly to wash ourselves of the red clay that smeared us from head to foot … and the blessed relief that Toby no longer smelt like a tanner's dog in soiled nappies. The hot bath that night was the sweetest I've ever had; the draught of whisky in front of a fire the most warming. And best of all the bright eyes of Toby and Ginny over the next few months as they revelled in the joy of adventure and peril overcome.

*

The final production before I left Ellesmere College was, fittingly enough, *The Tempest*, widely considered to be Shakespeare's last play, his farewell to the world of theatre. It is one of my favourite plays; no surprises there, considering it has as its central character the enchanter Prospero. Set as it is on an island, I wanted to do the play 'in the round' – that is, with the audience on all sides of the stage. To that end, I cut out a huge circle of canvas to create the stage and painted it in all the colours of the seaside: sandy whites, seaweed pinks, kelp browns and pearly greens. I also placed large trays of water at certain points around the stage so that bright spotlights shining on them could throw rippled reflections as shifting nets of light on the walls and ceiling of the theatre.

Toby played Caliban, of course; he had graduated from his Third Form performance as Puck and now brought his exquisite physicality to the role of brooding troll. As in the *Dream* all those years ago, he spent the first twenty minutes of the performance on stage but concealed from the audience, not wound into a tree this time but hidden in a sea chest that would have barely held a smallish beagle. When he came forth complaining of the cramps inflicted upon him by Prospero, the cramps needed no acting. Ariel was played by a serene girl called Alice with shining copper hair and an elfin face, who expressed many of her emotions and thoughts through the exquisite playing of a viola tucked under her chin.

To involve four more students who had auditioned for this play but for whom there were no speaking parts, I created the extra roles of four elemental sprites to do Prospero's bidding. These, I decided, should be sprites of water, air, earth and fire – indeed, the appearance of the students fitted admirably with these four elements. Ginny and Hannah were suitably willowy and fluid in their motions and appearance to play Water and Air. Edward was a potato-shaped lad who suited his role as an Earth spirit.

The fourth boy was a lad called Sam Curlewis; he had flaming red hair and a restless energy, so I assigned him the role of Fire.

It is a somewhat thankless task to have a non-speaking part in a play and still be expected to attend all rehearsals, but three of these elemental students took up the challenge gracefully. Sam, on the other hand, didn't. He had no real interest in working out how to play the part of a fire spirit. He often missed rehearsals, and when he did attend he was frequently disruptive. As opening night grew closer and closer, my patience got thinner and thinner. The last lead-up to any play is not a gradual slope to perfection but a swooping exponential curve, where three days before the entire play is an utter shambles, the next rehearsal is a stumbling cripple of a performance, dress rehearsal is deeply disappointing – and then comes first night, when everything clicks into place and the magic happens.

It was at the dress-rehearsal stage that I was at my most maniacally dangerous. The performance was slow and flat, cues were being missed, props forgotten, lighting effects weren't working and one particular scene, supposedly the most dramatic in the whole play, was as tepid and uninspiring as tapioca. This is the scene where a magical feast laid out for the hapless noblemen vanishes with a clap of thunder and Ariel appears in the form of a terrifying harpy. In the midst of lightning flashes and whirling demons, Ariel accuses them of their former crimes and declares that they are now about to be punished by the long-vanished Prospero. This is where I was hoping to use my four elemental sprites to help Ariel create a terrifying scene of whirling chaos: dashing water waves, tornados of whirling air – *well done, girls!* – tumbling boulders of earth – *good job, Edward* – and ... *and where the hell is Fire? Fire?? Curlewis? This is your scene! Why aren't you on!!*

When Sam was located and loped unapologetically onto stage, his limp attempts to be fiery consisted of nothing more dramatic than wiggling his fingers as though he were trying to hypnotise a rabbit. I called a halt to the rehearsal and chewed my lip thoroughly, trying to contain my impatience. 'Sam, I have cast you as the ancient spirit of Fire, the elemental force at the heart of the sun, the volcano, the forest conflagration in all its fury. I have not cast you as the ancient elemental spirit of three-day-old porridge. You've had three weeks to come up with something really good to represent fire. Opening night is tomorrow. We need something more than looking like a squashed earwig. It needs to be . . . well, *energetic*! Dangerous! Fiery, in fact.'

'What, like fire-breathing?' said Sam.

'Well, no, obviously not actual fire-breathing but—'

'Because I can, you know. I taught myself last summer.'

'You . . . what?' I really had no time for this.

'Fire breathing. 'T's easy, innit?'

'Are you telling me that you know how to fire-breathe and you have only just now chosen to inform me of that?!'

'Well, yeah, you never asked.'

'Get out of here!!' I bellowed. 'Get out of here and be back in twenty minutes with whatever sodding stuff you need to show me that you can fire-breathe! Go!'

None of the cast had ever seen me really lose my temper before. I was white-faced and shaking, filled with enough wrath to play a hundred vengeful harpies. Sam took one look and scarpered out the door. 'Right,' I said, 'Let's move on. Act Three. And let's see some pace.'

Thirty minutes later, Sam was back with a can of something flammable, a rag tied to a stick and a lighter – and sure enough, demonstrated the skill of fire-breathing like a pro, sending up great plumes of red flame from his mouth with each breath. Now we were cooking with gas – or whatever it was in the can; I didn't like to ask. Suddenly, the harpy scene had wings, so to speak.

My sound technician dug out a CD of *Carmina Burana* and played it at full volume throughout, the costume ladies ran up a devil's cloak in flaming orange in record time and with Sam breathing great gouts of fire within an inch of the actors' noses there was no need for me to exhort them to act terrified. The scene became the highlight of the show.

On the final night, Sam's parents were in the audience, and I bustled up to them afterwards to bask in the customary glow of praise one usually receives from parents who have seen their son or daughter transformed from the grunting teenager seen at home to the dazzling star of the stage. The praise from Dr and Mrs Curlewis was perfunctory; they were clearly keen to address a matter dearer to their hearts.

'Mr Mackinnon, we cannot help being somewhat perturbed that your coaching of Sam has involved something as hazardous as fire-breathing. Why were we not informed that this was part of the Drama curriculum?'

Before I could splutter out some sort of explanation, another set of parents had swept up to congratulate me on the play, something I would usually revel in had they not been so effusive about the harpy scene and all that wonderful fire-breathing. 'Fancy!' the Watsons burbled. 'It looked so daring! And in a school play and all! You don't see that too often, do you?'

Dr Curlewis did not seem to share their enthusiasm. 'Surely some sort of permission form should be in order in the case of dangerous activities?' he asked acidly.

'Dangerous?' said my friend Ross Bassenthwaite, sweeping up from behind with a pint of ale from the foyer bar. 'Bloody marvellous,' he chuckled. 'Just what Shakespeare needs, eh?'

Undeterred by this tide of opinion, Mrs Curlewis chimed in. 'Because let me assure you now that if a permission form had been forthcoming, we would not have signed it. We are considering registering a formal complaint with the school but feel it only courteous to register our disappointment with you in person first.'

By the time I had tried simultaneously accepting the compliments of Ross and the Watsons while making little shooshing noises whenever they mentioned the fire-breathing, Dr and Mrs Curlewis had swept off and I didn't get a chance to explain. Toby Larkin was nearby, however, and had heard this exchange. I turned to him to let off some indignant steam.

'Really,' I spluttered. 'Sam's parents are blaming me for teaching him how to fire-breathe. I didn't get to explain to them that this was a skill he picked up on his own somewhere. Ah well, he'll tell them no doubt. Still …'

'Hmmm,' murmured Toby, looking thoughtful. 'I'm not sure of that.'

'What do you mean? Surely he'll set them straight?'

'I doubt it. Sam had never fire-breathed in his life before three days ago.'

'What? But he told me he could …'

'Yes, I know. He was just doing that to wind you up. He knew it would make you cross.'

'You mean, he … he … ?'

'Yep, he just didn't realise how cross. When you yelled at him to get the stuff pronto and show us his fire-breathing, we'd never seen anything like it. Sam was so frightened he ran off to the library and found a book on how to do it. Amazing what you can find in a library …'

'You mean … ?'

'Yep. He learnt it from a book on the spot, stole a can of petrol from the maintenance shed and tried it out for the first time in front of us all at the dress rehearsal. Quite good for a beginner, don't you think?'

I was flabbergasted. And appalled. But I was also a tiny little bit proud. As a teacher, I had finally arrived. Why, I could be even more frightening than the thought of self-immolation; that was surely a useful trick to have up my sleeve.

*

After the play was over, as a sort of treat for the main actors, we drove over to Pistyll Rhaedr one glorious afternoon of summer, shortly before the school year ended. I remember this as one of the loveliest times I spent with students while at Ellesmere. The hills at the head of the valley were purpling with heather, the fields along the winding valley bottom were striped with gold furrows where the hay lay waiting to be collected. The waterfall itself sparkled like a snowy torrent as it fell from its craggy height and thundered into the dark pool below. Flanking it on either side were those loveliest of trees, grey-trunked beeches, lifting their fan-vaulting high above, canopied with the jewel-green leaves of their foliage.

We scrambled up to the top of the cascade and looked right down the valley, which wound away into a blue-gold distance. Larks sang in the summer air. Alice, the girl who had played Ariel with such grace, draped herself on a slanting pine tree near the cliff's edge – it could have been the very cloven pine in which her spirit had been imprisoned by the foul witch Sycorax. Toby clambered ape-like around the rock stacks, climbing into every crevice and playing at Caliban. My Prospero, a tall dark-eyed boy of great gravity who would later go on to become one of the UK's premier trapeze acrobats, stood gazing out over the valley lost in thought. It was a timeless scene; somehow, the fiction of the play overlay the reality of the landscape. These students – children really – had taken on themselves the power, the grace, the burning intensity of the roles they had so recently played, and it still clung about them like a shining skin. Not for the last time did I marvel at how fortunate I was to have been a part of their lives, a part of the magic that has not yet faded at that age into the commonplace affairs of adulthood.

And as I stood there, I recalled that visit I had made years earlier, when Nina Scarlatti had first arrived and we had come here on a day of spring snow and primroses under bare trees. That treasure hunt she had suggested. A good idea indeed. And now it was time to get busy.

Chapter 26

What can promote innocent mirth, and I may say virtue, more than a good riddle?

—George Eliot, *Middlemarch*

There is in life an element of elfin coincidence, which people reckoning on the prosaic may perpetually miss.

—G.K. Chesterton, *The Innocence of Father Brown*

The treasure hunt took a year to devise. For me, this glorious final year acted as a summation of all that I had loved and explored while at Ellesmere College. Every free weekend, every afternoon at a loose end, every midnight hour saw me either driving around the local countryside to climb church towers, examine stained-glass windows, note down inscriptions on brass plaques or tombstones, delve into Shakespearian texts or construct elaborate riddles involving chess pieces or tarot cards. The final aim was to produce nine large paintings, to be gifted to the school on my departure, containing all the clues, both written and visual, to enable eager, curious minds to discover the whereabouts of a treasure worth the seeking.

I decided that the quest needed some sort of character to act as a narrator, and the obvious choice was Jack de Crow. He had long since departed the College for wider skies, but when I remembered how he had stolen my housemaster's gold pen, the housemaster's wife's ruby earrings and Lord knows how many other trinkets of jewellery from around the place, Jack seemed an obvious candidate for a cheeky character with a hidden hoard to discover. Indeed, the opening rhyme started practically writing itself:

> Jack Micawber Phalacrocorax
> Magister Mordicorvus De Crow
> Lived at the College to my certain knowledge
> A hundred and something summers ago . . .

Some treasure hunts can be solved by sitting in an armchair, puzzling over the provided clues. I wanted something different, something that would get students hopping on their bikes and cycling down country lanes, to clamber down tunnels, visit crypts by moonlight or climb tall towers to spot a distant landmark, all as instructed in riddling verse by that master of mischief, Jack de Crow. Rather than leave clues written on paper at each new location which risked being lost or damaged, I found ingenious ways to use plaques, inscriptions, dates and milestones set indelibly in the landscape as ciphers to solve the next clue in the paintings.

I wish I could tell you of all the twists and turns the treasure hunt took, but to do so would be to write a new novel. Suffice to say that the finished quest was the richest congeries of imagery, adventure, history, myth and literature it is possible to conceive. They were an amalgam of all my Ellesmere days, and each of these gems linked by painted images and playful verses: the stained-glass figure of Saint Oswald with his raven in the College chapel and the carved wooden mice on the pews, pointed out by the gentle Edwin Appleby six years previously.

THE
IV
THE JUNGLE BOOK
RUDYARD KIPLING
The Psalms of David
POST
Hickory ickory here they run!
Count them creeping one by one
Some on the side and one in the centre
Bishop Hatto dare not enter!
Here sits Jack in the shadowed night
His Master stained with silver light
Seeks for the voice of a noble poet
"I can't get on until I know it!"
Suddenly then at the Dick
A Voice rings out with si
"Where City and Town a
Village meet,
There is the Poet you've com
to seek"
The Poet's La said to Jack
A starting point is what you lack.
I saw in a reflective mood
A Knight who by the Bluebell Wood
Gazed at the dark horizon far
And upwards to the Northern Star
(In degrees and minutes read
Through what angle did he raise
He gazed at the Northern Star that
Then turning a quarter to the right
Beyond the fields and woods he saw
Two miles hence... or a fraction more
As the Crow doth fly, a Ho
Go thence!" she cried.
Jack gave a nod.
"Your view of life," he cawed, "is
But off he flew to find the Churc
And so continued with his search.

Hickory dickory, here they run!
Count them creeping one by one.
Here sits Jack in the shadowed night,
His master stained with silver light.

A grandfather clock chiming midnight in the haunted moonlight of the ante-chapel; Tennyson's Lady of Shalott who saw the world in a mirror; the giddy heights of the Breiddens, where Betty Bombadil had so nearly brought about my bloody demise . . . and restored me to my senses. An exploration of the tarot deck with all its strange and compelling archetypes:

And Mage and Man and Star and Tower,
They too go dancing, prancing by . . .
But their numbered steps are of equal power
To the Sun, the Moon and I.

Which takes us in a neat loop via the oddity of Psalm 46 to the Bard himself; and so to his luckless prince in *The Merchant of Venice*, who chose the golden casket and found only a gilded skull in the lottery of love.

The Psalmist's hidden Master
Is trying to bring to mind;
What did the Dark Prince choose there
And what did the Dark Prince find?

From that revelation to Melverley's magpie church (where I would later wash up on the early days of my dinghy voyage) to find a golden skull on a memorial plaque: the trail of clues was labyrinthine in the extreme.

A remote chapel in a Snowdonian valley whose font was carved with ancient runes; a chess problem centred around Whittington Castle as one of the white rooks on a board that overlaid the Shropshire plain:

> Jack flew over the chequerboard plain and spied the
> land below,
> Five long leagues from North to South, as straight as the
> flying Crow.
> Fulke the Knight in his Castle White; the Bishop of
> Melverley Green;
> A Blackened Tower at Eleanor's Bower; at Winifred's
> Well, a Queen;
> A King that looked to the stars above, and sure as he was
> a crow,
> Four cawing cousins on every side, in sable and in snow.

The list goes on and on, and each of those items could be unpacked to reveal more and more intricate details of enchantment and synchronicity, like ever tinier and more elaborately carved Chinese boxes nested one within another, seemingly without end.

*

But what of the actual treasure, the prize, the reward for anyone persistent enough to follow this bizarre golden thread of clues? I had at first thought to bury some jewelled trinket, the sort of thing Jack de Crow might genuinely have stolen from a jewellery box left unattended on a lady's dressing table. However, it soon became apparent to me that the complexity of the quest demanded a more significant prize, so I decided that it should be a quest for the ultimate treasure – the Grail itself.

I have long been fascinated with the Holy Grail and, indeed, all things Arthurian. My childhood reading of *The Once and Future King* had hooked me firmly into the world of King Arthur, that mysterious figure of royalty and nobility who lived who-knows-when and who-knows-where but who still exercises such a powerful hold on the hearts and minds of the English race. The Grail story, in particular, fascinates me with its rich imagery. My old Adelaide friend Tom and I had devised – and played endlessly when we should have been writing essays on Joseph Conrad or Patrick White – a board game set in a mystical forest of ever-changing topography, peppered with seductive Morgan le Fays, questing Red Cross Knights, holy hermits, white stags, Fisher Kings and the Grail itself shining out from the top window of a lofty forest tower like a beacon. Now it was time to take the Grail quest to a new level.

There was of course the small matter of the treasure itself. Having decided that the treasure should be a Grail of sorts, I would have to find a silversmith and commission them to make something suitable. This proved harder than I had imagined. Every silversmith I spoke to made it clear that earrings or brooches were about their limit and that anything as large and intricate as a jewelled chalice was beyond their scope. Yet again, Fate intervened in a most helpful fashion.

I was at the time directing a production of *The Pirates of Penzance* for the College and my leading actress, the girl playing Mabel, was a wonderful lass called Clarinda Honeywell. Clarinda was a superb singer built along the generous lines of many classical opera singers; she had a lively sense of humour and had no qualms about using her considerable bulk to bring to the role a wonderful comic grace, finding many an opportunity to smother Frederick's kisses in her ample bosom or to sit coquettishly on his knee, seemingly oblivious to his manly attempts to stifle his groans of agony.

The HILL of the SUN
The UNICORN
The HOLY GRAIL
The ARMOUR
The WITCH
The MIZ-MAZ
The TOWER
The FISHER KING
The SORCERER
The ROSE

As well as these intentional slapstick mishaps, the performance was not without its genuine alarums, which tested Clarinda's professionalism to the full. On opening night, Clarinda stood as directed, holding a regal pose upon a geranium-decked balcony while the policemen's chorus sang her praises below. I was somewhat irritated, however, to see a certain fidgetiness in her demeanour. Less than pleased at this, I stormed backstage at interval to demand a little more professionalism. To my chagrin, Clarinda explained what the problem had been. A small frog had sought the shelter of one of the geranium pots during its nightly watering out of the back of the theatre and had been inadvertently brought inside, hidden under the leaves. When the full glare of the spotlight flooded the balcony, it had instantly decided that it was no Kermit; the world of the limelight was not to its liking. Seeking some deep, moist crevice as a hidey-hole, it had dived straight down Clarinda's blouse. Far from ticking her off for an unpardonable case of the fidgets, I should have been congratulating Clarinda on the professionalism of maintaining her poise in the spotlight's glare for a full seven minutes while the frisky amphibian thoroughly explored her cleavage.

This professionalism was about to be tested again. In one scene in *The Pirates of Penzance*, we had a swing lowered from the ceiling on two ropes and Mabel would sit on this being pushed to and fro by Frederick as they sang an aria of undying love together. It was Clarinda's idea that, at the height of the aria, Clarinda's descending arc should propel her lover backwards off stage to vanish entirely into the wings, whence would emanate a muffled squeak as some poor stagehand got trampled, before Frederick emerged a second later still valiantly trying to sing while disentangling himself from some prop ivy and a fire bucket or two.

Offstage, however, Clarinda had an admirer, more toad than frog, a spotty stagehand called Roscoe, whose ardent affections she did not return. In her sweet-natured way, she tried to let him down gently, but Roscoe, like some villain in a Victorian melodrama, did not take this placidly. He started spreading horrid rumours about Clarinda, some of them amphibian-related, none of which the poor girl deserved. Indeed, she was so graciously forgiving of his behaviour that he became baffled with rage and decided to try something more drastic. The first I knew of it was when Toby Larkin – blessed Toby Larkin, who seemed to know everything that went on and never lacked the courage to step in when needed – came to me just before opening night and suggested I check out the rope swing carefully. Mystified at his cryptic warning, I did so … and discovered that the ropes holding the swing had been tampered with, the intention being that when Clarinda was at the height of her swing in the Second Act, the ropes would snap and send her hurtling like an infant hippopotamus into the orchestra.

The ropes were quickly and discreetly replaced, but it was noticed that Roscoe grew ever more gleeful as the swing scene approached. During the aria, in fact, he even sneaked out from backstage and came up to the lighting box to watch his dastardly plan eventuate – where he found me with some awkward questions to answer. Poor Roscoe. He broke down and confessed all. He went home for a few days and the matter was soon over. However, on the final night, Clarinda's parents came up from Wolverhampton to see their daughter's sterling performance and after the show came to congratulate me on the production. What is more, they had heard of the rope incident and the fact that I had managed to avert disaster and they started acting like the grateful parents in some music-hall melodrama.

'You saved our Clarinda's life, Mr Mackinnon,' Mr Honeywell intoned with awed sincerity. He had a Midlands accent and a face like an anxious walrus. 'Who knows what might have happened if those ropes had snapped and our Clarinda in mid-air? It makes us shudder to think of it, doesn't it, my pet? Shudder … and that's no word of a lie!'

I tried to demur, but they were having none of it. 'If there's anything we can do for you, anything at all, you've only to ask. Name your price, young man, name your price.'

I tried to shake off the feeling that I had saved Clarinda from being tied to the railway tracks and was now expected to ask for her hand in marriage. I sought to change the topic. 'So, what do you do, Mr Honeywell? Where does Clarinda get her acting skills from? Are you in theatre yourself, Mr Honeywell?'

'Oh Bernard, please, call me Bernard. No, I'm a jeweller by trade. Antiques. Silver mostly. Cups, chalices and the like. But enough about me. You saved our Clarinda's life, you did, and if there's any way we can be of service—'

I stopped him short. 'Well, actually, funny you should say that …'

*

Mr Honeywell did himself proud. The finished Jack de Crow Grail was fashioned from a solid antique silver bowl or wide chalice. Mr Honeywell took four designs I had created and engraved them in four panels on the outside of the chalice. These showed all sorts of elements of the treasure hunt: a tarot card Hermit, a clock and mice, a graven skull and Jack the jackdaw himself. Then he took wine-red garnets, pearly moonstones and bright turquoises

and set them about the beaded rim to make a handsome and ancient-looking treasure.

I went further. I had recently been given a great bag of broken costume jewellery by the amiable Mr Crabbe of the Ellesmere Antique Emporium – a reward, he said, in return for the immense pleasure he still got from regaling friends and customers with the story of the great Yeats hoax – and choosing the best pieces, I placed them in the chalice itself as a glittering hoard of gems and jewels such as might have been stolen by the thieving Jack de Crow. Indeed, I had so many of these brooches and chains, bracelets and earrings, that I found another use for them in a project I shall write of later.

The next thing to do was to decide upon a suitable hiding place. It may seem odd that this decision had still not been made, but I had devised the treasure hunt in such a way that the final resting place of the chalice could be anywhere I chose, with only the last few clues leading the seeker to the location of the prize. Indeed, I was adamant that this should be the experience of the successful treasure-seeker; armed with all the information garnered from the first eight paintings and their forays around the region, they should be presented with one final glorious bicycle ride following a chain of clues to some magical location unbeknownst to them until they arrived, spade in hand, and ready to claim the prize from its earthy tomb.

But where should it be? The waterfall of Pistyll Rhaedr? St Winifrede's Well? The slate mines of Cwm Penmachno? Or perhaps closer to home. I toyed briefly with the idea of burying it under the First XI cricket pitch and imagining with secret glee the sacred turf being turned over during midnight forays by hordes of avid treasure-seekers – a parting revenge for the hours I had spent there unwillingly over the last five years trying to put Chadwick's umpiring tips to good use.

Eventually I decided simply to ride out into the countryside on a bike and see where fortune led me. One bright Sunday morning on the day of the equinox – September 21st – I set off, a small backpack stuffed with sandwiches and a notebook, and soon I found myself heading west from the College and striking the Llangollen Canal not a mile from the school gates. Along this canal runs a towpath, and it struck me as a perfect road to adventure: a secret winding way shunned by motorists and the hurrying world, ducking under motorways, ambling by old inns and sleepy lock-cottages, fragrant with a thousand wildflowers and always the glint of water at one's side – bulrushes, watercress, kingcups and waterlilies, moorhens and mallards and the occasional bright gleam of a kingfisher – the Fisher King himself – leading the Grail-seeker onwards. Indeed, it would later be along this very route that the final clues of the completed treasure hunt would lead the successful seeker, and the starting place was to be that very fairy hill, beech-crowned, where I had sat all those years ago, piping unawares to the Midsummer moon and the wide-eyed Daniel May. But that morning I knew nothing of the trail ahead – only that it offered promise and adventure at every turn.

To my growing delight, the canal wound its way towards the blue hills of Wales, where magic and myth lie over every wood, on every hilltop, in every stone. Two hours' riding brought me to a landscape considerably more dramatic and Arthurian than the flat plains around Ellesmere. A long dark tunnel takes the cyclist boring through a wooded hill and out onto a great aqueduct spanning a valley. Here, barges float high above the Llangollen valley and the swift and beautiful River Dee; here, I, too, floated

on my magic steed, pedals pumping, wheels a whirring glitter. Beyond this aqueduct, the canal turns up the Llangollen valley and creeps along the thickly wooded hillside, perched impossibly halfway up the steep slope, becoming ever narrower and darker as it approaches its terminus in the iconic Welsh town of Llangollen. The towpath ends at a fine old church with a tall steeple, but it still didn't feel the right place to bury my treasure.

As I lingered there looking around for some obvious waymark, a goldfinch flew across the graveyard in a flash of scarlet and gold. It had been feeding on the summer thistle-heads that grew against the tombstones but now flitted up the hill beyond the churchyard. I have written before of how special these little birds are to me. So the sighting of this little harlequin was enough for me. I took the steep winding lane up which the goldfinch had flown and soon found myself looking down into a smaller valley that wound northwards. Immediately to my right rose a great hill

crowned with a broken ruin. This is the Castell Dinas Brân, a steep hill covered with russet bracken and a swathe of pinewoods above where sit the broken remains of an ancient castle. To my left, the lane wound down past a white gate and an old farmhouse to a wide field – and there on a mound of grass stood a tall carved stone. It looked very ancient; a few lines of writing could be barely made out beneath the mustard-coloured lichen. This was it. This was where I would bury the Grail, here where the shadow of the stone fell at midday upon the Equinox. A glance at my Ordnance Survey map told me that this was called the Pillar of Eliseg: a mysterious name, something straight out of an Alan Garner book or a Welsh legend. My watch showed that it was midday, so I placed a distinctive stone right on the spot where the shadow fell, so I could come back later and bury the treasure in the correct place. My goldfinch had led me aright. Now all I had to do was devise the last few clues as a way of leading an eager treasure-seeker to this spot by the very route I had just followed.

(As a side note, a few months later I was to be bowled over yet again by a series of staggering discoveries, which has confirmed my belief that where treasure hunts are concerned coincidences, synchronicities and serendipitous connections come tumbling from the fabric of the cosmos like lemmings from a precipice. Judge for yourself.

Some weeks after my departure from Ellesmere College in my little yellow dinghy *Jack de Crow I* found myself within hailing distance of Marlborough, the new home of *Jack*'s namesake, the kindly Mr Du Croz and his wife Mary. Over afternoon tea in their elegant living room, I browsed through a book on their coffee table, a book called something like *The Sacred Places of Britain*. It was all there: Stonehenge, Iona, Glastonbury Tor – a score of familiar names. But then one particular page caught my eye. There was a photo that was strangely familiar, a tall stone pillar on

a mound of grass. In the background rose the distinctive shape of a hill capped with the jagged crown of its castle ruins. In growing wonder, I read the commentary.

Here in the Vale of Llangollen stands the mysterious Pillar of Eliseg, whose origins and purpose are lost in the mists of time. An inscription on the stone marks this as the monument to a certain Owain Ddantgwyn, whom certain scholars now identify as the best historical candidate for the legendary King Arthur.

I blinked at the improbability of it. I seemed to have buried my Grail in the very shadow of a monument to Arthur himself. I read on …

An excavation of the mound in the 1800s unearthed nothing but a gilded skull … – and I recalled with a start that one of the clues at the very heart of my treasure hunt had involved a golden skull on a church plaque and, leading to it, a reference to the Prince of Morocco and his discovery. But there was more.

The connection with the court of King Arthur is made perhaps more plausible by the pillar's proximity to Dinas Brân, which has long been connected to the Grail legend as the castle of the Fisher King …

My tea grew cold unheeded as I considered the staggering implications of all this. Utterly unwittingly, I had hidden my mock Grail within bowshot of a castle said to be the location of the legendary Grail, at the foot of the only known memorial to the best contender for the genuine King Arthur – and sharing a hidey-hole with a gilded skull. Why, my Grail even had a skull inscribed on its silver sides, one of the designs engraved there by the amiable Mr Honeywell.

I was later to find that the same scholar who had identified Owain Ddantgwyn as the best contender for the historical Arthur had discovered intimate connections between the real historical Grail and Whittington Castle, Fulke FitzWarren, the Hawkstone Park obelisk with its 153 steps, the eagle of Saint John, the Book of Psalms and the tarot cards, every one of which I had used unwittingly in this treasure hunt.

Perhaps you won't be surprised that I have since wondered if there is something about the act of setting a treasure hunt that taps into some magic deeply embedded in the landscape. Can historical acts of mystical significance that happened centuries ago somehow set up resonances in the very stones, streams, woods and horizons which are able to shape a receptive mind a thousand years later? I felt the tables turned. I felt like one doomed to see in a mirror-glass, the Lady of Shalott, to see everything reversed. I hadn't been setting a treasure hunt. I was being set one – and the prize was the Holy Grail itself.

But it was the last comment in the Du Crozs' coffee-table book, thrown away almost as a footnote, that still astounds me the most. It is a trivial fact and will mean nothing to the forensic Arthurian artefact hunter or the serious historian, but it means the world to me and makes me realise that my choice of hiding place for the treasure of Jack de Crow has been made in regions and by forces way beyond my own far-from-gilded skull. It is the

fact that the Welsh name *Dinas Brân* means, of all things, 'Crow Castle'.)

But whichever Muse it is that arranges such toils of grace and leads me to think, like Daniel May before me, that I somehow tread the borderlands between twilit enchantment and the plain pastures of daylight reality, she must be that very Muse who shows a sense of balance and humour in all her works. It is she that balances the high mysteries revealed to Tamino with the comic buffoonery of Papageno, matches the enchantments of Titania in her bower with the asinine swaggering of Bottom. And I, too, was not to escape this age-old pattern. For all the wondrous serendipity and high enchantment of the day, there was an element of pure bathos to the rest of that afternoon. Shortly after leaving the Pillar of Eliseg, I was cycling along a laneway heading homewards when I was suddenly stricken in both legs simultaneously by a terrible cramp. Now it may seem astonishing, but I had never experienced cramp before. As both of my legs stiffened and became useless, I could do nothing but topple slowly off my bike and fall headfirst into the lane-side ditch. I lay there wondering what on earth was happening to me. Had the sandwiches I had just eaten poisoned me? Had I been bitten by an unseen adder? Was there some malign power at work trying to prevent me from completing my quest to hide the Grail? With Alan Garner fresh in my mind, I glanced around to see if I could spot some fat, robed figure chanting medieval Latin at me; his terrifying Selina Place, the Morrígan herself, come to paralyse me with her dark arts.

After a minute or two, the cramps passed and I was able to hop back on the bike, though somewhat more warily now. My heart was racing and my brow was sweating, but I took deep calming breaths until I had restored myself to a sense of placid normality. I pushed off, wheeled blithely fifty yards down the lane, came to the slightest of rises, which demanded a bit of pedal action ... and toppled off into the ditch, both legs immobilised with crippling cramp once more.

This happened seven more times over the next hour. My progress was slow and erratic, and I was glad I had chosen not to cycle the towpath to get back home. If I had, each bout of cramp would have risked sending me helplessly into the murky waters of the canal rather than into the relatively harmless – though often nettle-strewn – depths of the roadside ditch. On the sixth topple, as I lay there face down on the verge moaning softly to myself and wondering if I would make it back alive, I heard the *clip-clop* of hooves approaching. A few seconds later, a pair of horsewomen loomed over me, glancing down from a great height.

'Drunk!!' snorted one. 'Disgusting!' agreed her friend – and they trotted off smartly before I could explain that no, I was just on my way back from burying a treasure, a Holy Grail if you will, ma'am, a goldfinch led me there you see ... which on a moment's reflection would, I realised, only have served to confirm the lady's diagnosis beyond doubt. Besides, I had other things to contend with. I'd lain there paralysed long enough for a small colony of earwigs to start making a nest up my trouser leg, and a badly placed nettle had swiped me across the eyes as I fell, bringing me out in a colourful rash. Once the cramp had passed, I'd need to strip to my underwear and find a dock leaf or three before I could comfortably tackle the remaining fifteen miles back to College.

Chapter 27

Parting is such sweet sorrow . . .
—William Shakespeare, *Romeo and Juliet*

There were only a couple of weeks to go before the end of the school year and my time to depart the school for good. It was in that last two weeks that on a visit to Shrewsbury I found myself gazing at the swift green waters of the River Severn as it flowed away beneath the Welsh Bridge and started to daydream of the possibility of sailing away from the College in a tiny jollyboat. It was in the last two weeks that I investigated the little yellow upturned hull of an abandoned Mirror dinghy lying in the buttercups on the shores of Whitemere. It was in the last two weeks that I idly mentioned to Nina Scarlatti a half-joking idea that it might be good to auction off all my possessions for charity so I could row away into the sunset with nothing to my name but a tin whistle and a pith helmet – *ha, ha!* – and then came back from a weekend away to find that with characteristic alacrity, Nina had taken me at my word. My flat was stripped bare and every single thing I owned was now on display in the school theatre, each with a lot number ready to be, indeed, auctioned. Nina had rallied her obliging partner Turm, and between them they had organised the whole thing.

And so I come at last to my departure from Ellesmere. As readers of my previous work will know, this took the form of me rowing away in a little Mirror dinghy, yellow-hulled and scarlet-sailed, borrowed from the College Sailing Club on the shores of Whitemere. I had painted the name on her bows and transom – *Jack de Crow* of course – and had enlisted the aid of the amiable Kiwi Turm to cart the boat over to a place I had chosen as my launching place; the canal near the waters of Colemere, shining on that tranquil September evening.

Oddly enough, only three days ago I came across a number of photos of that occasion that I had never seen before, given to me by Nina, now a highly successful teacher in a respectable Melbourne school and still good for a laugh – though I do tend to wear thicker jumpers these days when she is in a playfully belligerent mood. With amazed delight I recall all the faces that thronged the little humpback bridge that evening. They are all there: Stanley Pinkerton the Head of Maintenance, who just the week before has finally turned up to remove those filing cabinets from the North Pole sitting room. He is leaning over the parapet and saying something unintelligible in his Staffordshire accent which sounds like, 'Gart ferret! Blacky lidder port! Hoody darn tit, eh?' His wife, Pamela, who has forgiven me at last for my reprehensible betrayal at the auction all those years ago, is waving a tiny lace hanky and has pressed a farewell piece of dry sponge into my hand to snack on later.

Even the gloomy Brian the Iron is there. The previous day I had bumped into him as I was saying my farewells to the office staff. I'd already said goodbye to Captain Powlett-Price – a somewhat frosty farewell as he had just heard about Sam Curlewis's fire-breathing in the recent *Tempest* production and felt the need to remind me of various Health and Safety issues regarding the use of the school theatre; this, despite the fact that I was about to depart for good.

Escaping from the bursar, I'd run straight into Brian the Iron in Miss Pike's office and inwardly sighed. I couldn't stomach another blast of hostility; my encounters with him over the last six years had convinced me that he nursed a deep loathing for me, expressed by resentful blood-hound eyes, a pursed mouth as sour as a withered lemon and a grim silence punctuated only by sighs of irritation as I had apologised my way through an explanation of what I had needed in the way of ironwork props for my plays. To my astonishment, this final encounter in the office was markedly different. 'Oh, deary me,' he lilted in cheery tones. 'I've heard you're off, isn't it, into the wide blue yonder!' His Welsh voice was full of warmth and kindly regret. 'I'm right sorry to hear it, boyo. I've loved our little chats down in my workroom over the years, so I have. All those swords and such like. Brightened my week, they did. Such a pity you're going, it is. You'll be missed and that's no word of a lie!'

I was somewhat astonished. 'Er … well, thank you, Brian. Um … you seem chirpy today, if you don't mind me saying so. Um …'

I didn't add, 'unlike your usual surly, miserable, black-souled self, you grimy embittered dwarf', of course, but Brian guessed what I was thinking.

'I know, I know. It's a miracle. The truth is, I went to the doctor a few weeks back and he worked out I was gluten intolerant. He made me give up bread and whatnot and I can't believe the difference. I couldn't understand how everyone else could be so bloody cheerful all the time. I thought they were just pretending. Now I've given up gluten, I'm a new man. Makes you think, doesn't it, boyo? Makes you think …'

And after shaking my hand heartily and blowing Miss Pike a kiss, he had waltzed out of the room executing a lamb-like heel-kick on the way out. Down the corridor, we could hear him strike up 'Men of Harlech' in a tuneful whistle. Miss Pike and I had looked at each other in some astonishment. Then …

'I think I might suggest Captain Powlett-Price visits an allergist. What do you think?'

And on that note, I had smiled again at Miss Pike's primly acid wit and left her to her task of soothing the irascible temper of the bursar next door.

The popping of a champagne cork brings me back to the bridge, here and now over the canal, where an impromptu party is beginning to happen. All my colleagues of the last six years are there: Michael and Donna and young Bess and little Seb, now six years old. (I am later to hear that after I rowed off, Seb burst into tears on the way back to the College in the car and delivered the following heartfelt *cri de coeur*: 'He was such a good man!' The epitaph-like finality of my godson's outburst was perhaps prompted by witnessing my erratic steering of the rowboat along a darkening canal and a comment on the likely imminence of my drowning that very evening.)

Others are there too. Nina Scarlatti and Turm, of course. Ross Bassenthwaite, trying to refrain from comment at my pith helmet. Felix Arne, relaxed and sardonic; Arthur Beagle, gloomily predicting disaster. Ernest Wimborne, Bruce Bamford, Mr Witherspoon, Mr Pebmarsh and . . . and of course they are nothing like the sore-headed bears or fussy pedants I have portrayed them as in these pages. They are my friends and colleagues, passionate, eccentric, demanding in their fields just as I have been. That is, they are teachers. The students of Ellesmere should count themselves fortunate to have been under their guidance. And of course, there are students there as well – Ned Marlow and Toby Larkin, Clarinda Honeywell, Sam Curlewis, Archie Hobbs – and the ghosts of the departed Skelligs: Walter, Nick, Katy and Jonathan – and Edwin Appleby from all those years ago – and Daniel May is probably there too, having made himself invisible by some new bit of wizardry.

It feels odd to be finishing a book with a scene that started a previous book, and I will not try to recapture here the trembling excitement of that farewell, the fragrance of the autumn leaves, the cool Madonna blue and primrose of the late afternoon sky. There was for me no heaviness of departure; indeed, only an extraordinary lightness and impatience to be off. Even Betty Bombadil had given me her blessing to depart in peace by dying suddenly at Whitemere just the week before. Furthermore, all my goods and chattels had been sold off at the charity auction, thanks to Nina's energetic efforts, and I was sailing away free and unburdened. It had especially pleased me that Toby Larkin had set his eyes on – and purchased in that auction – the little silver ship of Skillibladnir, the symbol of the Philosophy Club over the years that had always managed to lighten the darkness and set the soul free to fly to the ends of time and space and thought. As a teacher, one should never have favourites, but it is fair to admit that young Larkin had encapsulated all that I loved the best about the students I taught over the years. There was something about Toby's independence of thought, playfulness and lively curiosity that had appealed enormously to me ever since I had first cast him as Puck a few years previously. Indeed, I had been flattered recently when he had rung me one half term and had asked me to describe my maze design over the phone. He had just been given permission to add some feature to his parents' garden and rather than going for something like a garden gnome or a birdbath, he had decided with characteristic ambition to see if he could construct my entire spiralling labyrinth in gravel and miniature hedges. It was for this reason that I decided to choose him as the starting point of a little project that had been growing in my mind over the last month or two.

You may remember that I had had the good fortune to take possession of a large bag of jewellery from the helpful Mr Crabbe and that I had taken the best pieces and used them as part of the hidden hoard of Jack de Crow. But what was I to do with all the leftover pieces of jewellery? Toby's enquiry about my maze had suggested an idea.

I had long thought how nice it would be if someone would set me a magical treasure hunt, a quest of the same enchantment and complexity as the one I had just spent a year devising for the students of Ellesmere College. I had even wondered if it was possible for me to set a treasure hunt for myself – before deciding that this was a paradox too far even for me. But now, the bag of jewels and brooches and golden chains combined with a wine-red velvet cloth recently purchased came together to form something quite promising. Here's what I did.

I took the velvet square, which was about the dimensions of a card table, and spent three days stitching all the leftover jewels onto it with gold thread to form my maze design. Happily, I had enough chains and strings of pearls to use for the spiralling loops. I took apart a bracelet consisting of eight identical topazes the colour of sherry, each set in silver, and used these to define the eight cross pieces. A beautiful round moonstone with an opalescent sheen sat at the heart of the design and a myriad of other gems adorned the loops at intervals – cairngorms, diamante brooches, agate rings, tiger-eye cufflinks, paste sapphires and rubies and emeralds, glittering in a spiral galaxy of flashing colour.

Then I wrote a letter in calligraphy on some high-quality paper designed to last. It read:

> Here You have the Jewelled Cloth of the Maze of the World's Heart.
>
> He who would Find his Way Inward to the Heart of Desire must ever turn Outwards. He who would be First must be Last. He who would Save his Life must Lose it.

This Treasure is therefore Yours for a Year and a Day, no More, no Less.

You shall then pass this Jewelled Cloth and this Letter to a Soul of Like Mind, and They shall become the new Keeper of the Maze for a Year and a Day, after which Time They too shall seek a Worthy Keeper of this Treasure.

Thus shall this Gift pass ever Onward from Person to Person of Good Heart until Its Maker seeks to find It once more.

Go Peacefully.

I decided that Toby Larkin would be the first recipient of this Jewelled Maze-Cloth. My hope was that he would faithfully follow the instructions on the parchment and within a year and a day find someone to pass the Cloth on to. Hopefully that person would be someone like-minded, someone who would understand the childish delight of passing on a secret treasure to someone they admired for the same qualities.

In this way, I hoped to achieve the seeming impossible, namely to set a treasure hunt for myself, to be completed some time far in the future. When I am feeling jaded with life, when the comforts I have cocooned around me have become suffocating, when the joys of an accustomed palate begin to pall and I am restless for adventure, I shall set off to track down the Jewelled Maze. I shall go and hunt down Toby, wherever he might be by then, and ask him who he thought to pass it on to. Assuming Toby doesn't say, 'Oh, that old thing, we've been using it as the dog's blanket for years now,' he will rack his brains, search through the dark and backward abysm of time to recall the name of a once-bright soul – and so I shall set off again, tracing the invisible clew left by the labyrinth from household to household, person to person, zigzagging to and fro across the world as my footsteps doubled to and fro through the whiteness of snow all those years ago. And what treasures I will find along the way; such minds and hearts scattered like gems along the golden threaded way.

But that is all for the future. How to start the process off?

Having completed the Jewelled Maze-Cloth, I decided that simply handing it to Toby would not be in the proper spirit of things, so I took a different approach. I had recently discovered that behind the altar of the Chapel of Saint Oswald's at the College was a stone trapdoor. I had explored this with great excitement thinking it might be ideal to use as part of the Chalice quest, especially if it led to some hitherto unexplored crypt. I had crawled along this tunnel at the time to discover that it ended twenty feet away in a brick cul-de-sac and was simply an access tunnel to the underground heating.

Useless though this was for the purposes of the larger Quest, it seemed to me an ideal place to hide the Jewelled Maze-Cloth. With barely days to go before I sailed away in my little dinghy, I crawled down the tunnel and hid the cloth and the parchment letter addressed to Toby in a leather bag at the very end. So when it came to the launching of *Jack de Crow* at the little canal bridge in Colemere Woods, it was good to have Toby there. In fact, it was Toby, my faithful Puck, my loyal Caliban, who helped me slide the dinghy into the water and saw me safely into the boat. As I clasped his hand in a final farewell, I whispered to him, 'In the Chapel. Behind the altar. The tunnel. There's a gift for you.' Then a champagne cork popped somewhere overhead, a cheer erupted from the gathered crowd and I didn't catch what Toby said in reply. A shove from an eager foot sent me gliding away from the bank and it was too late. I was off, bish-bashing my way down the canal with those unfamiliar oars until the shadows of Blakemere Wood swallowed me up in the blue dusk.

I often write as though these well-crafted moments of poignant departures or enchanted revelations drop sweetly into being like a ripe peach into the hand of a summer-drowsy child but to be honest, almost nothing I do ever goes off without a hitch of some sort. Two miles from Colemere Woods, the canal runs into the inky blackness of a tunnel. I was already considerably spooked by the dankness of the evening and the proximity of Blakemere, home to the Gollum-like Jenny Greenteeth, so the prospect of entering three hundred yards of pitch-black tunnel had my heart beating faster and my breath coming in quickened gasps. I was halfway through the tunnel, scraping Jack badly along the invisible concrete of the tunnel towpath and rather wishing I had remembered to pack a torch, when a hoarse voice out of the pitch-blackness frightened me half-to-death. I scooped wildly with an oar, dug too deep, the dinghy spun around and hit the far side of the tunnel with a splintering crack and I rocked wildly to a standstill, straining to see and hear whatever it was that had uttered that sepulchral whisper.

It spoke again.

'The Chapel? A tunnel? What tunnel? There isn't a tunnel, is there? What do you mean, tunnel?'

For a boy who had excelled so vividly on the stage over the years, Toby certainly knew how to ruin a dramatic moment. So much for the mysterious parting words of an adventuring knight to his faithful squire. Failing to understand me properly, he had jumped on his bike, raced along the main road and chosen the centre of the Blakemere Tunnel to intercept me to clarify matters. I repeated the instructions in clipped and well-enunciated tones with perhaps a hint of asperity in my voice. Toby responded with a cheery 'Oh. Righto!' before melting silently into the darkness as I resumed my rowing once more. It was a further irritation to discover, on emerging from the tunnel five minutes later into the open night air that in the kerfuffle, I had turned through 180 degrees and had rowed straight out the same end of the tunnel

I had entered some ten minutes earlier. It was with an understandable sigh of resignation that I turned on my oars and headed back into the darkness once more.

Chapter 28

I always pass on good advice. It is the only thing to do with it. It is never of any use to oneself.

—Oscar Wilde, *An Ideal Husband*

When I was just about to start my teaching career, my father and I walked down to the edge of the lake at Jindabyne and he asked if he could give me just one piece of advice. As a teacher and educator of many years' standing, I knew he would be itching to give me bucketloads more advice than just this one piece he had in mind, but he was wise enough to know that sometimes less is more. I reluctantly accepted his offer and waited resignedly. I knew what it would be; something like, 'Do your lesson plans,' or 'Keep up with your marking.' These were the things I knew would need working on and which he was so very good at. *Yes, Dad. Thanks, Dad. I'll try not to disappoint you.*

When the advice came, I was surprised by it. It was simply this: 'Sandy, like your students. Like them. Walk into each class and give off the resounding impression that you are happy to see them, that they are – secretly of course – your very favourite class. That doesn't mean you won't have to get cross with them sometimes, bring them into line, expect high standards. You will, and frequently. But you must always give them the idea that you are doing that because you feel they are likeable enough to be worth holding to account. And when you come across a student you really cannot like – and you will, very rarely – that's the boy or girl you must convince that out of all of them, he or she is really your favourite. Do that and you can't go far wrong.'

I was astonished by this advice, from my father of all men. As a teacher he was conscientious rather than inspiring. He was serious and studious: certainly not one of those teachers who is enormous fun or wildly eccentric. On approaching his lessons, you knew you were in for a steady and informative ride without histrionics. His focus always appeared to be on well-turned-out worksheets, good note-taking and assignments marked in a thorough and timely fashion. And yet, as I reflected on knowing him as a teacher and as the Headmaster of the school I attended, I realised that he had also followed his dictum – 'Like your students' – every day. In all the years I knew him as a teacher or Headmaster, I never once heard him express contempt or distaste for a single student, never heard him refer to them in a sneering or exasperated way. Occasionally, sure enough, a parent – or an inept or recalcitrant staff member – would set him fuming over the dinner table, but he loved his students. It showed in the way he would stop and chat with them in the quadrangle, twinkle at them when they showed success on the playing field or stage, beam in a knowing avuncular way when they admitted to some folly, giving the impression that he had known all along – and it shows through in the number of loving comments I still receive from old friends and past students of his some five years after his passing away.

The other memorable thing said to me once about teaching was from someone who has appeared in these pages from time to time, albeit reluctantly no doubt. It was years and years ago, after we had both finished our first few years of teaching, and Tom and I were reflecting on our lives as teachers so far. We were up Brownhill Creek at the time, having cycled there one apple-green evening to recapture boyhood memories. No treasure hunts were currently being inflicted on either of us. No stories were coalescing around us. No magic of the sort that I have hinted at in these pages. But the stars were coming out, and one star – a planet probably – already hung in the west like a great drop of molten gold. The air had the sweetness of spring; a wild apple tree nearby was clouded with white blossom as we lay on the grass laughing at some ridiculous story from the working week just past: a boy who had said something inadvertently hilarious, perhaps, or the laughable inability of the Deputy Head to explain the new bell system to the entire school.

'But it is bloody wonderful, for all that, isn't it?' said Tom. 'For all the marking and the yard duties and the lesson plans that no one ever reads, and the surfie dudes in the back row who are way cooler than we'll ever be, it's like ... well, it's like having constant access to the Well of Eternal Youth.'

'How do you mean?' I asked, chewing a grass stem and listening to the distant carolling of magpies in the Seven Pines.

'Well, *we* get older year by year. *We* teach the same thing over and over again – "*i* before *e* except after *c*"; light and dark imagery in *Romeo and Juliet;* "it's spelt *d-e-f-i-n-i-t-e*, for God's sake, de-fin-*ite*, how could it possibly be de-fin-*ate*, you pelican?" ... and so on. And it's all old to us. But not to them. They're always thirteen, always fourteen, always fresh and new – and they don't know that brilliant way of explaining apostrophes, or what iambic pentameter is. They don't even know how *Romeo and Juliet* ends, for Pete's sake! I had a girl burst into tears the other day when she found out that Romeo kills himself – and you realise all over again just how awful that is. You become thirteen again, year after year. And that's a bit brilliant.'

He was right. That observation was made after only three years of teaching, but even now, after almost four decades, it holds true. The Well keeps bubbling up, generation after generation:

young souls, keen minds, loving hearts, ridiculous enthusiasms, immoderate passions – they keep coming in through the classroom doors, year after year, ready to tackle *Animal Farm* for the first time and fall in love with satirical allegory; ready to discover the multilayered intricacies of Pascal's triangle or the golden ratio; ready to approach the question, age-old but fire-new to them, 'Is what I see as green what you see as green – and if so, how could you ever prove it?' Or just ready to say, 'What? Treasure hunts? Mazes? I love that stuff. I didn't know teachers liked that sort of thing . . .'

And the words of my father and the words of Tom that evening work their alchemy together. It is the loving that unlocks the Hesperidean spring, and so I have tried to love my students. Not always, and never enough. But I have tried, even when that has meant straying from the curriculum a tad. And who wouldn't, when these boys and girls, these scholars and sporting heroes, these actors and musicians, these poets and philosophers, tricksters and troupers and daydreamers and dunces, have for nearly forty years now been providing me with daily draughts of the waters of Eternal Youth?

Afterword

It is astonishing to me that one of the frequent comments made to me by readers who have just finished one of my travel books is along the lines of, 'Gosh! What a tale! But none of it's true, right?' – which always leaves me a little dumbfounded. Of course it's true. It's a memoir, a true-life travel tale and is advertised as such. If I weren't confined to the parameters of truth, there would have been a lot more dragons, a lot more rescuing of downtrodden folk from evil tyrants and a few modest episodes where I come across as a handsome and saucy demigod between the sheets. So yes, my tales are true, and so is this one.

Except … I must make a few disclaimers. One is that I have changed the names of almost every character within these pages with the exception of one or two about whom I remain entirely complimentary and who, besides, have already appeared under their own names in previous books. Sometimes I have taken the liberty of conflating a couple of individuals into one character for artistic economy; at other times, for the same reason, I have used anecdotes or even characters from other schools where I have taught over the years.

I must apologise in advance for any offence I might cause as I have striven to create caricatures for the sake of liveliness. 'If we shadows have offended,' says Puck, before neatly sidestepping any censure by that time-honoured schoolboy device 'Then I woke up and it was all a dream …' I will not attempt to be quite so slippery, except to say this: if any of my ex-colleagues or students reading these pages suspect that they are the model for that absentminded dimwit, waspish pedant, bullish oaf or blimpish colonel, they may rest reassured that in every case I was thinking of someone quite different in a very different school who just happened to fit the role. Not them at all, deary me, no. The very thought …

For the truth is that I was very blessed to be at Ellesmere College at a time when the staff and students were a particularly amiable lot: eccentric at times, passionate about their own contributions to the life of the College, clashing heads occasionally in the mad scramble of everyday life, but always finding time to be extraordinarily warm and welcoming to a stray Antipodean who washed up on their dandelion shores. I hope none will think that this book is how I repay such friendship. It is a true memoir – but also a nonsense, a farce, a daydream and, in response to my six very happy years at that place, a love letter of sorts.

Puck was an artful dodger and not to be trusted. I prefer to put my trust in the gracious Duke, also of the *Dream*, and with him fervently hope of these pages that 'never any thing can be amiss, When simpleness and duty tender it'. Amen to that.

A.J. Mackinnon, the River House

Also by
A.J. Mackinnon

blackincbooks.com

A couple of quiet weeks sailing the River Severn was the intention. Somehow things got out of hand – a year later I had reached Romania and was still going . . .

Truly hilarious books are rare. Even rarer are those based on real events. Join A.J. Mackinnon, your charming and eccentric guide, on an amazing voyage in a boat called Jack de Crow.

Equipped with his cheerful optimism and a pith helmet, this Australian Odysseus in a dinghy travels from the borders of North Wales to the Black Sea – 4900 kilometres over salt and fresh water, under sail, at the oars, or at the end of a tow-rope – through twelve countries, 282 locks and numerous trials and adventures, including an encounter with Balkan pirates. Along the way he experiences the kindness of strangers, gets very lost, and perfects the art of slow travel.